RECENT RESEARCHES IN THE MUSIC OF THE BAROQUE ERA, 160

Charles Avison

Concerto Grosso Arrangements of Geminiani's Opus 1 Violin Sonatas

Edited by Mark Kroll

Concerto Grosso Arrangements of Geminiani's Opus 1 Violin Sonatas

Recent Researches in Music

A-R Editions publishes seven series of critical editions, spanning the history of Western music, American music, and oral traditions.

Recent Researches in the Music of the Middle Ages and Early Renaissance
   Charles M. Atkinson, general editor

Recent Researches in the Music of the Renaissance
   James Haar, general editor

Recent Researches in the Music of the Baroque Era
   Christoph Wolff, general editor

Recent Researches in the Music of the Classical Era
   Neal Zaslaw, general editor

Recent Researches in the Music of the Nineteenth and Early Twentieth Centuries
   Rufus Hallmark, general editor

Recent Researches in American Music
   John M. Graziano, general editor

Recent Researches in the Oral Traditions of Music
   Philip V. Bohlman, general editor

Each edition in *Recent Researches* is devoted to works by a single composer or to a single genre. The content is chosen for its high quality and historical importance and is edited according to the scholarly standards that govern the making of all reliable editions.

For information on establishing a standing order to any of our series, or for editorial guidelines on submitting proposals, please contact:

A-R Editions, Inc.
Middleton, Wisconsin

800 736-0070 (North American book orders)
608 836-9000 (phone)
608 831-8200 (fax)
http://www.areditions.com

RECENT RESEARCHES IN THE MUSIC OF THE BAROQUE ERA, 160

Charles Avison

Concerto Grosso Arrangements of Geminiani's Opus 1 Violin Sonatas

Edited by Mark Kroll

A-R Editions, Inc.
Middleton, Wisconsin

For Gordon Dixon and the Avison Ensemble

Performance parts are available from the publisher.

A-R Editions, Inc., Middleton, Wisconsin
© 2010 by A-R Editions, Inc.

All rights reserved. No part of this book may be reproduced or transmitted in any form by any electronic or mechanical means (including photocopying, recording, or information storage and retrieval) without permission in writing from the publisher.

The purchase of this edition does not convey the right to perform it in public, nor to make a recording of it for any purpose. Such permission must be obtained in advance from the publisher.

A-R Editions is pleased to support scholars and performers in their use of *Recent Researches* material for study or performance. Subscribers to any of the *Recent Researches* series, as well as patrons of subscribing institutions, are invited to apply for information about our "Copyright Sharing Policy."

Printed in the United States of America

ISBN-13: 978-0-89579-671-4
ISBN-10: 0-89579-671-6
ISSN: 0484-0828

♾ The paper used in this publication meets the minimum requirements of the American National Standard for Information Sciences—Permanence of Paper for Printed Library Materials, ANSI Z39.48-1992.

Contents

Acknowledgments   vii

Introduction   ix
   The Italian Concerto Grosso in England   ix
   The Composers   ix
   The Music of the Edition   xii
   Notes on Performance   xii
   Notes   xiv

Plates   xvii

  1. Concerto in G Major (from Sonata in A Major, Op. 1, No. 1)
     I. Grave; Allegro; Adagio; Allegro; Adagio   1
     II. Allegro   7
     III. Grave   17
     IV. Allegro   17

  2. Concerto in D Minor (from Sonata in D Minor, Op. 1, No. 2)
     I. Adagio   24
     II. Allegro   27
     III. Adagio   33
     IV. Allegro   35

  3. Concerto in E Minor (from Sonata in E Minor, Op. 1, No. 3)
     I. Adagio; Allegro; Adagio; Tempo giusto; Adagio   44
     II. Allegro   51

  4. Concerto in D Major (from Sonata in D Major, Op. 1, No. 4)
     I. Adagio   62
     II. Allegro   64
     III. Grave   72
     IV. Allegro   73

  5. Concerto in B-flat Major (from Sonata in B-flat Major, Op. 1, No. 5)
     I. Affettuoso   79
     II. Vivace   82
     III. Grave   90
     IV. Allegro   91

  6. Concerto in G Minor (from Sonata in G Minor, Op. 1, No. 6)
     I. Affettuoso   98
     II. Adagio   103
     III. Allegro   105
     IV. Andante   114

7. Concerto in C Minor (from Sonata in C Minor, Op. 1, No. 7)

   I. Grave   123
   II. Allegro   125
   III. Grave   128
   IV. Allegro   129

8. Concerto in B Minor (from Sonata in B Minor, Op. 1, No. 8)

   I. Affettuoso   134
   II. Vivace   136
   III. Adagio   140
   IV. Vivace   142

9. Concerto in F Major (from Sonata in F Major, Op. 1, No. 9)

   I. Vivace   147
   II. Andante   151
   III. Allegro   152

10. Concerto in D Major (from Sonata in E Major, Op. 1, No. 10)

   I. Adagio   159
   II. Allegro   161
   III. Adagio   165
   IV. Allegro   167

11. Concerto in D Minor (from Sonata in D Minor, Op. 1, No. 12)

   I. Amoroso   172
   II. Allegro   174
   III. Adagio; Allegro   177

Critical Report   183

   Sources   183
   Editorial Methods   183
   Critical Notes   185

Acknowledgments

I express my sincere gratitude to Gordon Dixon, director of the Avison Ensemble of Newcastle upon Tyne and founder of the Charles Avison Society, for his invaluable help with this project. Gordon first invited me to come to Newcastle to study, perform, and edit the material in the newly acquired workbooks of Charles Avison, and arranged for copies of the manuscript to be sent to me. He has also asked me to provide material for the Avison Ensemble's ongoing series of recordings and performances of the repertoire from these workbooks, and continues to offer assistance and information with unfailing generosity and patience. I am equally grateful to Ellen Golde, who played a significant role in the project. She introduced me to Gordon and the people who support his efforts, helped arrange my initial performance and research visits to Newcastle, and continues to serve as a vital communication link between myself and the Avison Ensemble. I express my thanks to the staff of the Newcastle City Libraries, Local Studies Collection (now the Newcastle Collection), where the workbooks are housed. They too could not have been more helpful and kind in responding to my questions and requests. My appreciation also goes to Professor Wendy Heller and Professor Carol Lieberman. They both read the introductory material for this edition, and their excellent comments and suggestions improved the final product immeasurably.

Introduction

The Italian Concerto Grosso in England

It is somewhat ironic that one of the leading exponents of the Italian concerto grosso during the eighteenth century was an Englishman who may have never set foot on the Italian peninsula. Charles Avison (1709–70), who was born and died in Newcastle, England, composed more than fifty concerti grossi, as well as chamber music, vocal music, accompanied keyboard sonatas, and keyboard concertos. Although not as prominent as his contemporary George Frideric Handel (1685–1759), Avison can justly be considered the most important English composer of concertos. His contributions to the genre include not only original compositions, but also orchestral transcriptions of works such as Domenico Scarlatti's keyboard sonatas. The music of this edition, eleven concerti grossi based on Francesco Geminiani's opus 1 violin sonatas, falls into this latter category.

Neither the popularity of the Italian concerto grosso style among the British nor Avison's success as a composer of concertos should come as a surprise. England has often provided fertile soil for the transplantation of continental musicians and musical styles, particularly during the last quarter of the seventeenth century and throughout the eighteenth. During this period, performers and composers began to flock to the British Isles to take advantage of the rising number of public concerts, the growing affluence of the British Empire, and a relatively free-enterprise system that encouraged individual initiative and the earning of considerable amounts of money. Italian violinists seem to have been particularly welcome visitors. The English had developed a strong preference for the violin in the late seventeenth century, especially after King Charles II reclaimed the English throne in 1660 after years of exile in France. There Charles had the opportunity to hear the *Vingt-quatre violons du roi* of his host and rival King Louis XIV, and upon his return home, the English monarch placed his support firmly behind the instrument.

Despite the Francophile leanings of Charles II, however, the die was cast in favor of the Italians with the 1682 publication in England of Arcangelo Corelli's Sonatas for Violin and Basso Continuo, op. 1. From that moment on, Corelli (1653–1713) became the musical idol of the British. As Roger North described the situation in 1728, "Corellys first consort . . . cleared the ground of all other sorts of musick whatsoever; by degrees the rest of his consorts & at last the conciertos came, all which are to the musitians like the bread of life."[1] The appearance of Corelli's Twelve Concerti Grossi, op. 6, in England during this period had a similar—if not greater—impact on the development of English musical style, since these concerti established the model for all subsequent works in the genre. They also enjoyed enduring popularity throughout the eighteenth century. Writing in 1789, Charles Burney observed that "the *Concertos* of Corelli seem to have withstood all the attacks of time and fashion . . . they preclude criticism and make us forget that there is any other Music of the same kind existing."[2]

Corelli had not simply "cleared the ground" for his own music, however; it seems he had also paved the way for other Italian violinist-composers, many of whom streamed across the English channel on the coattails of their illustrious Roman countryman. Some of the Italian musicians who appeared in the British Isles during this period only made brief visits, as did Francesco Veracini (1690–1768) in 1714 and 1733. Others chose to stay, including two actual pupils of Corelli. One was Pietro Castrucci (1679–1752), who moved to London in 1715 and served as leader of Handel's opera orchestra for twenty-two years. The other was Francesco Geminiani (1687–1762), who arrived in 1714 and would go on to play a larger musical role in his adopted country than any of his Italian compatriots. The concerto grosso style brought by these Italian violinist-composers found no more devoted advocate in England than Charles Avison.

The Composers

Charles Avison

Charles Avison[3] was baptized on 16 February 1709 at St. John the Baptist Church in Newcastle upon Tyne, a bustling town of industry and commerce in northern England.[4] The son of Richard and Ann Avison, Charles probably received his early musical training from his father, who was a member of the Newcastle Corporation's town waits.[5] This organization, which could trace its roots back to the thirteenth century, had initially been established to provide watchmen for the town. By the time of Charles Avison's birth, however, their duties were essentially musical: the waits performed when required for official town functions and supplemented their income by playing at weddings, fairs, and funerals.[6]

Avison likely obtained further musical instruction while serving in some capacity for Ralph Jenison (1696–1758), a merchant and patron of the arts who was a member of parliament for Northumberland from 1724 to 1741 and Newport, Isle of Wight, from 1749 to 1758. It was Jenison who received the dedication to Avison's first published work, the Sonatas for Two Violins and a Bass, op. 1 (ca. 1737).[7] In addition to his work with Jenison, Avison probably studied with a Colonel John Blathwayt (or Blaithwaite), who had served for a time as director of the Royal Academy of Music, and who was the dedicatee of Avison's Six Concertos, op. 2.[8] Burney and other commentators assert that Avison traveled to Italy at some point during his early years, but no records exist to confirm this claim.[9] Nevertheless, Italy—or, more accurately, Italians—played an important role in Avison's career, particularly after he moved to London in the early years of the 1730s, and probably late 1733, where he met Geminiani.[10] Though Avison never mentioned it specifically in his numerous writings, he probably studied with the Italian master during this period.[11]

By 1735 at the latest, Avison had returned to Newcastle, where he would remain until his death in 1770. Avison's tireless activities as composer, teacher, conductor, and entrepreneur in his native city established him as the leading musical figure of northern England. His first position in Newcastle was as organist of St. John the Baptist, the very church in which he had been baptized. Although appointed on 13 October 1735, Avison could not begin his duties until Christmas of that year—or perhaps as late as 24 June 1736, when the newly acquired organ had become playable.[12] He left St. John's only four months later, on 20 October, to succeed Thomas Powell as organist at the larger St. Nicholas Church—a position that enabled Avison to double his yearly salary to £40.[13] It was also during this period that Avison became involved with a series of subscription concerts in Newcastle, quite possibly as the founder. The inaugural performance took place at the Assembly Room in the Groat Market on 1 October 1735; by 1738 Avison had been appointed the director of the series, now named the Newcastle Musical Society.[14] Avison would hold this position, as well as that of organist of St. Nicholas, for the rest of his life.

Although the Newcastle Musical Society thrived during subsequent years, an advertisement in the *Newcastle Journal* suggests that Avison struggled at times to find a sufficient number of players in the city to fill out his orchestra: "Any person that can play well upon the Violin and Hautboy and tune a Harpsichord, will meet with very good encouragement, upon applying to Mr. Charles Avison, in Newcastle upon Tyne."[15] Despite the apparent shortage of qualified musicians, the Society provided Avison with opportunities to make his most important musical contributions as a composer, performer, and entrepreneur. Avison likely premiered his arrangements of Domenico Scarlatti's harpsichord sonatas on the series in 1743, and he may have performed the arrangements of this edition there as well. In a 1751 performance under the Society's auspices, he was the first to introduce British audiences to Jean-Philippe Rameau's *Pièces de clavecin en concerts*.[16] Vocal music also appeared on the programs of the subscription concerts, including the oratorio *Ruth*, which Avison had composed in collaboration with another Italian émigré wandering the British Isles during this period, Felice Giardini (1716–96); Avison's arrangement of madrigals by Carlo Clari; and works by Handel.[17] In light of Avison's strong connections to Francesco Geminiani, it is striking that Geminiani's name is absent from the programs of all of Avison's concerts. Nevertheless, evidence strongly suggests that Geminiani, or at least his music, did appear in Newcastle.[18]

Avison also maintained an active teaching studio in his home, where he taught organ, harpsichord, flute, and violin on Mondays and Fridays between nine and six.[19] Among his students were various members of the nobility, such as Lady Milbanke, to whom Avison dedicated his Eight Concertos, op. 4, and who became a professional harpsichordist. Another student, Lady Blackett, received the dedication of Avison's Six Sonatas for the Harpsichord with Accompanyments for Two Violins and Violoncello, op. 5.[20]

As an organist, harpsichordist, teacher, conductor, and concert promoter, Avison was clearly quite busy in Newcastle. Nevertheless, he did find time to collaborate with a number of prominent musicians. Avison's close friend, the cellist John Garth (1721–1810), lived conveniently in the neighboring town of Durham, and together they presented a series of concerts in Durham resembling those of the Newcastle Musical Society, often sharing players and guest artists.[21] Another of Avison's collaborators was a man now better known as a scientist rather than as a musician: the astronomer Sir William Herschel (1738–1822). Although renowned as the discoverer of the planet Uranus, Herschel was also an accomplished musician; he performed in Avison's subscription concerts during the 1760–61 season, as well as in the concerts at the Spring Gardens in Newcastle.[22]

Avison's advocacy of Italian music and musicians is underscored by his collaboration with Giardini, who had earned the respect of all those who heard him play. Burney, for example, called him "the greatest performer in Europe."[23] Avison held a similarly high opinion of Giardini; he frequently hired him to play in the concerts of the Newcastle Musical Society during the 1750s and 1760s, and, as mentioned earlier, worked with him on the oratorio *Ruth*.[24] Avison was particularly effusive about Giardini in his 1752 treatise *An Essay on Musical Expression*, praising "the Brilliancy and Fullness of his Tone, the Sweetness, Spirit, and Variety of his Expression, his amazing Rapidity of Execution, and Exuberance of Fancy, joined with the most perfect Ease and Gracefulness in the Performance."[25] A further confirmation of Avison's esteem for Giardini is a singular act of generosity: Avison acted as the agent in purchasing Corelli's own violin and gave it as a gift to Giardini. According to Burney's account of the event, "the favorite instrument upon which Corelli himself had played, was brought hither soon after his death by Corbet, an Englishman, and remained many years in the possession of a gentleman at Newcastle, at whose decease it was purchased by the late Mr. Avison for Giardini, whose property it still continues."[26]

As Avison's reputation spread, and as the large network of friends and colleagues he maintained and nurtured grew and prospered, it was inevitable that he would receive employment opportunities outside of his beloved Newcastle. From a lengthy letter signed "Marcellinus" and printed in the *Newcastle Journal* of 17 March 1759, we learn that Avison had received an offer quite early in his career, in 1735, to become organist at York Minster, and that others opportunities followed: a teaching post in Edinburgh; the invitation to succeed Johann Christian Pepusch (1667–1752) as organist of the Charterhouse in London in 1752; and two positions in Dublin between 1733 and 1740 on the recommendation of Geminiani.[27] Unfortunately, no further documentation exists to substantiate these claims.

Despite these employment offers, Avison chose to remain in Newcastle, where he was obviously satisfied with both his professional situation and personal life. His marriage to Catherine Reynolds on 15 January 1737 was apparently a happy one, marred only by Catherine's untimely death on 15 October 1766. They had nine children, but only three survived into adulthood: Jane (1744–73), Edward (1747–76), and Charles (1751–95).[28] Avison died in Newcastle on 9 or 10 May 1770, and the obituary printed in the *Newcastle Courant* on 12 May 1770 succinctly described his modest and attractive personality and the esteem in which he was held: "His loss is greatly lamented by all that had the pleasure of his acquaintance, for he was much valued for the amiableness of his private character as admired for his skill in the profession, and for his excellent compositions."[29]

Charles Avison and Francesco Geminiani

As already noted, Avison was a passionate advocate of the Italian concerto grosso style, particularly as practiced by Corelli and Geminiani. In the preface to his Twelve Concertos, op. 9 (1766), he wrote that he had "endeavored to avoid the rapid style of Composition now in vogue . . . Its Reign will not be of long continuance . . . If any Person doubt the Force of this Truth . . . Let him attend to a Concerto of *Corelli* or *Geminiani*." Although Avison greatly admired Corelli, Geminiani occupied a more important and immediate place in Avison's world, both professionally and personally. Indeed, the strong and mutually beneficial relationship between the two musicians—one a somewhat temperamental, well-traveled Italian émigré, the other a true-blooded Englishman who probably never left his native country and remained close to the town of his birth—warrants further examination.

For his part, Avison rarely lost any opportunity to extol the virtues of his teacher and friend. In his *Essay on Musical Expression,* he described Geminiani thus:

> THE Public is greatly indebted to this Gentleman, not only for his many excellent Compositions, but for having as yet parted with none that are not extremely correct and fine. There is such a Genteelness and Delicacy in the Turn of his musical Phrase, (if I may so call it), and such a natural Connection in his expressive and sweet Modulation throughout all his Works, which are every where supported with so perfect a Harmony, that we can never too often hear, or too much admire them.[30]

More incendiary was Avison's claim that Geminiani was a better composer than that English icon, Handel. Calling his teacher "the greatest in *instrumental Music,*" Avison praised "the admirable GEMINIANI; whose Elegance and Spirit of Composition ought to have been much more our Pattern; and from whom the public Taste might have received the highest improvement, had we thought proper to lay hold of the Opportunities which his long Residence in the Kingdom has given us."[31] Not surprisingly, the veiled assault on Handel elicited howls of protest and inspired some heated literary exchanges. Chief among these was the book-length rebuttal to Avison's *Essay* that William Hayes published in January 1753, the *Remarks on Mr. Avison's Essay on Musical Expression*. The following month Avison responded with his own lengthy rejoinder to Hayes, *A Reply to the Author of Remarks on the Essay on Musical Expression,* published on 22 February 1753.[32] The debate created lasting animosities and warring camps on both sides, and it was never resolved to anyone's complete satisfaction.[33]

Despite the controversy that the *Essay* precipitated, Avison nonetheless continued to admire the works of foreign musicians, lavishing praise on composers such as Rameau, Domenico Scarlatti, and C. P. E. Bach. But pride of place was always reserved for Geminiani, as we read in Avison's preface to his Six Sonatas for the Harpsichord with Accompanyments for two Violins and Violoncello, op. 8 (1764):

> Among the various Productions of foreign Composers for the Harpsichord, the Sonatas of SCARLATTI, RAMEAU AND CARLO-BACH have their *peculiar* Beauties. The *fine Fancy* of the Italian—the *spirited Science* of the Frenchman—and the German's *diffusive Expression* are the distinguishing Signatures of their Music. But if we examine the Lessons of GEMINIANI we shall find them fraught with *every* Beauty, and therefore, worthy of the Attention of Those who would improve a true taste, and acquire a graceful and fluent Execution.

Geminiani always responded in kind when dealing with Avison, as we have seen in his reported recommendations of Avison to the posts in Dublin in 1733 and 1740. Geminiani's warm feelings also extended to his student's family. For example, when Geminiani visited Avison in 1760 to hear his thirteen-year-old son Edward play, he wrote "My friend, I love all your productions. You are my heir. This boy will be yours . . . to raise up geniuses like him is the only way to perpetuate music."[34]

Avison deeply mourned the loss of his friend when Geminiani died in 1762. He expressed his feelings with particular eloquence six years later in the following testimonial published in Newcastle's *Literary Register, or Weekly Miscellany:*

> On viewing a portrait of the late celebrated GEMINIANI.
>
> WHILE contending nations alarm the world abroad and interior commotions at home, I peruse *thy* pacific page, and

wonder where the powers of music are fled, not to harmonize the passions of men; yet still the dulcet strains will live in congenial souls, to smooth the path of life which providence has given to lovers of harmony.[35]

The Music of the Edition

Avison scored his arrangements of Geminiani's opus 1 for the same seven-part ensemble that he employed for all his large-scale concerti: a *concertino* group consisting of two violins, viola, cello, and harpsichord; and a *ripieno* ensemble of first and second violins, cello, and bass. (For Avison's specific instructions regarding the number and proportion of these instruments, see the "Notes on Performance.") Like the Geminiani originals, the first six concertos are written in the multimovement *da chiesa* style, while the final five are *da camera*, featuring binary dance movements (though they are not labeled as such). For example, the final movements of the Concerto in C Minor (no. 7 in this edition) and Concerto in D Major (no. 10) are in standard gigue rhythm; the third movement of the Concerto in B Minor (no. 8) is an allemande; and the second movement of the Concerto in F Major (no. 9) uses sarabande rhythm. Avison seems to have arranged only eleven of the twelve solo violin sonatas in Geminiani's opus 1; there is no surviving transcription of Sonata no. 11.

Geminiani published numerous versions of his opus 1 violin sonatas, making it difficult to determine with certainty which edition or manuscript copy Avison used as the model for his concertos. The first edition of the sonatas was published by Richard Meares in 1716 and bears a dedication to Geminiani's first patron in England, Baron Johann Adolf von Kielmansegg (1668–1717).[36] Walsh issued an edition in 1719, which was reprinted around 1730, and a "corrected version" in 1739 (dedicated to "Dorotea Contessa di Burlington").[37] Here Geminiani made wholesale revisions to his own work, adding ornaments, dynamics, and other expressive markings, correcting figures in the bass, making changes to the embellishments, and even altering the melodies of the originals. To further complicate matters, a trio sonata arrangement of the last six sonatas of opus 1 was published by Walsh around 1742 as being composed by Geminiani. This edition, however, is essentially a reprint of the work arranged several years earlier by Geminiani's Italian countryman and colleague in London, Francesco Barsanti (1690–1772), apparently with Geminiani's full approval. [38]

The trail of competing versions of opus 1 does not end here. In 1757 Geminiani composed his own arrangements of these sonatas "for Two Violins and a Violoncello or Harpsichord with a Ripieno Bass to be used then the Violins are doubled," meaning that they could be performed as trio sonatas or with a larger ensemble. Moreover, the composer here made further revisions by adding ornamentation, altering the melodies, and inserting new musical material. Finally, selected movements from the opus 1 sonatas also appeared in arrangements for solo harpsichord in Geminiani's *Pièces de Clavecin* of 1743 and 1762.

Avison's concerto grosso arrangements feature both similarities to and divergences from the Geminiani and Barsanti models. For example, Avison divided the solo violinist's double stops between the *concertino* violins—much as Barsanti and Geminiani did in their trio-sonata arrangements. But the precise allocation of music between the two violin parts varied among the three composers, with Avison remaining relatively faithful to the melodic lines and other features of the original violin sonatas. Avison also transposed two of Geminiani's sonatas to different keys: Sonata no. 1 in A Major was transposed to G major, and Sonata no. 10 in E Major became the Concerto in D Major.

There are a number of more significant modifications, however, in Avison's concerto arrangements. The most striking variant is the final movement of the Concerto in G Minor (no. 6), an orchestral Andante followed by a set of two-part variations based on the harmonic progression of the Andante. The music for the orchestral Andante and the two-part variations is not found in any version of Geminiani's G-minor violin sonata on which the concerto is based. All of the sonatas conclude with the Allegro that stands as movement three in the Avison concerto arrangement. However, we do find the minuet and variations in three sources of Geminiani's keyboard music: the *Pièces de Clavecin* of 1743; a collection of minuets published by Geminiani ca. 1740; and Walsh's 1743 publication *HANDEL's Celebrated WATER MUSICK Compleat.* [39] Avison has therefore created his own final movement by orchestrating one of Geminiani's keyboard minuets, adding Geminiani's two-part variations to it, and rounding off the movement with a da capo return to the orchestrated minuet. These variations, moreover, are idiomatically written for the harpsichord, so it is safe to assume that they are intended for keyboard performance. Since the keyboard player was always assigned the task of realizing the basso continuo in every other orchestral work by Avison, either original or arrangement, the two-part solo harpsichord variations in the G-minor concerto stand apart from the rest of Avison's output.

Notes on Performance

In addition to his rich life as a composer and performer, Charles Avison was one of the most influential writers on musical aesthetics in the eighteenth century. Never shy about expressing his highly individual opinions in print, he often achieved a degree of notoriety with his writings. Avison threw down the gauntlet with particular force in his *Essay on Musical Expression,* in which he claimed that "expression" was more important than following the formal rules of composition. Avison also wrote more extensively than did almost any other composer of the baroque era about what he considered the proper performance of his music. His instructions, which we find in the prefaces to his published works and in the *Essay on Musical Expression,* are specific, uncompromising, and written in Avison's clear and unambiguous style. Performers today are therefore fortunate, for by following Avison's instructions, they can present a performance of his music that will come very close to one the composer himself would have recognized.

Avison provided a detailed description of the proper performance of concertos in the preface to his Six Concertos in Seven Parts, op. 3 (1751), and his comments are equally applicable to the music of this edition. Addressing matters of ensemble size, Avison described what he considered the ideal balance of instruments in his orchestra. The *concertino* group should consist of four solo players: first and second violins, viola, and cello. Since the cello part is fully figured, it is to be assumed that a harpsichord was part of the *concertino* group. Avison's *ripieno* ensemble was larger than one would first suspect. Ideally, it ought to include six first violins and four second violins, four cellos, and two double basses. As there are no figures in the bass line of the *ripieno*, it is unlikely that a second harpsichord was used in these concertos. Ever the practical musician, Avison was flexible about the number of players for the *ripieno*, noting that "a lesser Number of Instruments [in the *ripieno*], near the same Proportion, will also have a proper Effect, and may answer the Composer's Intention; but more would probably destroy the just Contrast, which should always be kept up between the *Chorus* and *Solo*." Avison cautioned against doubling any of the *concertino* instruments, since this "wou'd be an Impropriety in the Conduct of our Musical Oeconomy." He also defended the seemingly large number of cellos, answering critics who would think that they "wou'd be found too powerful for the *Violins*" with the rejoinder that "the [*concertino*] Instruments are in their Tone so clear, sprightly, and piercing, and as they rather gain more Force by this Addition, they will always be heard." He also insisted that a double bass always be used, "especially in a Performance of full Concertos, as they cannot be heard to any Advantage without that Noble Foundation of their Harmony."

Avison addressed almost every other aspect of performance practice in this preface, often with a sharp tongue likely honed from years of dealing with the amateur musicians who filled the seats of his orchestra. For example, he felt it necessary to ask for something that should have been taken for granted: players should study their parts and the score, and—above all—practice. "For Instance, how often does the Fate of a Concerto depend in the temerarious Execution of a Sett of Performers, who have never previously considered the Work, examined the Connection of it Parts, or studied the Intention of the Whole?" Performance and rehearsal levels must have been frustratingly low indeed in Newcastle at this time. Avison frequently complained that his players were unable to maintain a steady rhythm, and apparently even the soloists had difficulties in this regard; as Avison noted, "in the four principal Parts, there ought to be four Performers of almost equal Mastery; as well in regard to *Time,* as Execution; for however easy it may seem to acquire the former, yet nothing more shews a Master than a steady Performance throughout the whole Movement."

This same preface includes Avison's particularly cutting remarks about viola players, who, like today, seem to have had the reputation of being weak musicians. In what is perhaps the first viola joke in music history, Avison described the weakness of his violists and told us why he never dared giving them anything complicated to play. In his experience, violists have "one of the worst Hands," so much so that "it is from a Difficulty of finding a Performer, equal to what is required on this Instrument, that I have been induced to throw the principal Points, and Fugues of this Part into the Violoncello."

Avison also admonished players for their inability to realize the dynamics exactly as he wrote them. For example, he found it necessary to remind performers to keep "strict Regard . . . to the *Piano* and *Forte*" since they often "pass unobserved, or at all express'd, in so careless and negligent a manner as to produce little, if any, sensible difference to the Hearer." Avison also insisted that performers create a diminuendo simply by playing softer, rather than by reducing the number of instruments, criticizing "those lukewarm Performers, who imagine that diminishing the number of Instruments will answer the same End as softening the whole, to quit their Part when they shou'd rather be all Attention how to manage it with the utmost Delicacy." Elsewhere Avison warned "unexperienced performers" against making the very common mistake of slowing down in a diminuendo or speeding up for a crescendo.[40]

Avison further cautioned against excessive embellishment, particularly by members of the *ripieno* section. Here Avison was again unequivocal: absolutely no ornamentation should be allowed. "In every Part throughout the full Chorus, all manner of Graces or diminution of Passages, or Transposition of eight Notes higher, must be avoided; which some indiscrete Performers are but too apt to make use of . . . but these Gentlemen ought to consider, that by such Liberties they do not only disappoint the expecting Ear . . . but often introduce and occasion *Disallowances* in the Harmony." Performers during that time also seem to have indulged in the astonishing habit of playing *after* a piece had ended. Avison evoked the gods of Corelli and Geminiani to serve as the correct role models: "we sometimes hear Performers, the Moment a Piece is ended, run over their Instrument, playing a thousand Tricks. . . . What a dissonant Interval do these heterogeneous Fancies, or Excrescences of Music, afford to the experienced Ear, between the fine concerted Movements of a *Corelli* or *Geminiani!*"

As a virtuoso keyboard player, Avison not surprisingly devoted considerable attention and space to the proper performance on the harpsichord. His instructions, at least to players of modest accomplishments, were specific, numerous, and uncompromising: play the correct chords, keep a steady rhythm, do not fill in rests with extraneous embellishments or passage work, do not add connecting material to the first endings of repeated sections, and be discreet about the use of *acciaccaturas* and other techniques typical of harpsichord arpeggiation—especially if the harpsichordist is not a master of the instrument:

> As [the harpsichord] is only to be used in the Chorus, the Performer will have little else to regard but the striking just

Chords, keeping the Time and being careful, that no jangling Sound, or scattering of the Notes be continued after the *Pause* or *Cadence*.... The same Care is necessary at the return of each *double Strain,* when there are no intermediate Notes to introduce the *Repeat.* In fine, a profound Silence must always be observed, wherever the Composer has intended a general Respit, or Pause in the Work. I am the more particular in giving this Caution to Performers on the Harpsichord, as they are the most liable to transgress in this way; because their Instrument, lying so commodious to their Fingers, is ever tempting them to run, like Wild-fire, over the Keys, and thus perpetually interrupt the Performance.... The Use of *Acciaccatura* or sweeping of the Chords, and the *dropping* or *sprinkling* Notes, are indeed some of the peculiar Beauties of this Instrument. But these graceful *Touches* are only reserved for a Masterly Application on the Accompanyment of a fine Voice or single Instrument.

Avison was active during a period in which it is now generally (and incorrectly) assumed that keyboard players used a non-legato touch. Avison's advice about this aspect of performance practice, whether playing solo music or basso continuo, is characteristically clear and practical: harpsichordists should play legato. As we read in the preface to his Six Sonatas for the Harpsichord, op. 5 (1756),

> In regard to the Harpsichord; the Manner of Playing as described by the Term *Legato,* or chaining the Passages, by some *spirited Touch of the Finger,* is much more suitable to the Style of these Pieces, than that of the *Staccato,* or invariable marking of the Notes *by means of the Wrist* ... for however strange it may seem to assert, that different Performers give the same Harpsichord a very different Tone, the Fact is nevertheless true, and may be justly accounted for, from the different Methods of playing here noted, *i.e.,* either with, or without lifting the wrist.[41]

When grappling with questions of historical performance in Avison's concerti grossi, modern musicians should eagerly follow Avison's clear instructions. In doing so, they will be satisfying one of the principal tenets of historical performance: be faithful to the original intentions of the composer—in this case, Charles Avison.

Notes

1. Roger North, *The Musicall Gramarian,* ed. Hilda Andrews (London: Oxford University Press, 1925), 37; quoted in Norris Lynn Stephens, "Charles Avison: An Eighteenth-Century English Composer, Musician and Writer" (Ph.D. diss., University of Pittsburgh, 1968), 93.
2. Charles Burney, *A General History of Music From the Earliest Ages to the Present Period,* ed. Frank Mercer, 2 vols. (London, 1935; repr., New York: Dover, 1957), 2:442.
3. Further information about Avison's life and works are to be found in Jenny Burchell, *Polite or Commercial Concerts? Concert Management and Orchestral Repertoire in Edinburgh, Bath, Oxford, Manchester and Newcastle, 1730–1799* (New York: Garland, 1996); Pierre Dubois, ed., *Charles Avison's Essay on Musical Expression* (Aldershot: Ashgate, 2004); P. M. Horsley, "Charles Avison: The Man and His Milieu," *Music and Letters* 51 (1974): 5–23; Roz Southey, *Music-Making in North-East England During the Eighteenth Century* (Aldershot: Ashgate, 2006); Stephens, "Charles Avison"; and Roz Southey, Margaret Maddison, and David Hughes, *The Ingenious Mr. Avison: Making Music and Money in Eighteenth Century Newcastle* (Newcastle: Tyne Bridge, 2009).
4. The baptismal record reads, "Charles, Son of Richard Avison, musician, bapt. 16 Feb. 1708/9." Newcastle, St. John's Church *Parish Register.* Stephens, "Charles Avison," 1; and Southey, Maddison, and Hughes, *The Ingenious Mr. Avison,* 11.
5. Richard Avison (d. 1721) joined the waits in 1702. It was once thought that Ann Avison (d. 1749) succeeded her husband as organist at Gateshead Church upon his death, but this is now considered unlikely. See Southey, *Music-Making in North-East England,* 14 and 64; and Southey, Maddison, and Hughes, *The Ingenious Mr. Avison,* 126 n. 15.
6. The waits played primarily outdoors until the beginning of the seventeenth century, when records indicate that they also performed at indoor events. They therefore had to be extremely versatile and adept at playing a wide variety of instruments: loud winds such as trumpets, shawms, and sackbuts for the outdoor events, and strings, flutes, and plucked instruments for their indoor work. Nevertheless, one did not get rich being employed as a wait. Their salaries rarely rose above £5 per year, plus whatever they might earn from supplemental performances. Charles Avison therefore grew up in quite modest circumstances. See Stephens, "Charles Avison," 13.
7. Although he was a career politician, evidence of Jenison's patronage of the arts is confirmed by the number of works dedicated to him, such as Corelli's *The Score of the Twelve Concertos ... revised by Dr Pepusch* (London, 1732).
8. In the preface to his Six Concertos, op. 2, Avison wrote about the "valuable opportunities of improving" that he had received through Blathwayt's "generous assistance." Southey, Maddison, and Hughes, *The Ingenious Mr. Avison,* 48 and 129 n. 58.
9. Burney wrote that Avison "visited Italy early in his youth." Burney, *General History of Music,* 2:1013.
10. Southey, Maddison, and Hughes, *The Ingenious Mr. Avison,* 30.
11. Despite the absence of Avison's words of confirmation, several reliable sources make a reasonable claim that he was indeed Geminiani's student. An article in *The Newcastle Journal* of 20 March 1759 calls Avison a "disciple" of Geminiani, and William Hayes, in his *Remarks on Mr. Avison's Essay on Musical Expression,* stated that Avison had received "the principal Part of his Education from Geminiani." William Hayes, *Remarks on Mr. Avison's Essay on Musical Expression* (London: J. Robinson, 1753), 112. Burney added in his description of Avison's training that "having received instructions from Geminiani, a bias in [Avison's] compositions for violins, and in his *Essay on Musical Expression,* towards that master is manifest." Burney, *General History of Music,* 2:1013.
12. Information found in the Newcastle *Common Council Book* for 13 October 1735, fol. 296 and 12 July 1736, fol. 316, cited in Stephens, "Charles Avison," 7. See also Southey, Maddison, and Hughes, *The Ingenious Mr. Avison,* 34.

13. Newcastle *Common Council Book,* 20 October 1736, fol. 330. See Southey, *Music-Making in North-East England,* 16; and Stephens, "Charles Avison," 7.

14. We read of Avison's appointment as director of the series in the *Newcastle Courant* of 29 July 1738: "The Gentlemen who first promoted the SUBSCRIPTION CONCERTS, having resigned the management of it to Mr. Avison (and also intend to assist him with their Performance, etc.) he takes this Opportunity to inform the Town, that the Subscription will now be Half a Guinea; and each Ticket to admit two Ladies, or one Gentleman, as usual. As it is humbly hoped this Undertaking will meet with some Encouragement, Mr. Avison will take the Liberty (between this and Michaelmas) to wait on his Friends with Proposals." Quoted in Stephens, "Charles Avison," 21. The season consisted of twelve concerts presented every two weeks between early October and late March or early April. After 1757 they were held at Parker's Long Room. It was also in this year that a summer concert series was added, from April to August. The Newcastle Musical Society continued to present concerts after Avison's death, until it was disbanded in 1813. See Dubois, *Charles Avison's Essay on Musical Expression,* x–xiii.

15. Quoted in Stephens, "Charles Avison," 29.

16. Regarding the premiere of Rameau's *Pièces de clavecin en concerts,* Avison wrote in the *Newcastle Courant* on 21 September 1751: "there will be performed in every Concert, during this Season, select Pieces from the Works of M. RAMEAU, principal Composer to the Opera of Paris.... I shall also have the Pleasure of introducing to a Northern Audience, the Compositions of this celebrated Master, which, as yet, are but little known in England." Quoted in Burchell, *Polite or Commercial Concerts,* 283.

17. The appearance of Handel's music on programs of the Newcastle Musical Society undermines the allegation by Hayes and Burney that Avison did not like his music.

18. For further information, see Mark Kroll, "Avison, Geminiani and the Italian Connection," in *Charles Avison in Context,* ed. Eric Cross and Roz Southey (forthcoming).

19. From an advertisement in the *Newcastle Courant,* we learn that "Mr. Avison begs to acquaint his friends that Mondays and Fridays are set apart for his teaching in Newcastle ... he proposes to attend young Ladies on the harpsichord between the hours of nine and one in the forenoon—and—from two to six in the evening—he will teach the violin and German flute.... The terms are half a guinea per month (or eight lessons) and one guinea Entrance." Quoted in Dubois, *Charles Avison's Essay on Musical Expression,* xi.

20. Lady Milbanke was the wife of Sir Ralph Milbanke, fifth baronet. Lady Blackett was the wife of Walter Blackett, who occasionally served as Lord Mayor of Newcastle.

21. The Durham performances were held on Tuesdays, and those in Newcastle on Thursdays; Wednesdays were reserved for theater productions in both cities. After 1761, additional concerts were also presented in a room at the vicarage of St. Nicholas on Sunday evenings. Dubois, *Charles Avison's Essay on Musical Expression,* xii.

22. See Southey, *Music-Making in North-East England,* 211. For example, we find the following entry by Herschel in his *Chronicle:* "I went from Sunderland to Newcastle, where I attended the regular subscription concert of Mr. Avison, the organist, in which I engaged as first violin and solo player." William Herschel, *The Herschel Chronicle,* ed. Constance A. Lubbock (Cambridge: At the University Press, 1933), 18, quoted in Stephens, "Charles Avison," 28. See also Burchell, *Polite or Commercial Concerts,* 29 n. 15; and Southey, Maddison, and Hughes, *The Ingenious Mr. Avison,* 93–94. Herschel also served as a conductor, directing an orchestra in August 1761 at the Spring Garden Concerts in a program that included some of his own music. Herschel, *Chronicle,* 22, quoted in Stephens, "Charles Avison," 29.

23. Burney, *General History of Music,* 2:895. Giardini became well established in England. For example, he was governor of the Foundling Hospital and performed at the Bach-Abel concerts, Three Choirs Festival, and King's Theater. See Dubois, *Charles Avison's Essay on Musical Expression,* 66 n. 60.

24. For Giardini's appearances in the Newcastle Musical Society, see Southey, *Music-Making in North-East England,* 34–35. The oratorio *Ruth* was originally planned to be composed jointly by three men: Avison, Giardini, and William Boyce. However, Boyce was forced to withdraw because of illness, and Avison composed both first and third parts. This version of *Ruth* was performed on 15 April 1763, but when it was repeated on 13 February 1765, only Avison's music for part one was heard, while the remainder was composed by Giardini. In a subsequent performance on 25 May 1768, all three parts were by Giardini. Avison's music is now lost. See Dubois, *Charles Avison's Essay on Musical Expression,* xii and xlii n. 32; and Simon McVeigh, "Music and Lock Hospital in the 18th century," *Musical Times* 129 (1988): 235–40.

25. Charles Avison, *An Essay on Musical Expression* (London, 1753; repr., New York: Broude Brothers, 1967), 119–20.

26. Burney, *General History of Music,* 2:990. Southey, Maddison, and Hughes, *The Ingenious Mr. Avison,* 74.

27. The text of the letter reads as follows:

I have been told, when one organist was elected to serve at St. Nicholas', that he had a favourable prospect of establishing himself in London. But it seems his inclination to fix in Newcastle prevailed above all other considerations. I could never otherwise account for his refusing the offers that have since been made him. First, he had the offer to be organist of the Cathedral of York when it was given to Dr. Nares.... Soon after, Mr. Avison was applied to by Sigr. Geminiani, whose disciple he had been, to accompany him to Dublin, having a promise to succeed as organist to two churches vacant in that city.

Afterwards he had a proposal from Edinburgh to perform in the concerts there, and to teach upon the harpsichord, the proposers engaging to procure him two hundred pounds sterling per annum. Lastly, on the death of Dr. Pepusch he was desired by several gentlemen in London to offer himself a candidate for the place of organist in the Charter House ... but all of these opportunities of advancement himself he declined, though he had friends and character to support him.

Quoted in Stephens, "Charles Avison," 39–40.

28. Both Edward and Charles went on to become professional musicians and performed in their father's concerts in Newcastle and Durham. Edward (1747–76) was the more successful of the two. He succeeded his father at St. Nicholas and as director of the Newcastle Musical Society, but his career was cut short by his death at the age of twenty-nine. The less responsible of the two, Charles (1751–95) had a particular penchant for travel. He wandered as far as St. Petersburg, Russia, but ultimately returned to Newcastle to serve as organist at All Saints' Church and later at St. Nicholas, a post he held until his death. Charles also taught piano, but he died in debt. His household goods were sold six months after his funeral to satisfy his creditors. Horsley, "Charles Avison: The Man and His Milieu," 16; Southey, Maddison, and Hughes, *The Ingenious Mr. Avison,* 110–20.

29. Stephens provides the following explanation for the discrepancy in the date of death: "Since the newspapers in Newcastle were published on Saturdays at that time, Thursday would have been May 10. The St. Andrew's *Parish Record* gives the date as May 9. This discrepancy of one day would indicate that he died during the night of May 9. He was buried in St. Andrews Churchyard beside the remains of his wife on the day the obituary notice appeared." Stephens, "Charles Avison," 9.

30. Avison, *Essay on Musical Expression,* 104.

31. Ibid., 103.

32. A third edition of Avison's *Essay on Musical Expression,* a reprint of the second edition, appeared in 1775, as did a German translation of the first edition, published in Leipzig.

33. For example, as late as 1789 Charles Burney would write that Avison's "judgement was warped by many prejudices. He exalted Rameau and Geminiani at the expence of Handel." Burney, *General History of Music,* 2:7.

34. *Newcastle Journal*, 20–27 December 1760. Quoted in Horsley, "Charles Avison: The Man and His Milieu," 9.

35. *The Literary Register, or Weekly Miscellany* 1 (1768): 278. Quoted in Dubois, *Charles Avison's Essay on Musical Expression*, xiii and xlii n. 36.

36. Burney wrote that "In 1716 [Geminiani] published in London his first work, dedicated to Baron Kilmansegge [*sic*], consisting of Twelve Solos for the Violin, which though few could play, yet all the professors allowed them to be still more masterly and elaborate than those of Corelli." Burney, *General History of Music*, 2:991. Another edition was published by Meares in 1718 and announced in the *Daily Courant* of 8 August 1718.

37. Jeanne Roger (and Le Cene) also published an edition in Amsterdam (1722), and Le Clerc did the same in Paris in 1740. Burney tells us that he was aware of the Amsterdam edition: "these seem to have been previously published at Amsterdam, by Le Cene, of which edition I am in possession of a copy, beautifully engraved in copper." Ibid., 2:991n.

38. Hawkins claimed that Barsanti arrived with Geminiani in London in 1714, but David Lasocki questioned this assertion, citing the fact that Barsanti "does not appear in the list of six oboe players examined in 1720 for four posts in the opera orchestra of the Royal Academy of Music." Lasocki, rather, believed that Barsanti arrived some years later, probably in 1723. See David Lasocki, "Professional Recorder Players in England 1540–1740" (Ph.D. diss., University of Iowa, 1983), 846, cited in Enrico Careri, *Francesco Geminiani (1687–1762)* (Oxford: Clarendon, 1993), 8 n. 2. Another error made by Hawkins was his statement that Barsanti "made into sonatas for two violins and a bass, the first six solos of Geminiani." In fact, Barsanti arranged the last six sonatas. See Sir John Hawkins, *A General History of the Science and Practice of Music*, ed. Charles Cudworth, 2 vols. (Novello, 1853; repr., New York: Dover, 1963), 2:896.

39. This minuet and variations can be found in *Menuetti con variazioni composti per il cembalo da F. Geminiani* (ca. 1740); *Pièces de Clavecin Tirées des differens Ouvrages de M.ʳ F. Geminiani* (1743); and *HANDEL's Celebrated WATER MUSICK Compleat. Set for the Harpsicord. To which is added, Two favourite MINUETS, with Variations for the Harpsicord, By GEMINIANI* (1743).

40. In the preface to his Eight Concertos in Seven Parts, op. 4 (1760), Avison criticized those performers "with whom it is almost a general Practice to *abate* the *Time* where the Sounds are *diminished*; as also where the Sounds are *encreased* to *quicken* the *Time* . . . we should neither *retard* the *Piano,* nor *precipitate* the *Forte*."

41. In this same preface, Avison reiterates his remark about the proper technique to use on the harpsichord, especially when arpeggiating chords and adding acciaccaturas and other decorative notes: "the *Acciaccatura*, or separating the Chords, which are never to be struck at once, but swept from the lowest Note to the highest . . . in the quickest Succession, dwelling only on the Keys which express the Harmony . . . where the same Note is repeated in any quick Time . . . the Hand must either be raised from the Key, or the Key must be struck with different Fingers."

Plate 1. Charles Avison, Concerto in D Minor (from Francesco Geminiani, Sonata in D Minor, Op. 1, No. 2), first movement, measures 1–16. Newcastle City Library, Newcastle Collection, Charles Avison Archive, Workbook II, page 15. Reproduced with permission from the Avison Ensemble.

Plate 2. Charles Avison, Concerto in G Minor (from Francesco Geminiani, Sonata in G Minor, Op. 1, No. 6), fourth movement, measures 33–130. Newcastle City Library, Newcastle Collection, Charles Avison Archive, Workbook II, page 54. Reproduced with permission from the Avison Ensemble.

Plate 3. Charles Avison, Concerto in F Major (from Francesco Geminiani, Sonata in F Major, Op. 1, No. 9), first movement, measures 16–24, and second movement, measures 1–18. Newcastle City Library, Newcastle Collection, Charles Avison Archive, Workbook II, page 67. Reproduced with permission from the Avison Ensemble.

1. Concerto in G Major
I

From Francesco Geminiani, Sonata in A Major, Op. 1, No. 1

II

13

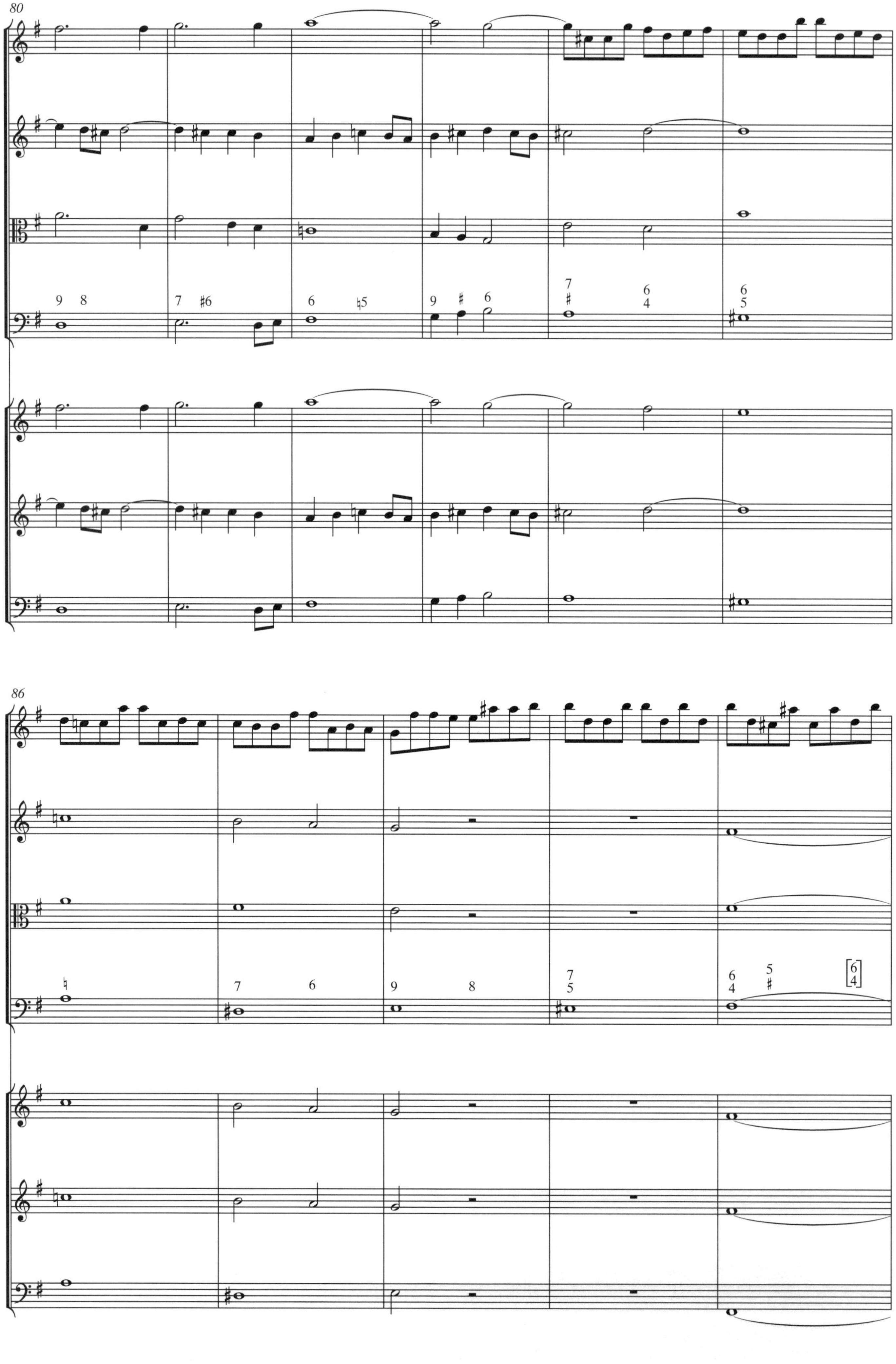
80
86

15

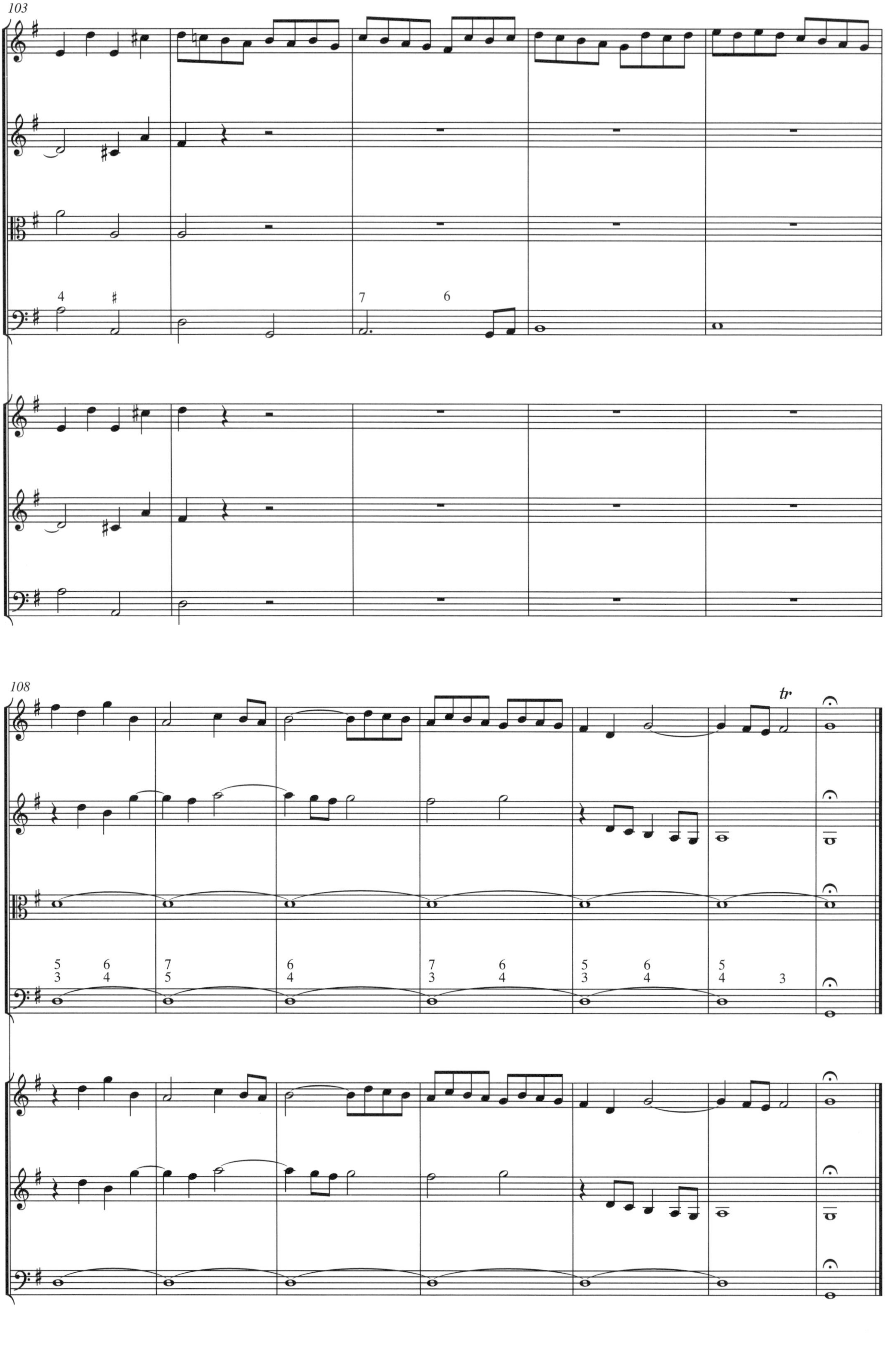
103
108
tr

III

IV

18

19

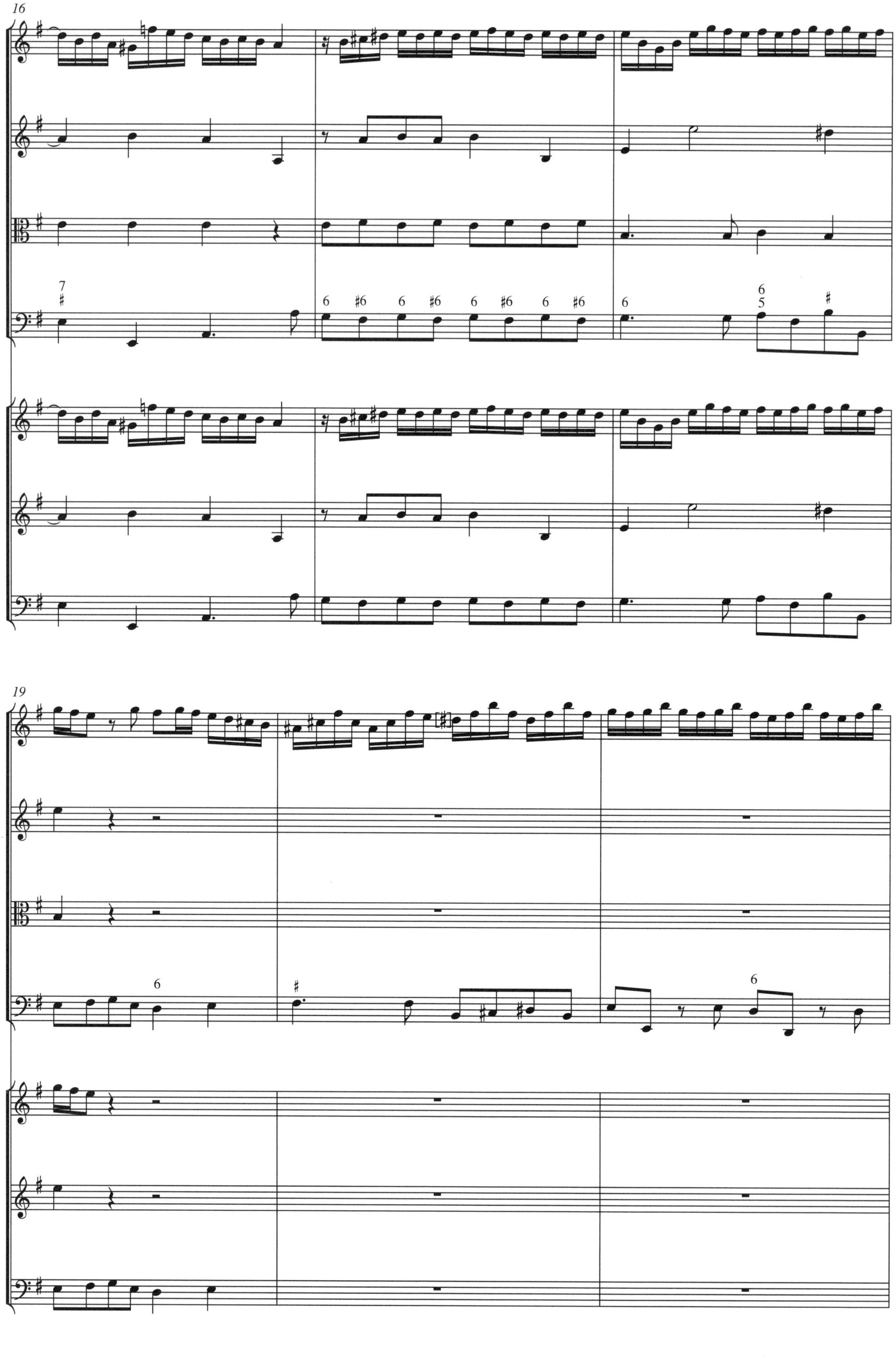
16
19

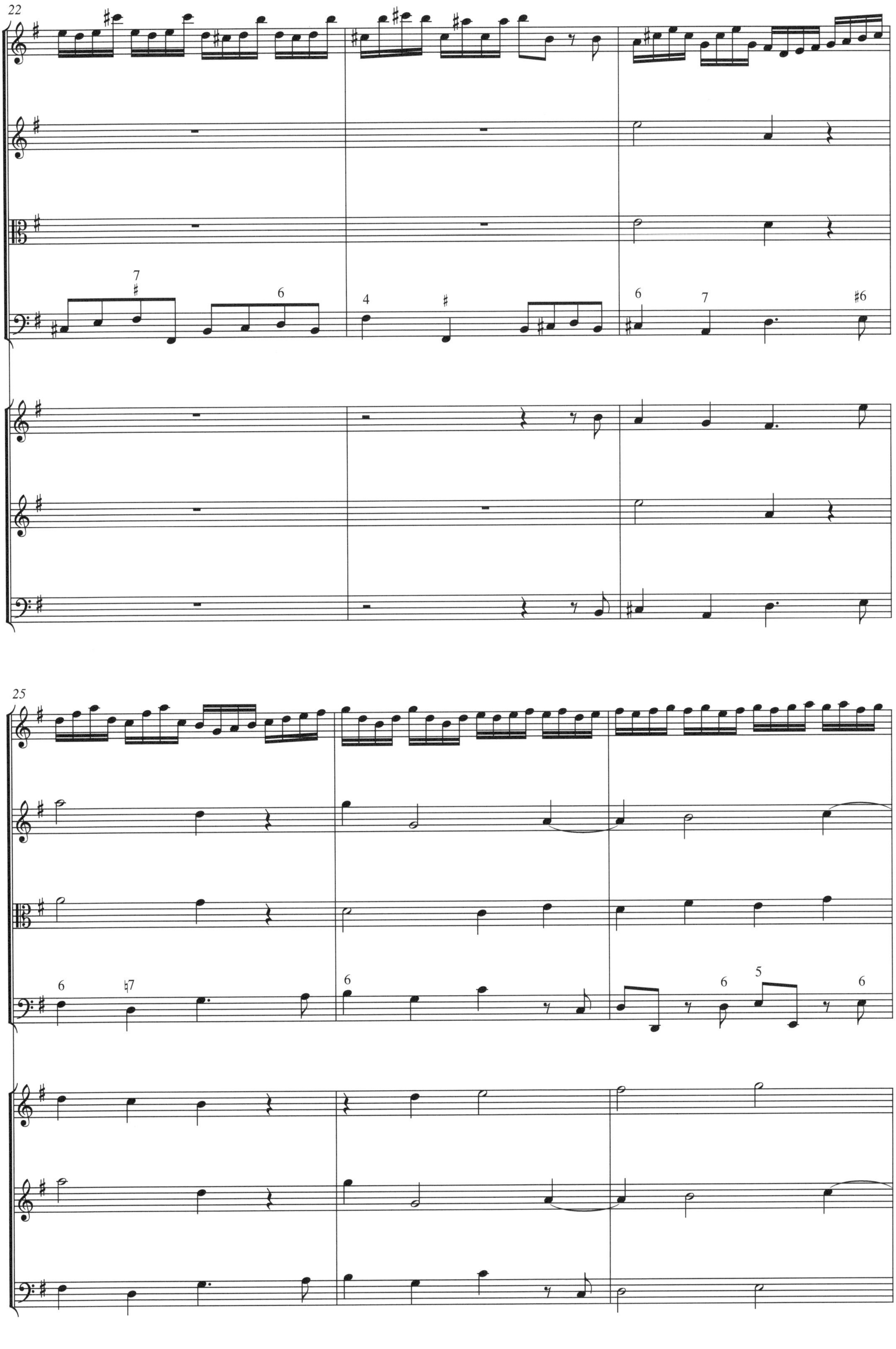
22
25

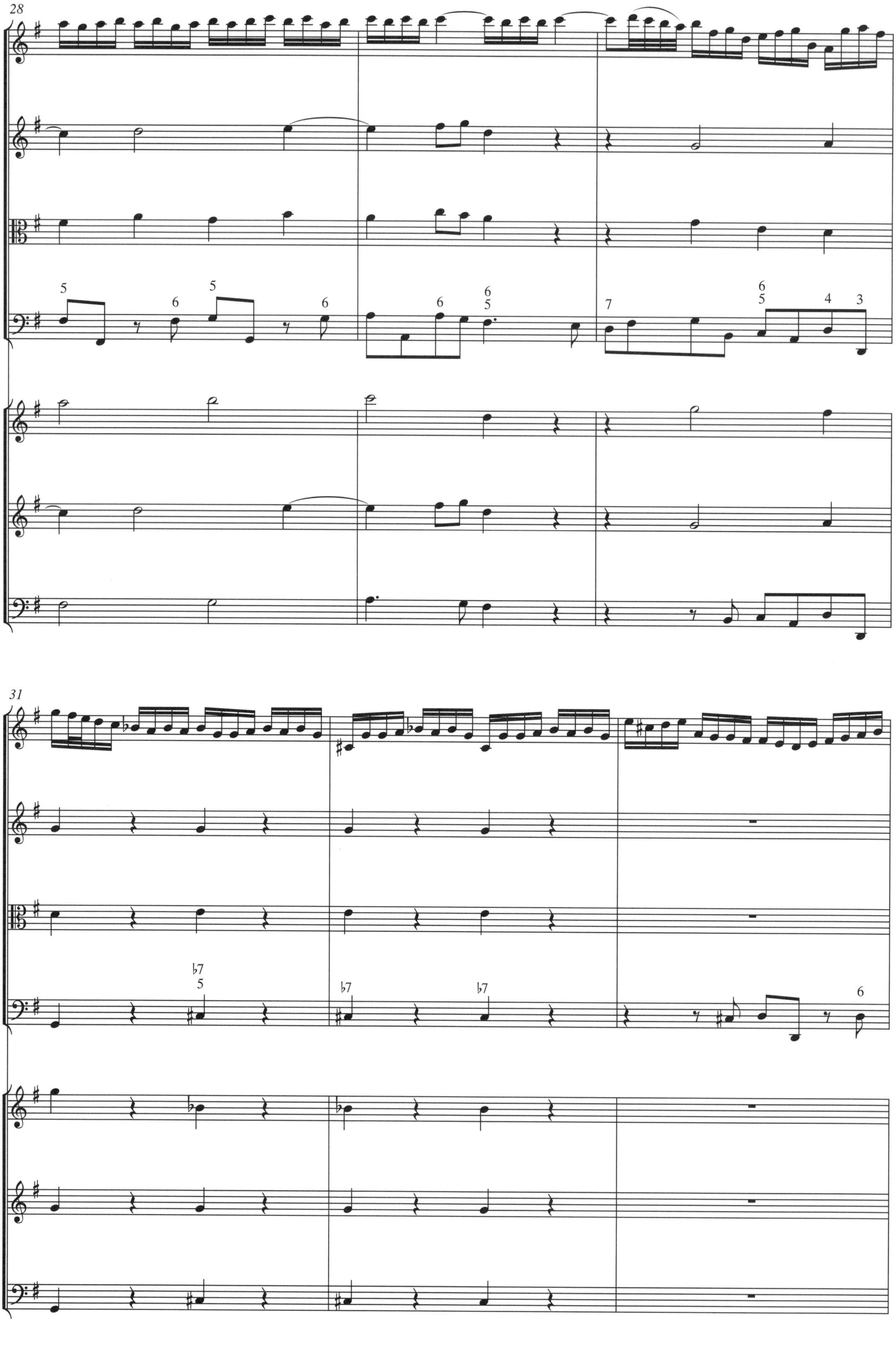
28
31

23

2. Concerto in D Minor

I

From Francesco Geminiani, Sonata in D Minor, Op. 2, No. 2

25

26

II

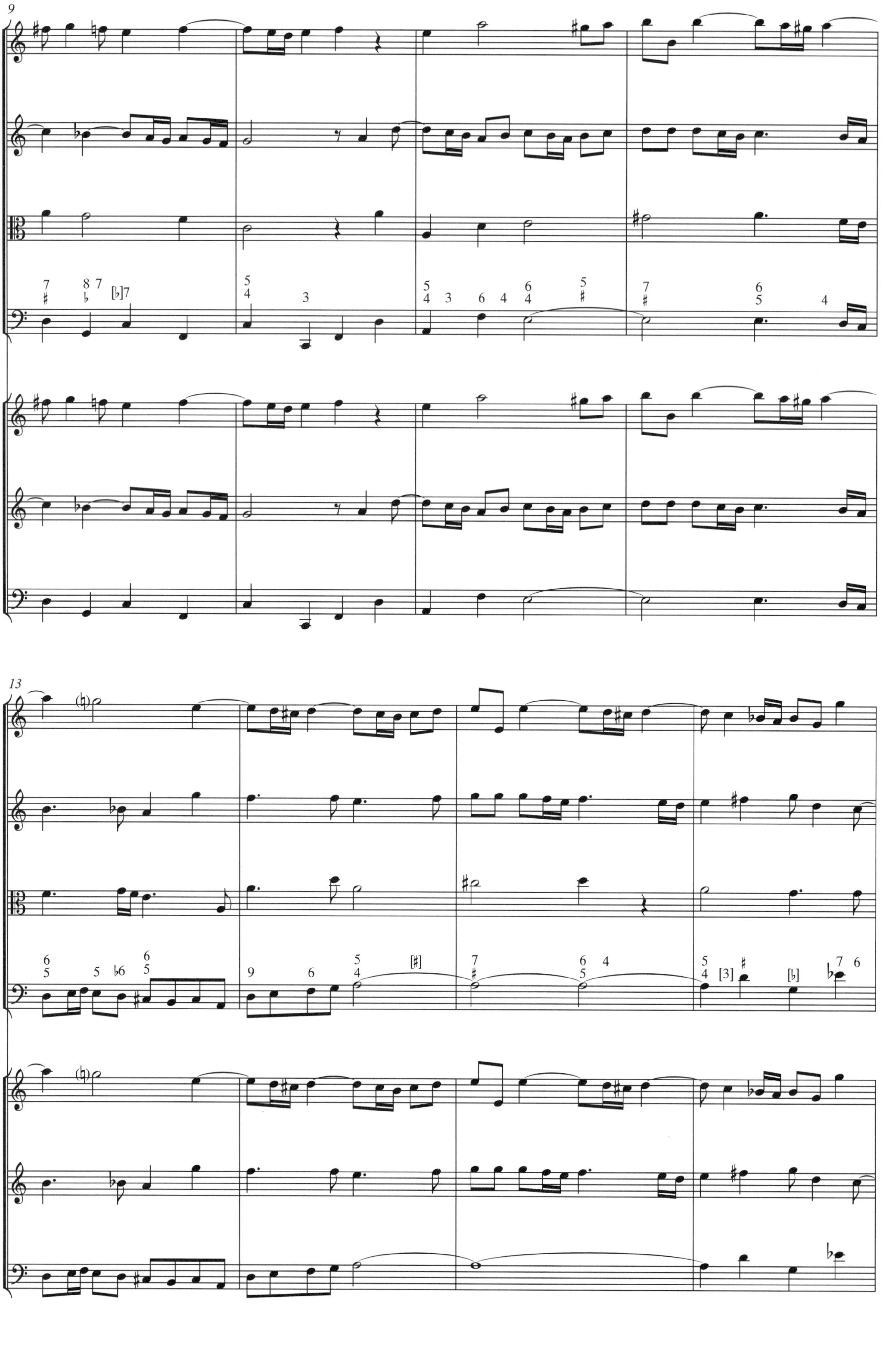

29

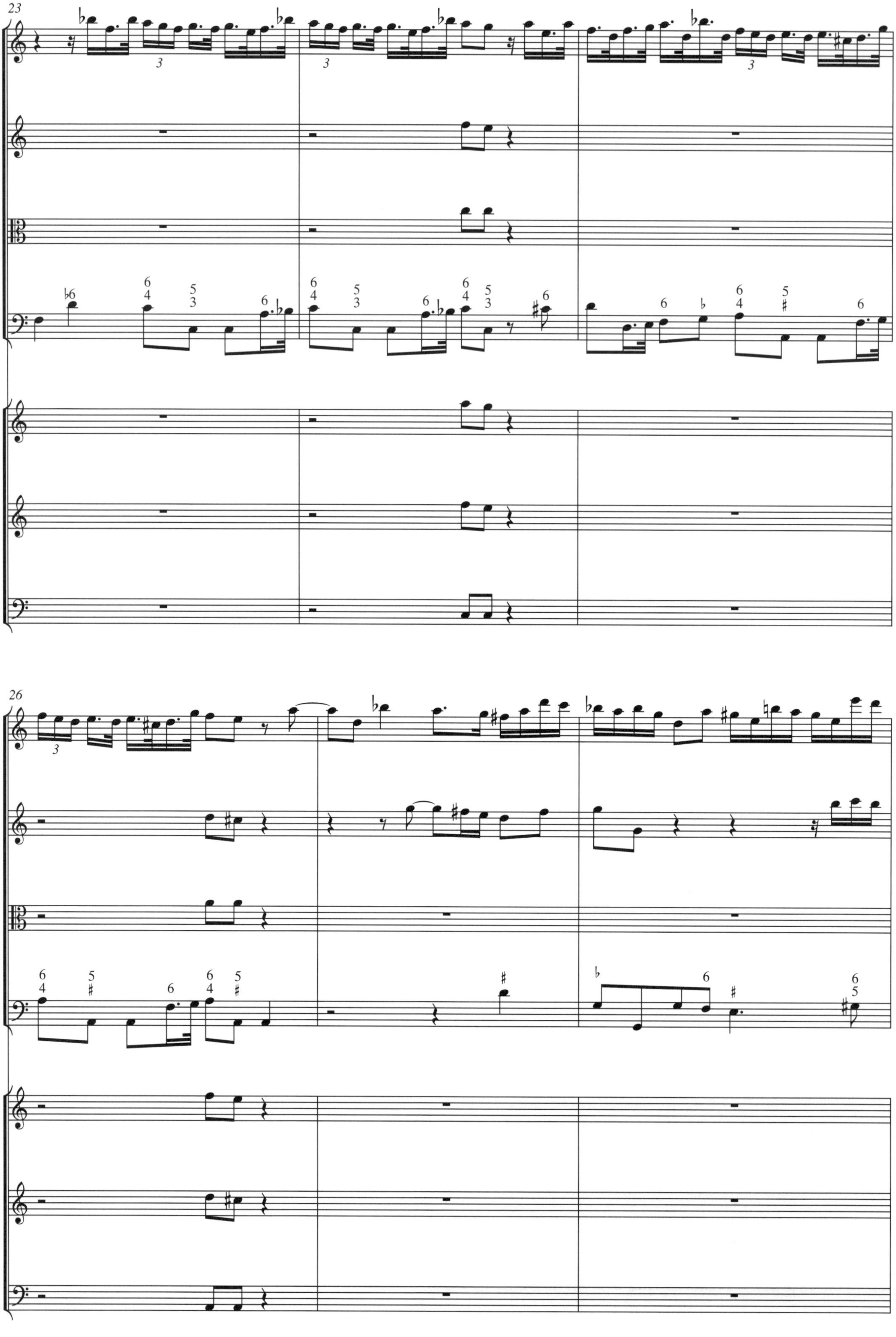
23
26

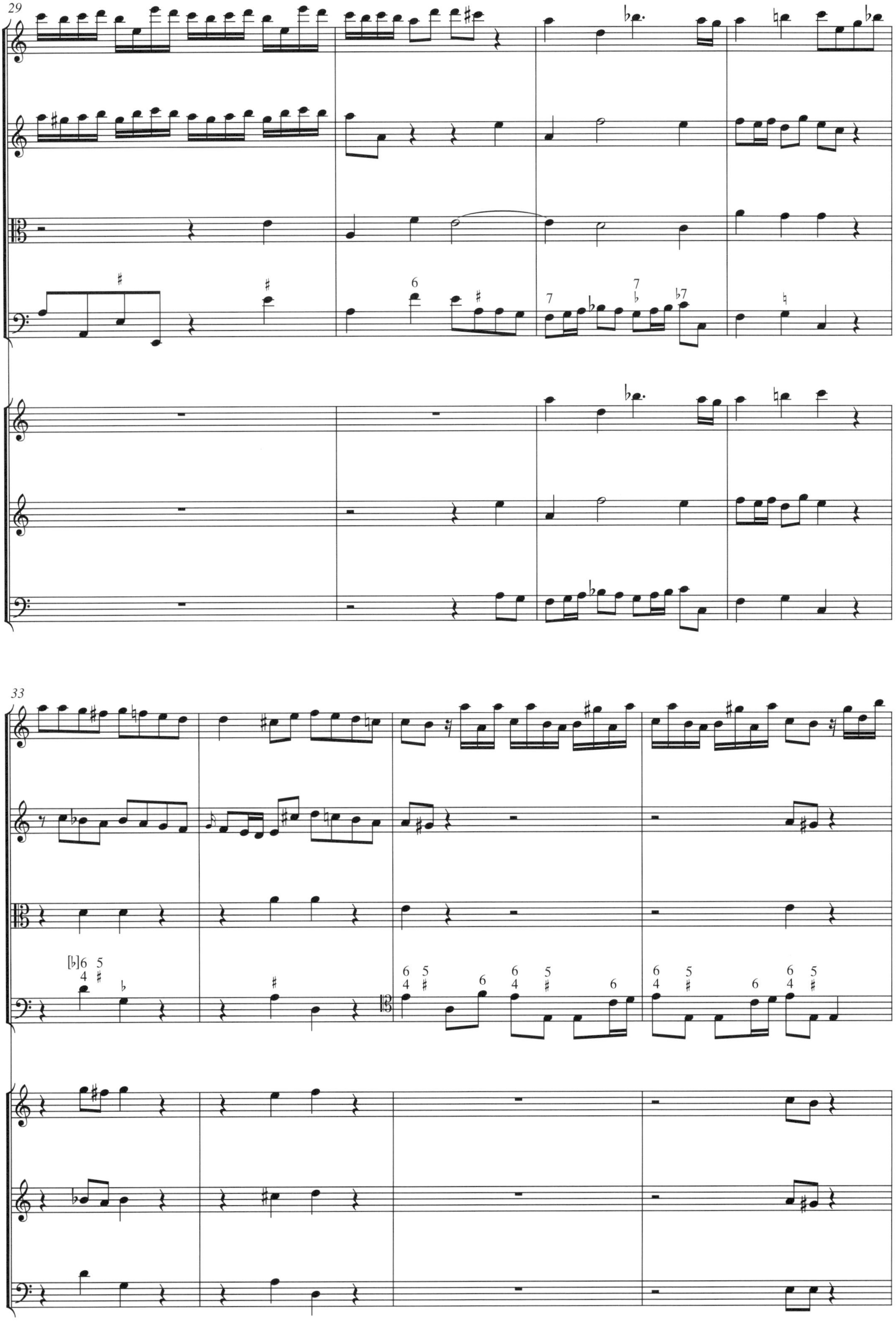

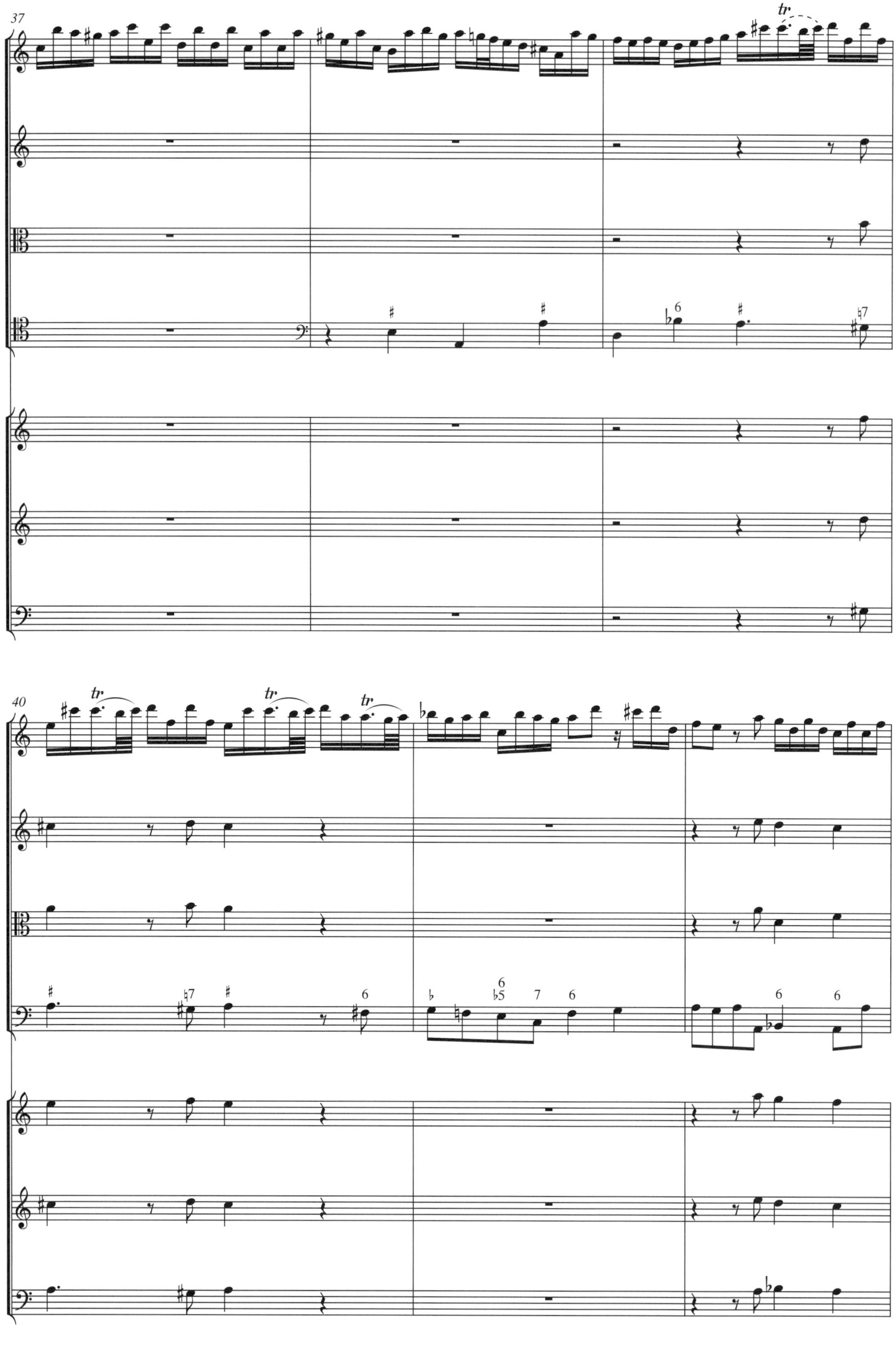
37
40

III

34

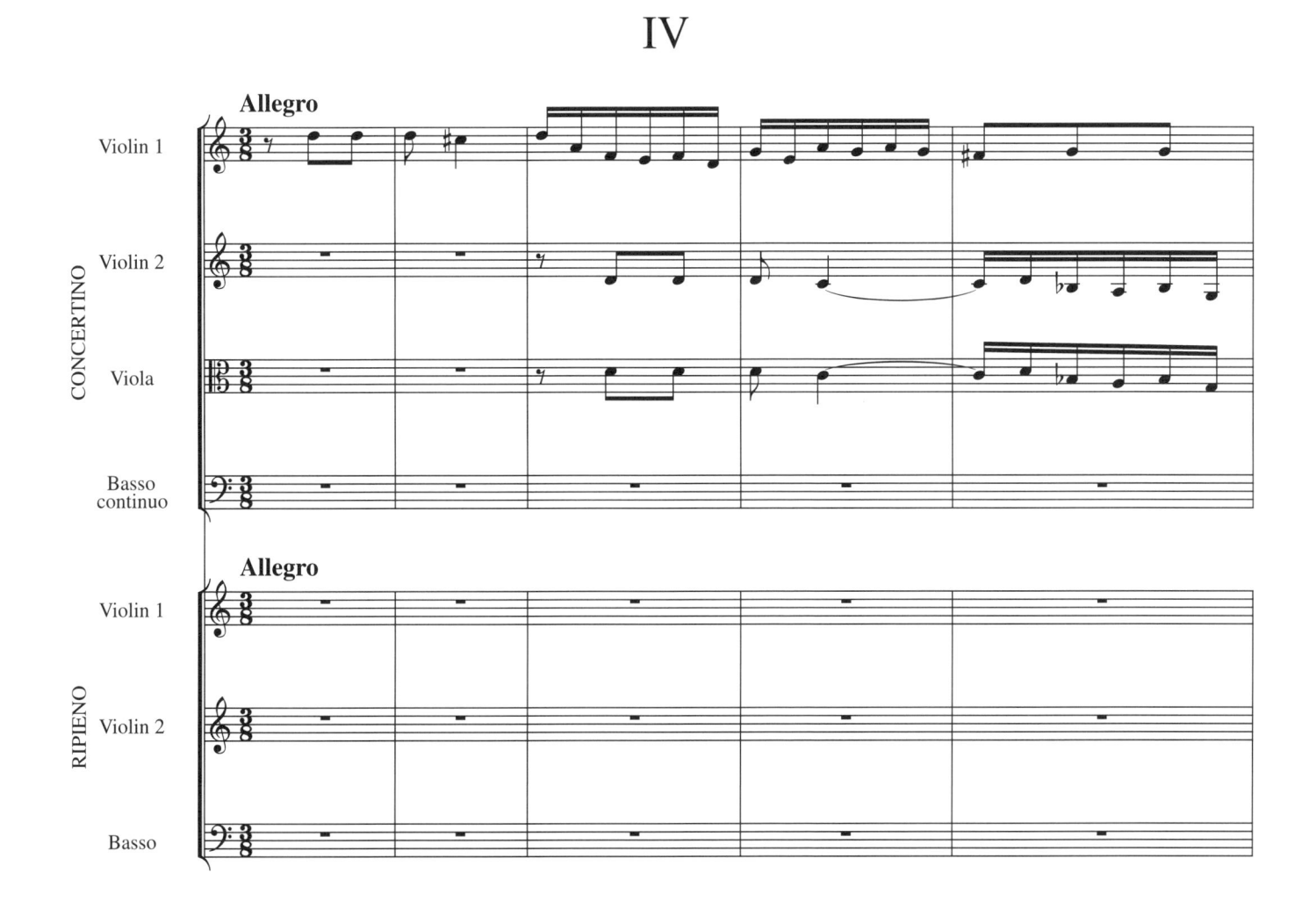

IV

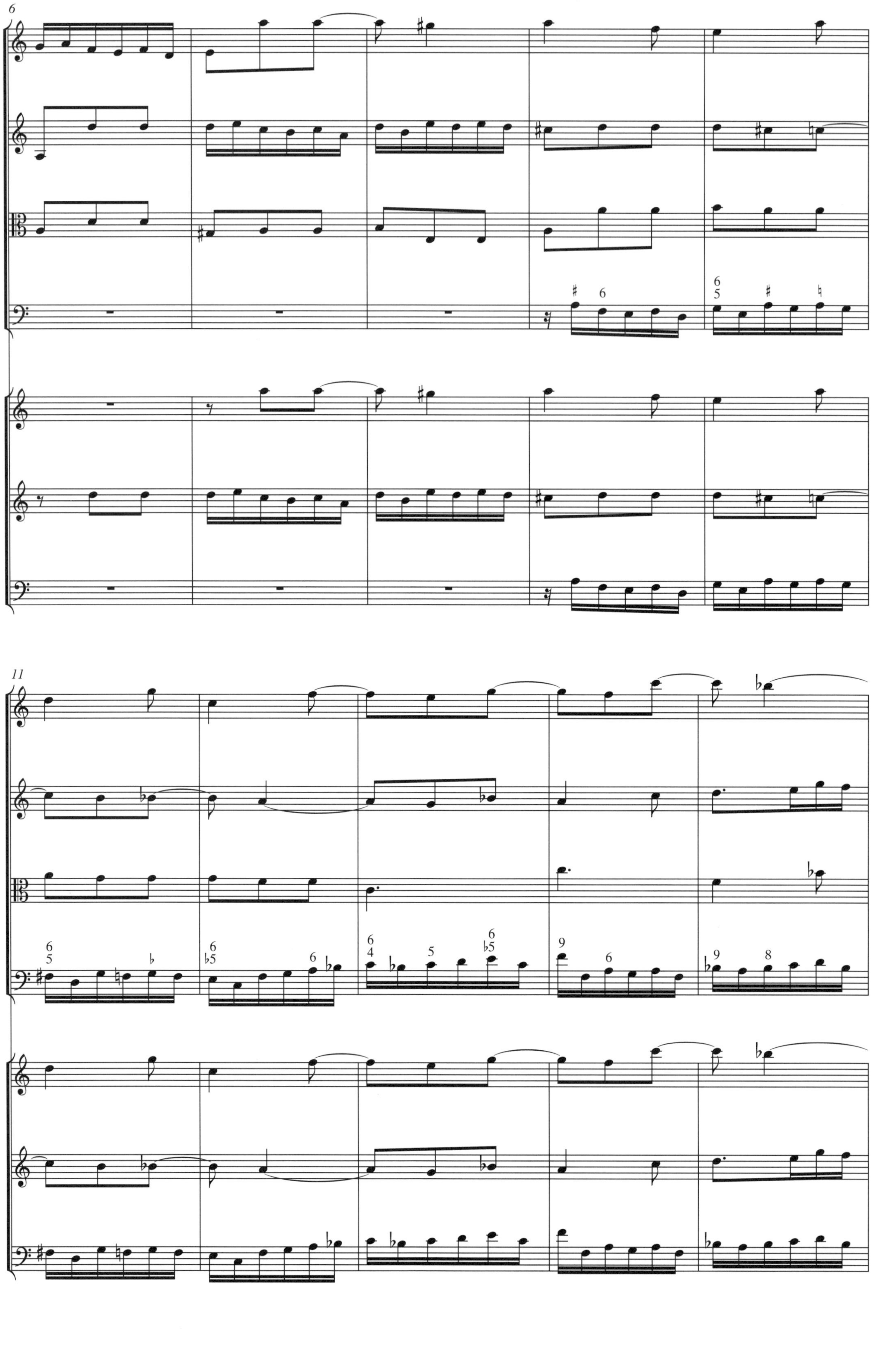
6
11

37

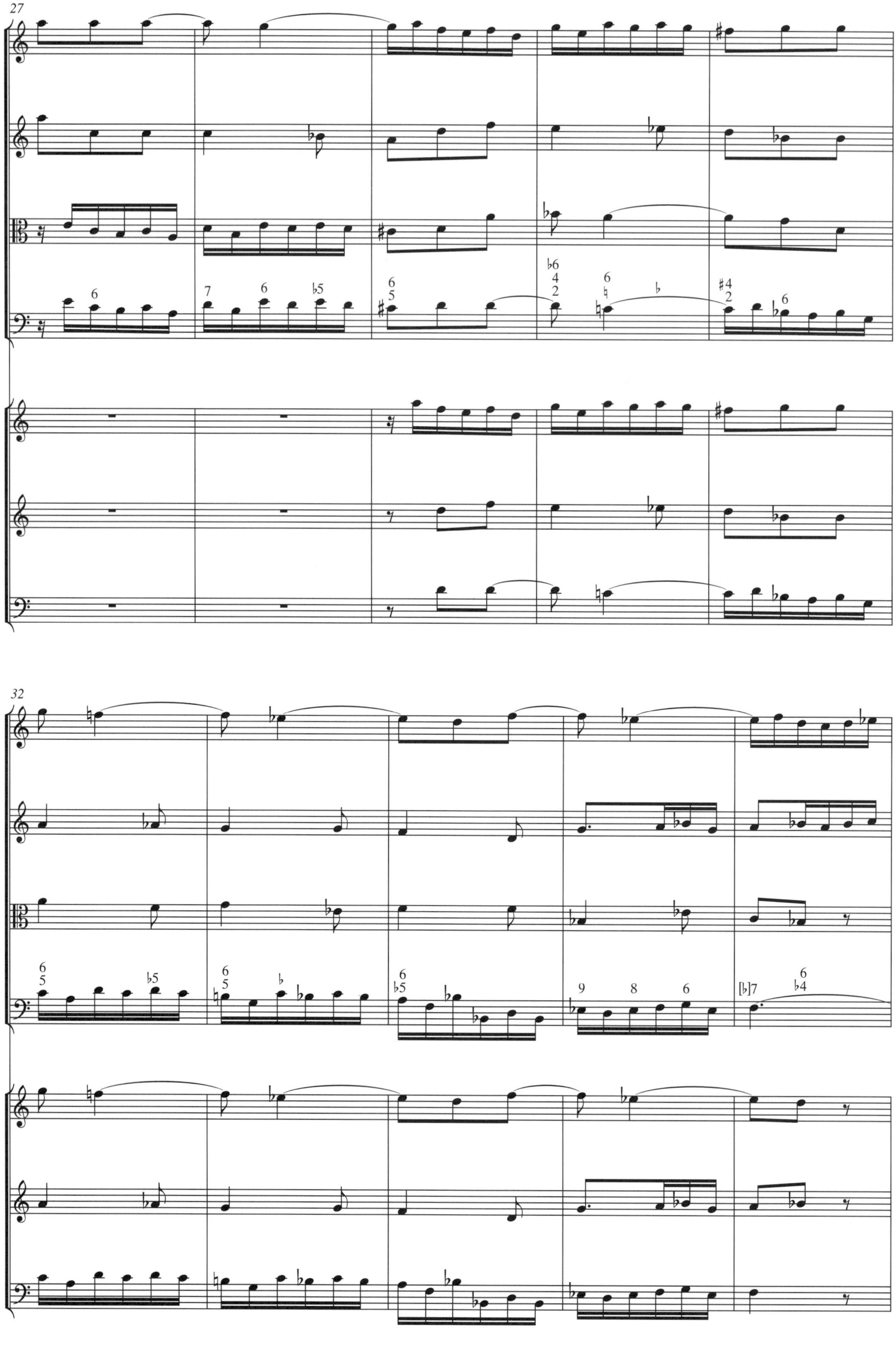
27
32

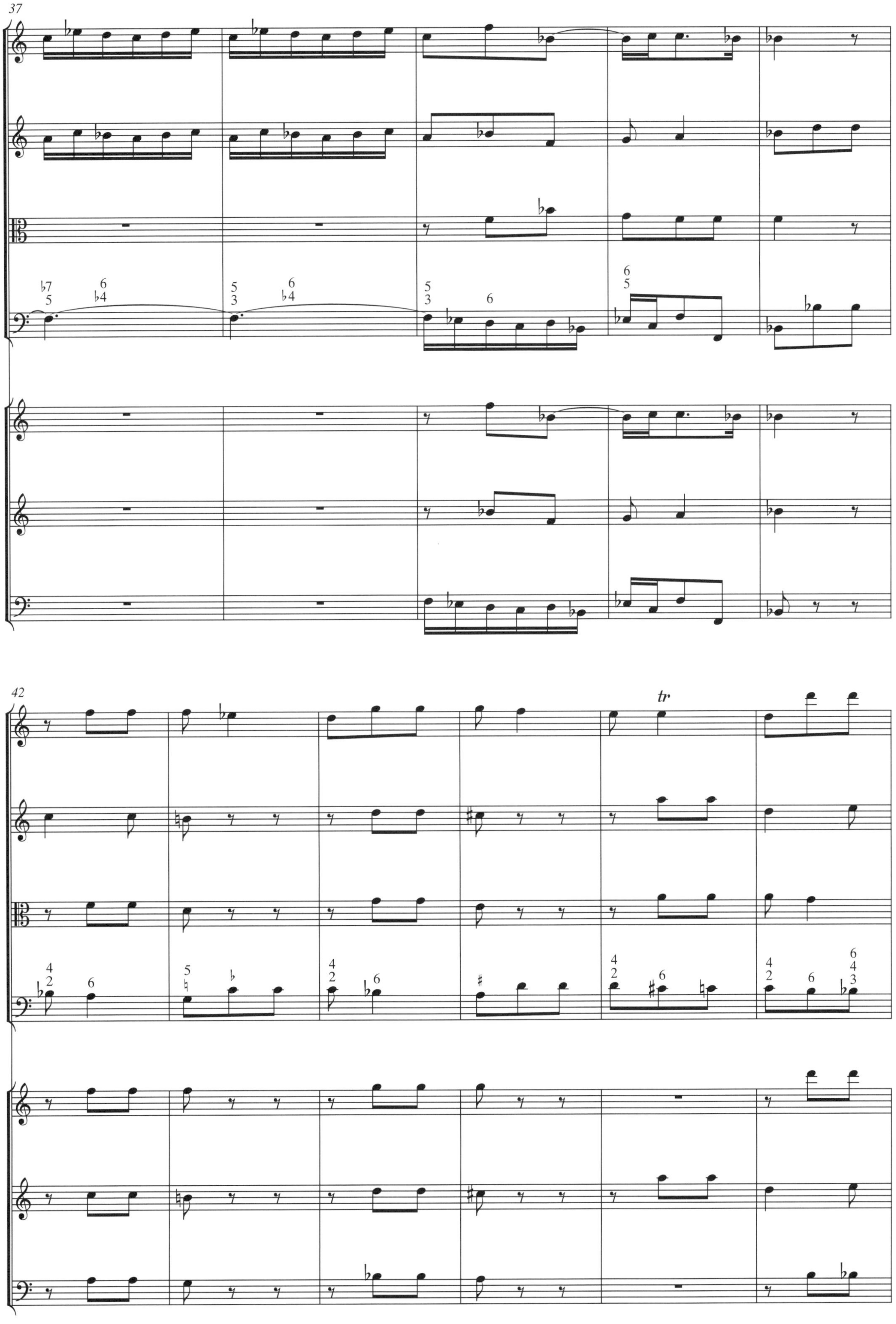
37
42
tr

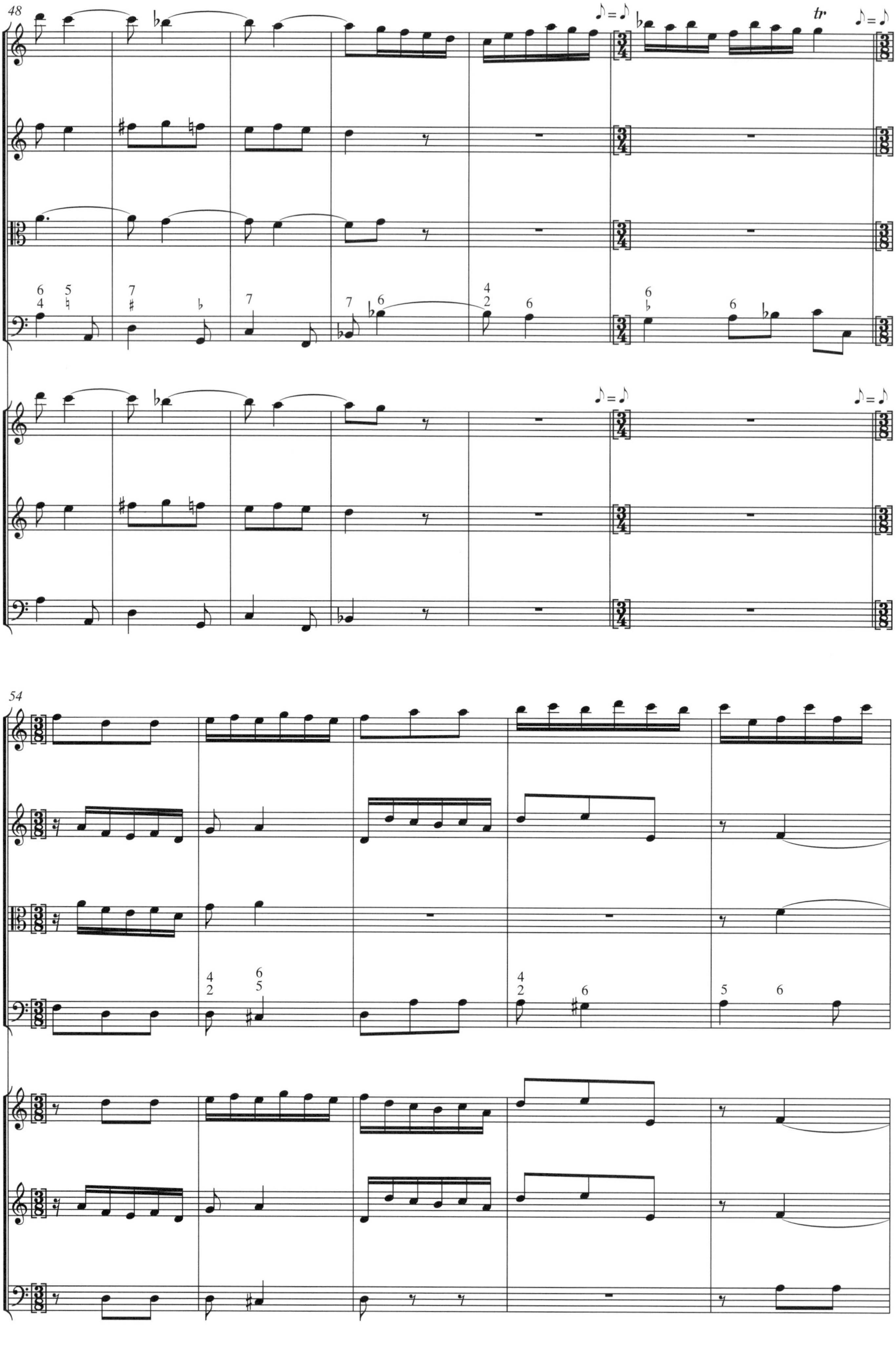
48
tr
54

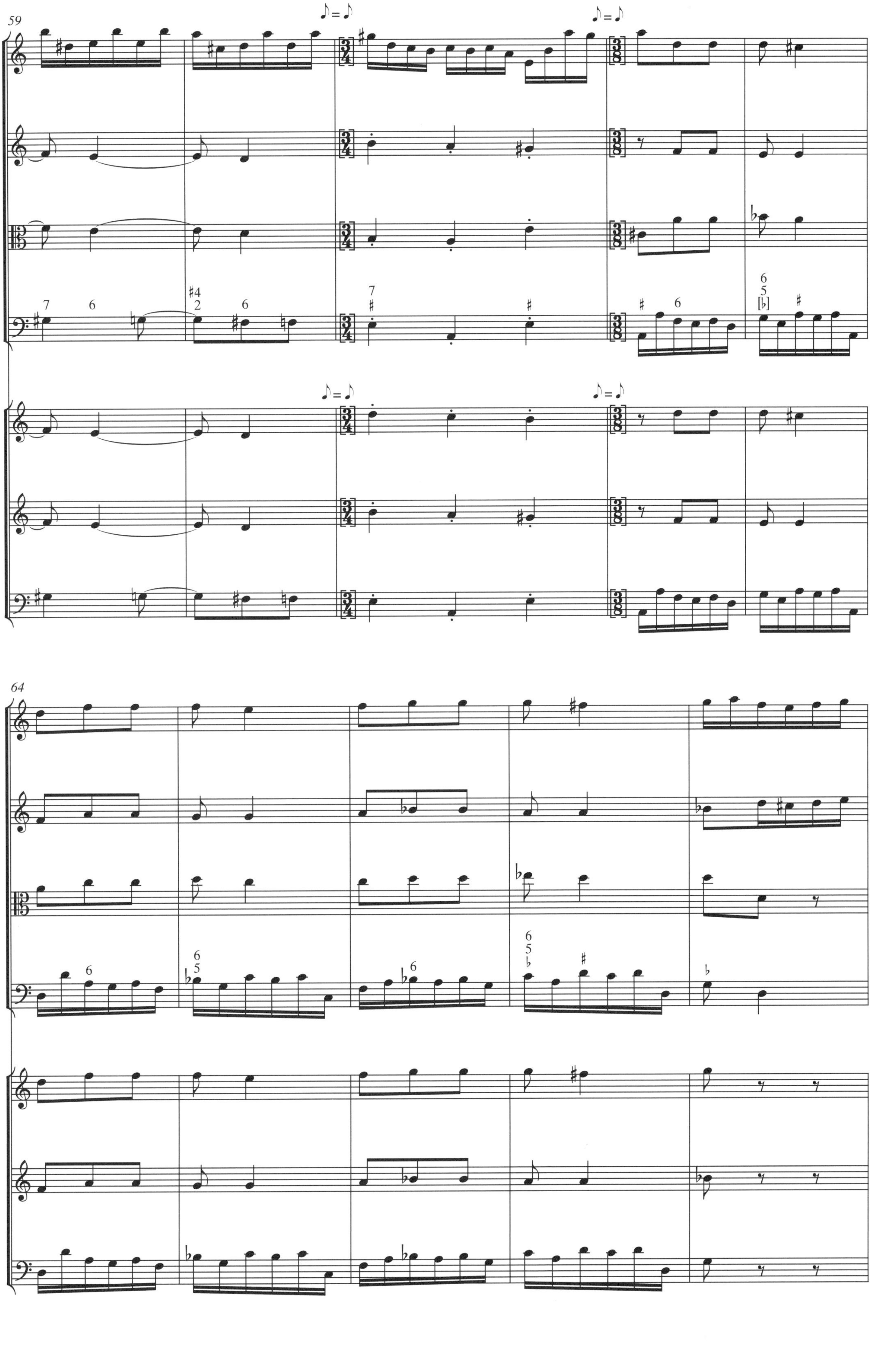
59
64

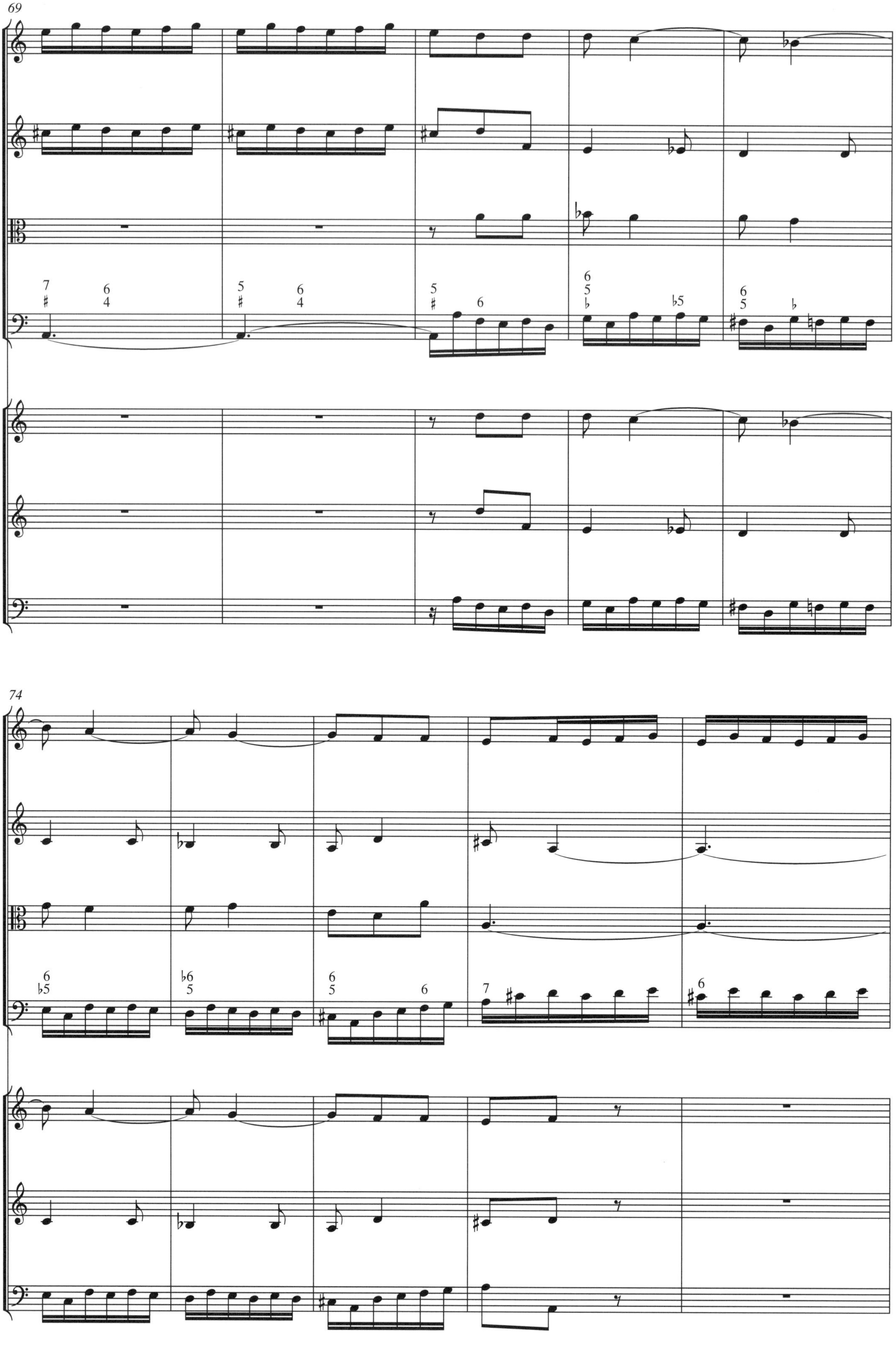
69
74

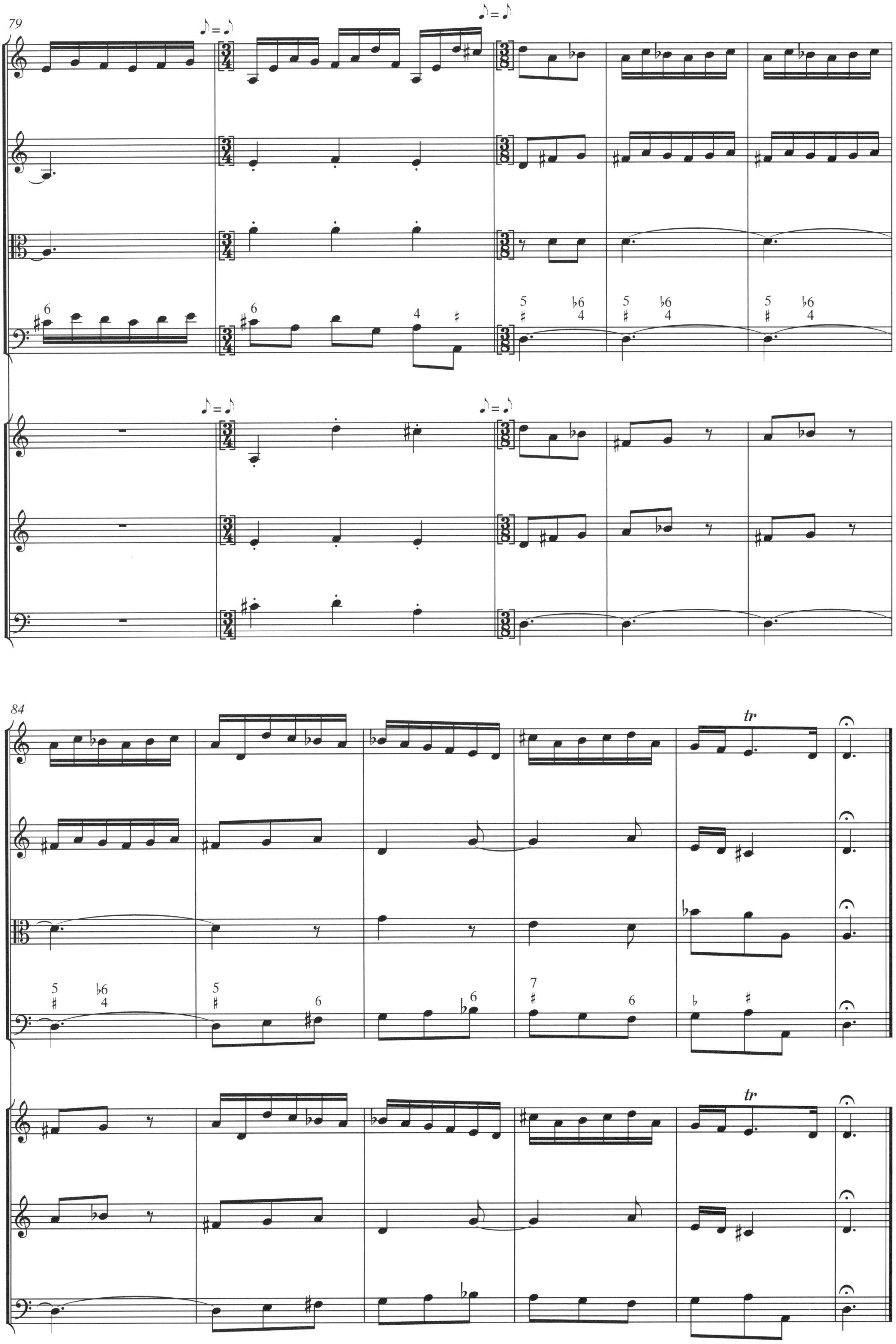

3. Concerto in E Minor
I

From Francesco Geminiani, Sonata in E Minor, Op. 1, No. 3

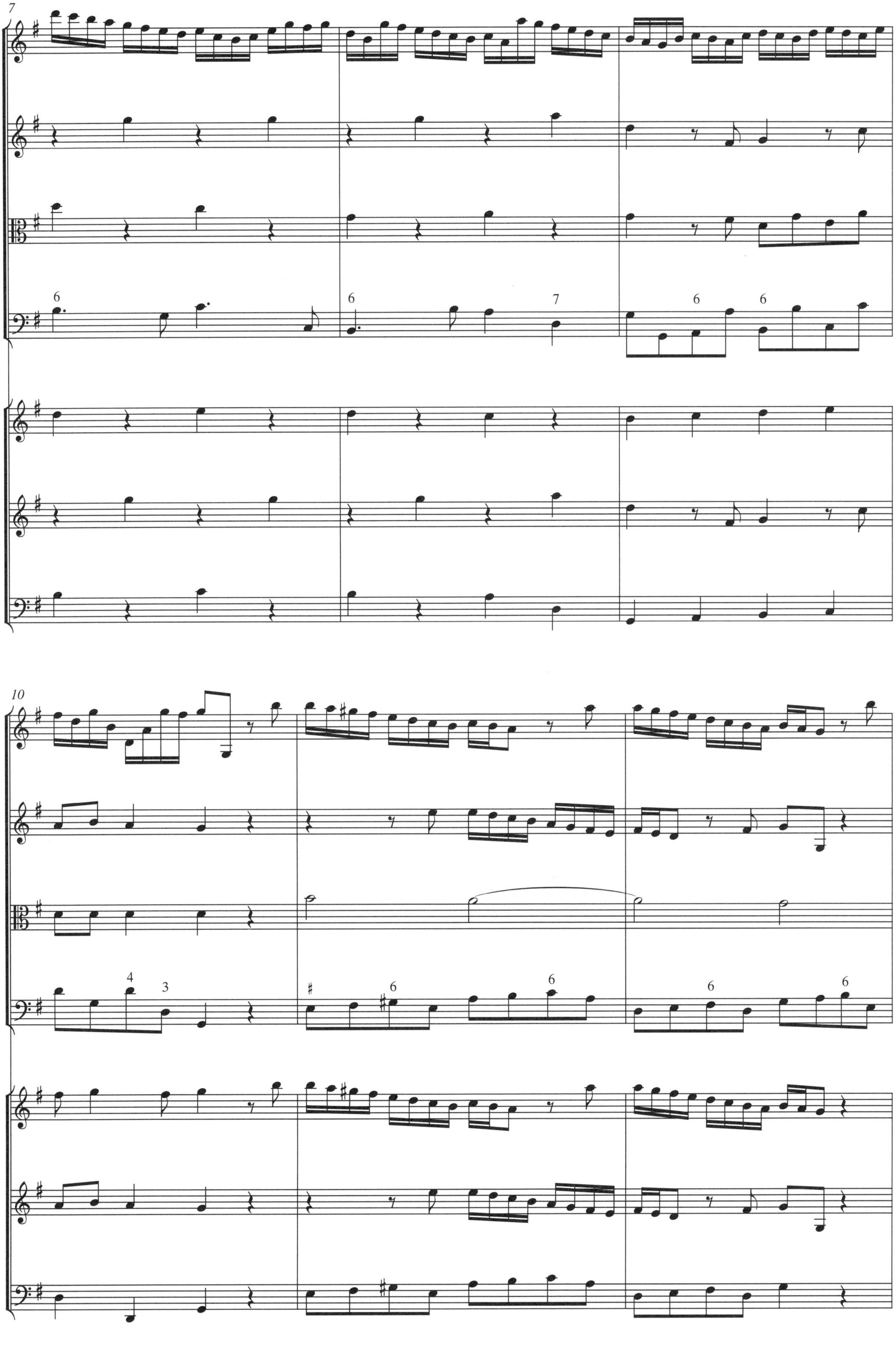

46

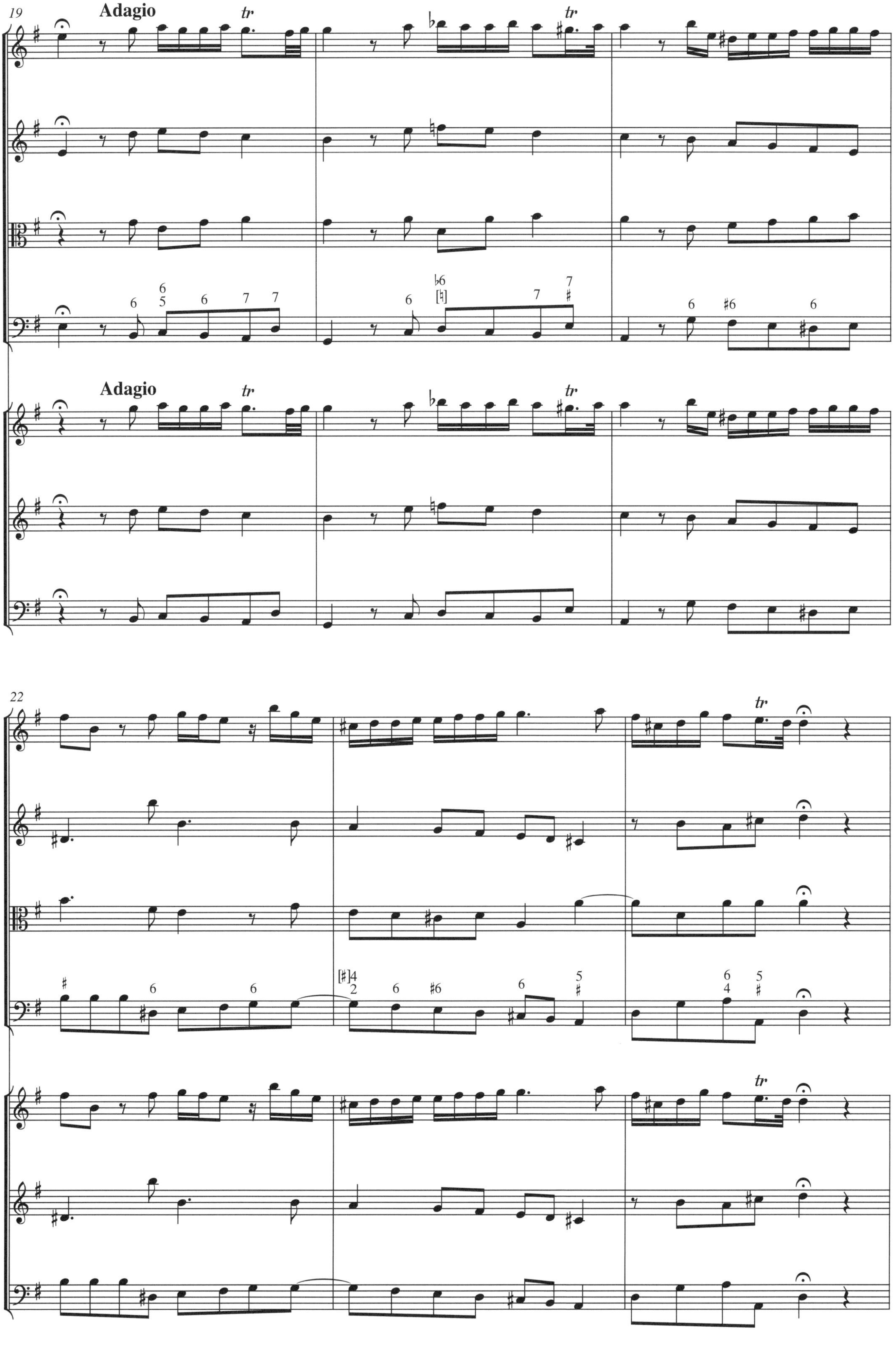
19
Adagio
tr
tr
Adagio
tr
tr
22
tr
tr

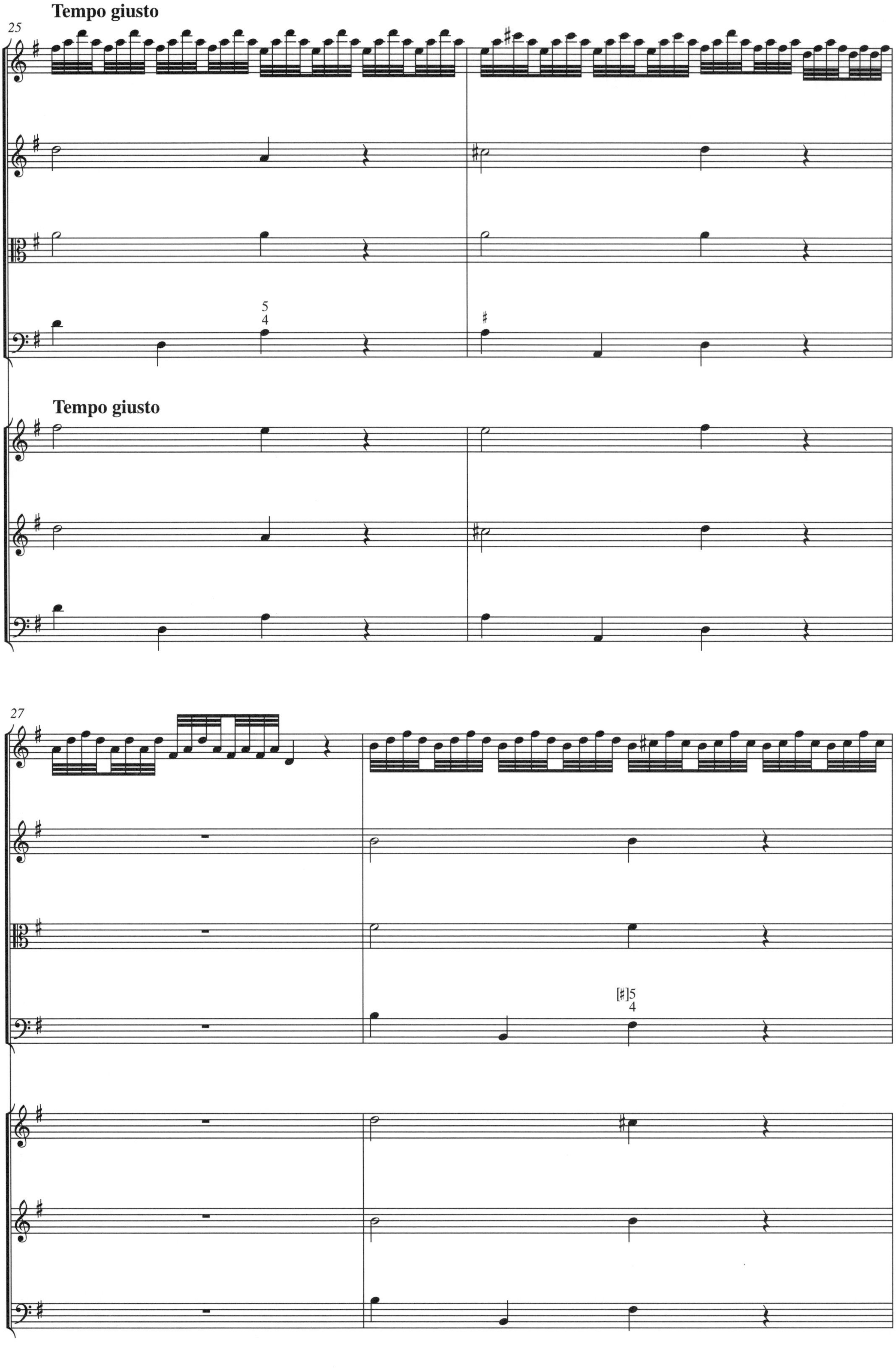
Tempo giusto
25
5
4
♯
Tempo giusto
27
[♯]5
4

49

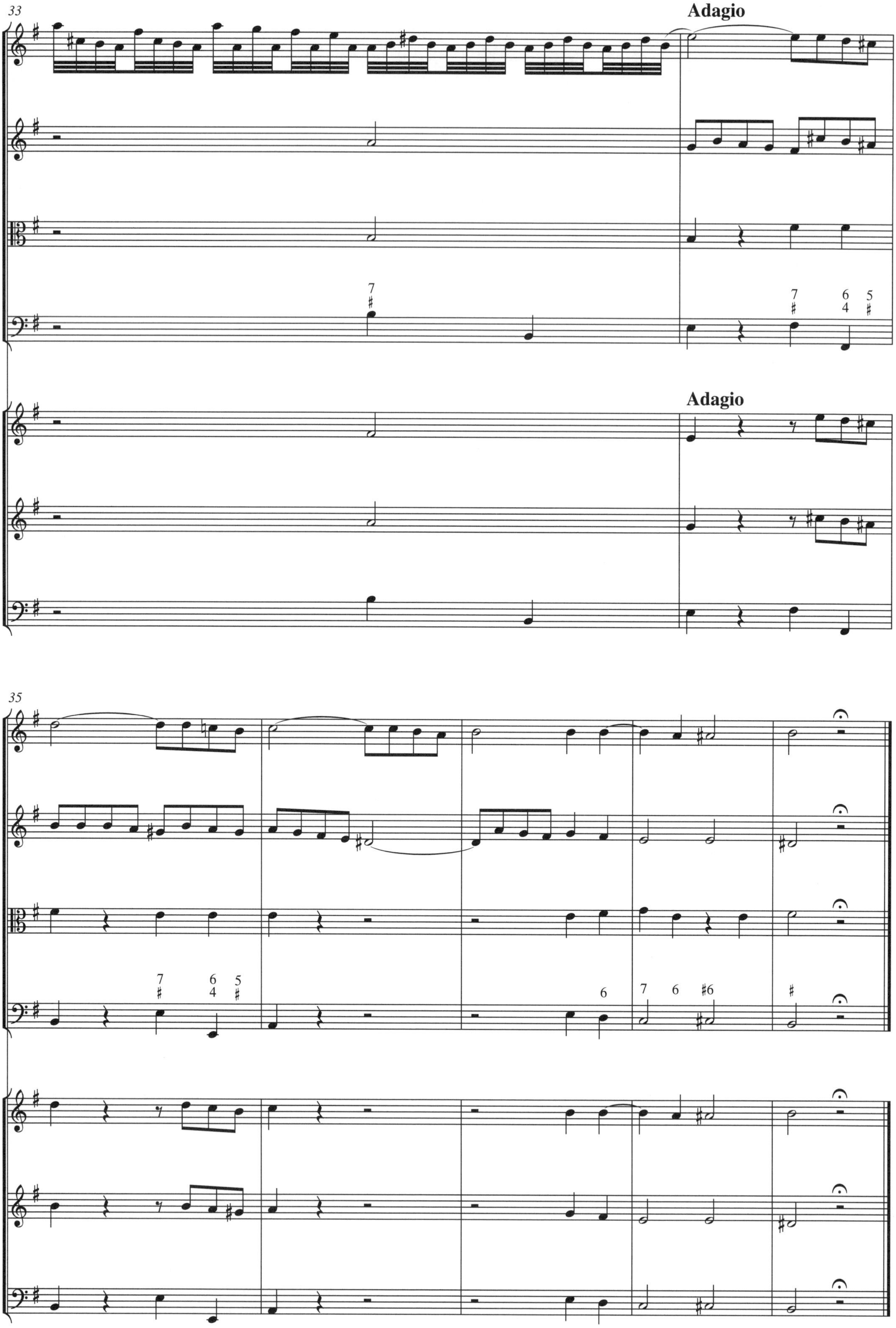
33
Adagio
Adagio
35

II

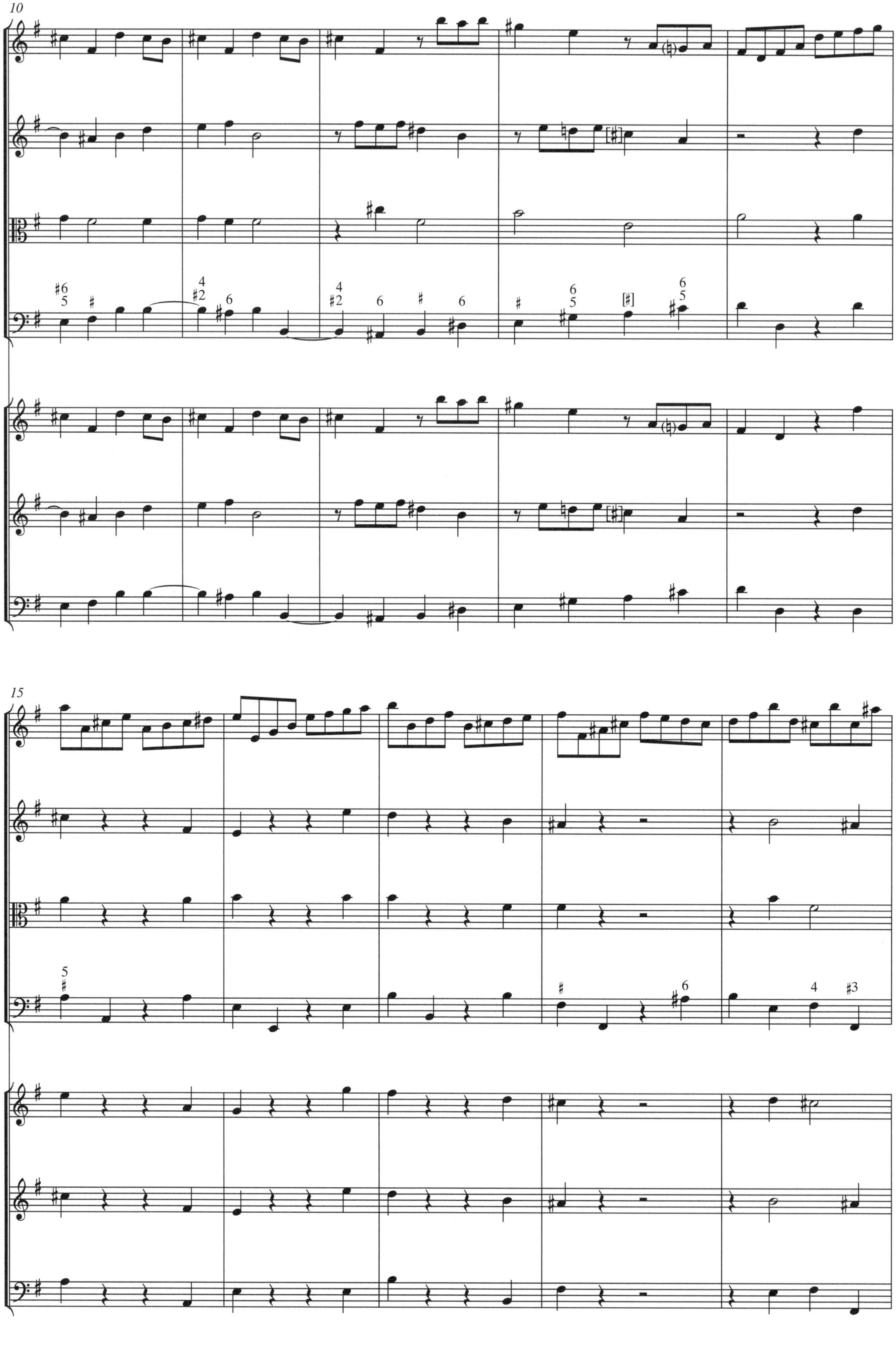
10
15

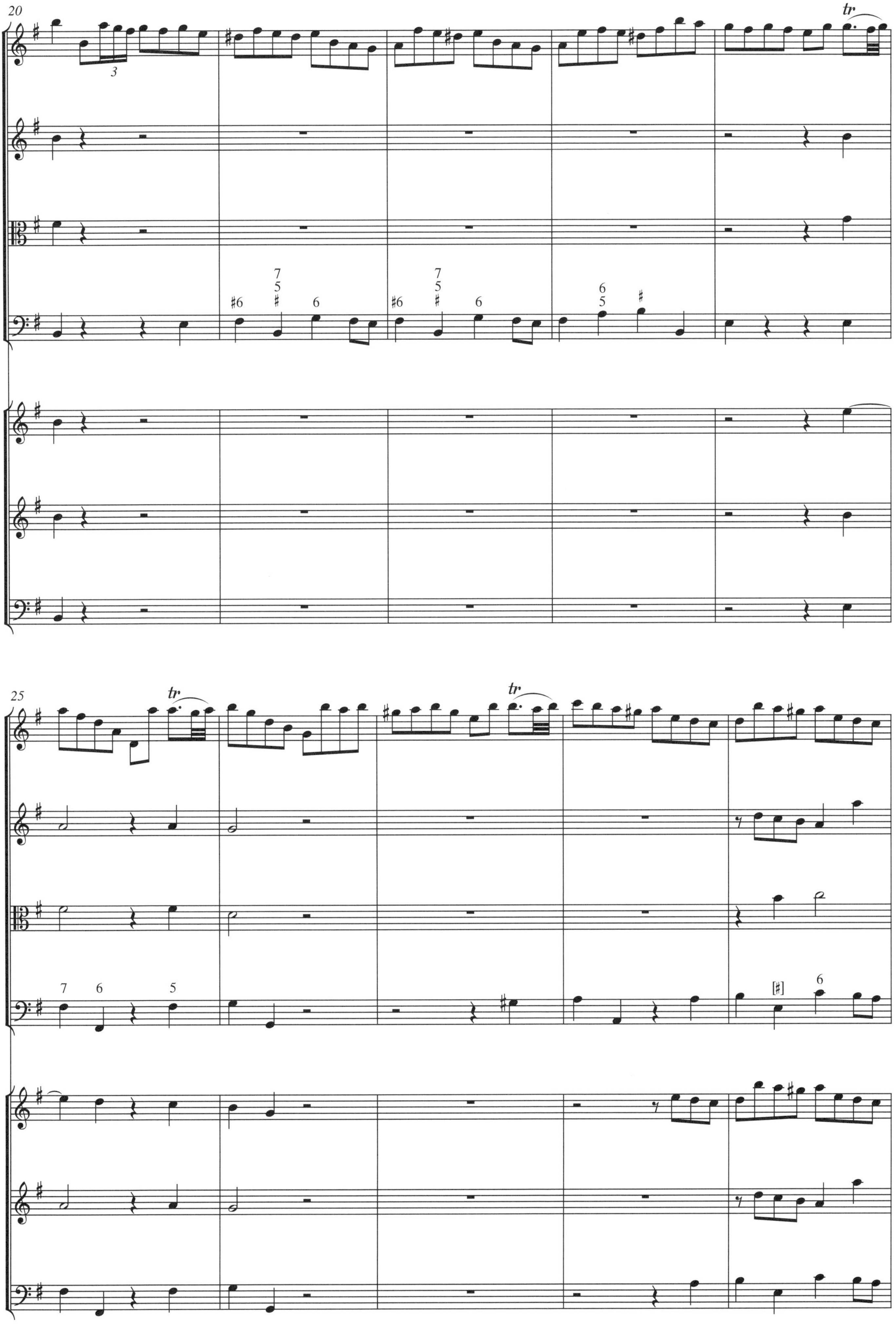
20
tr
25
tr
tr

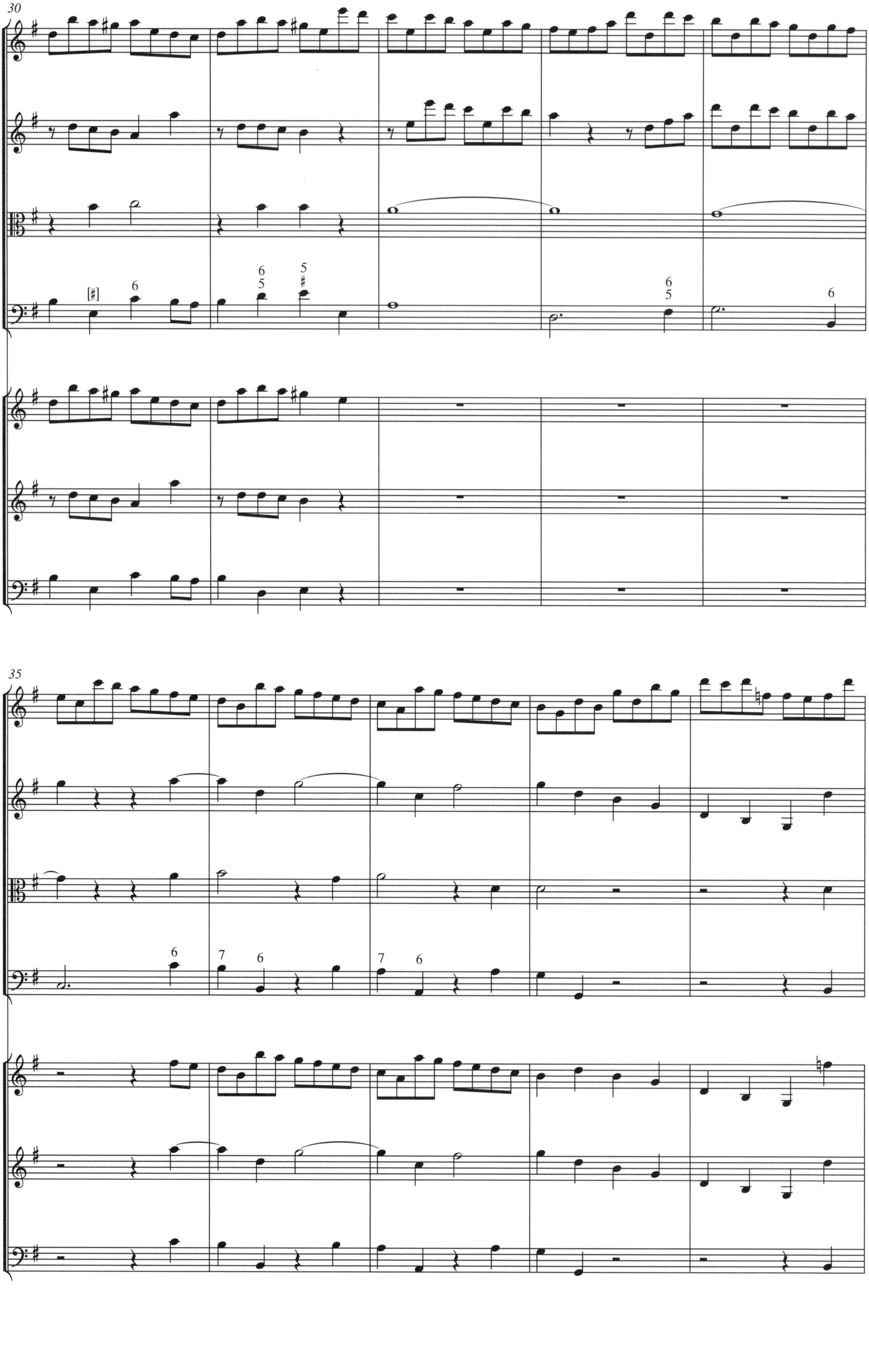
30
35

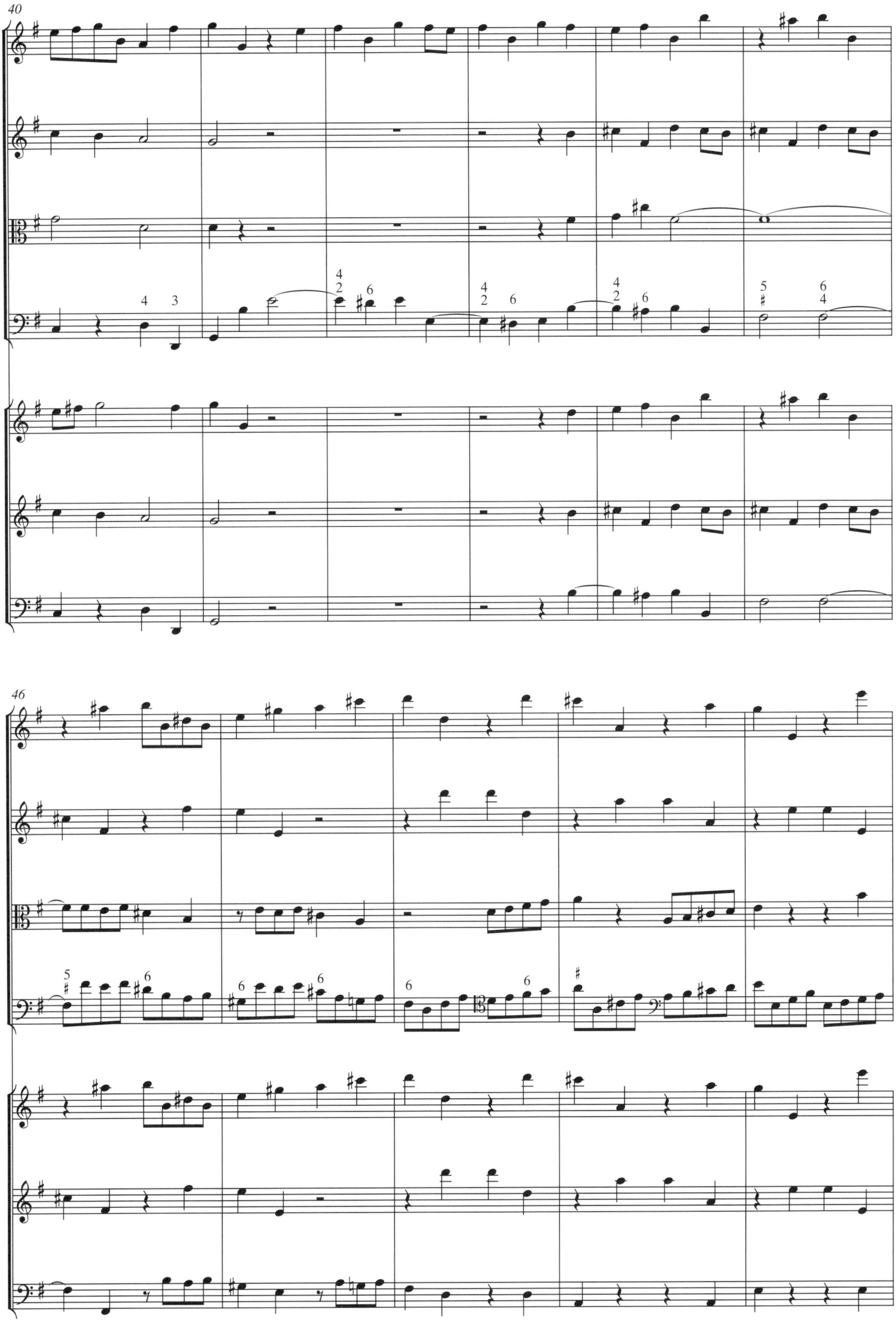
40
46

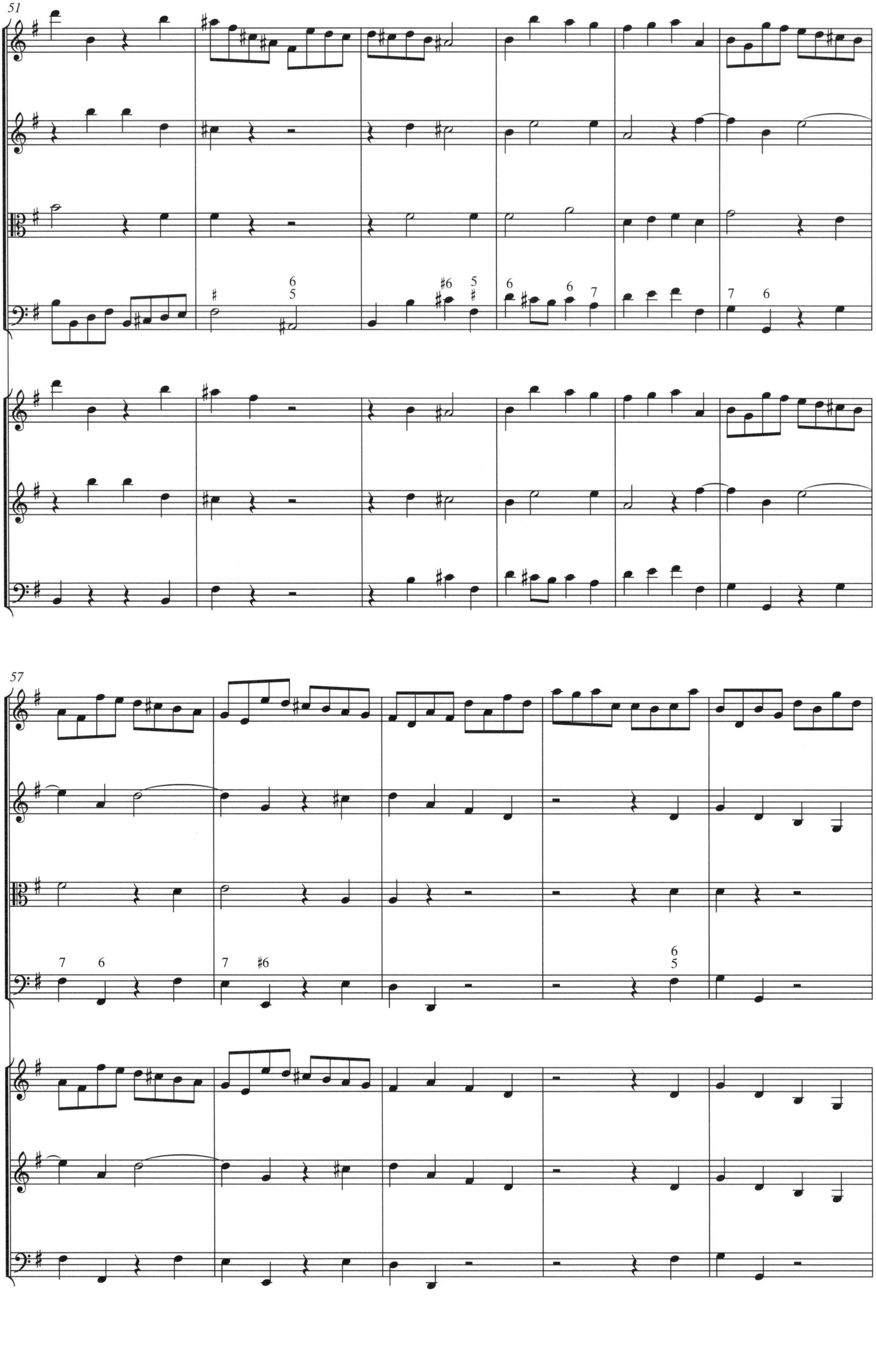
51
57

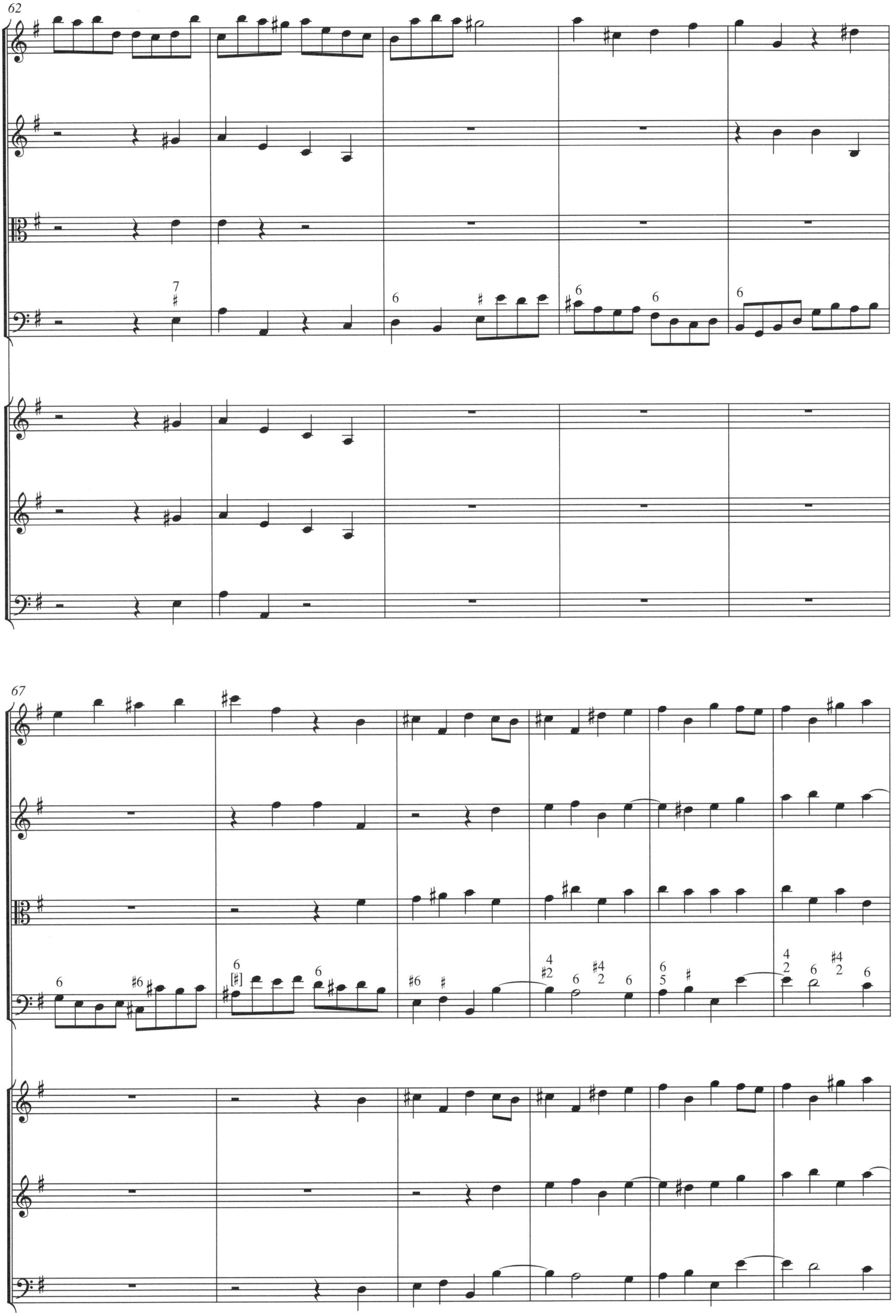
62
67

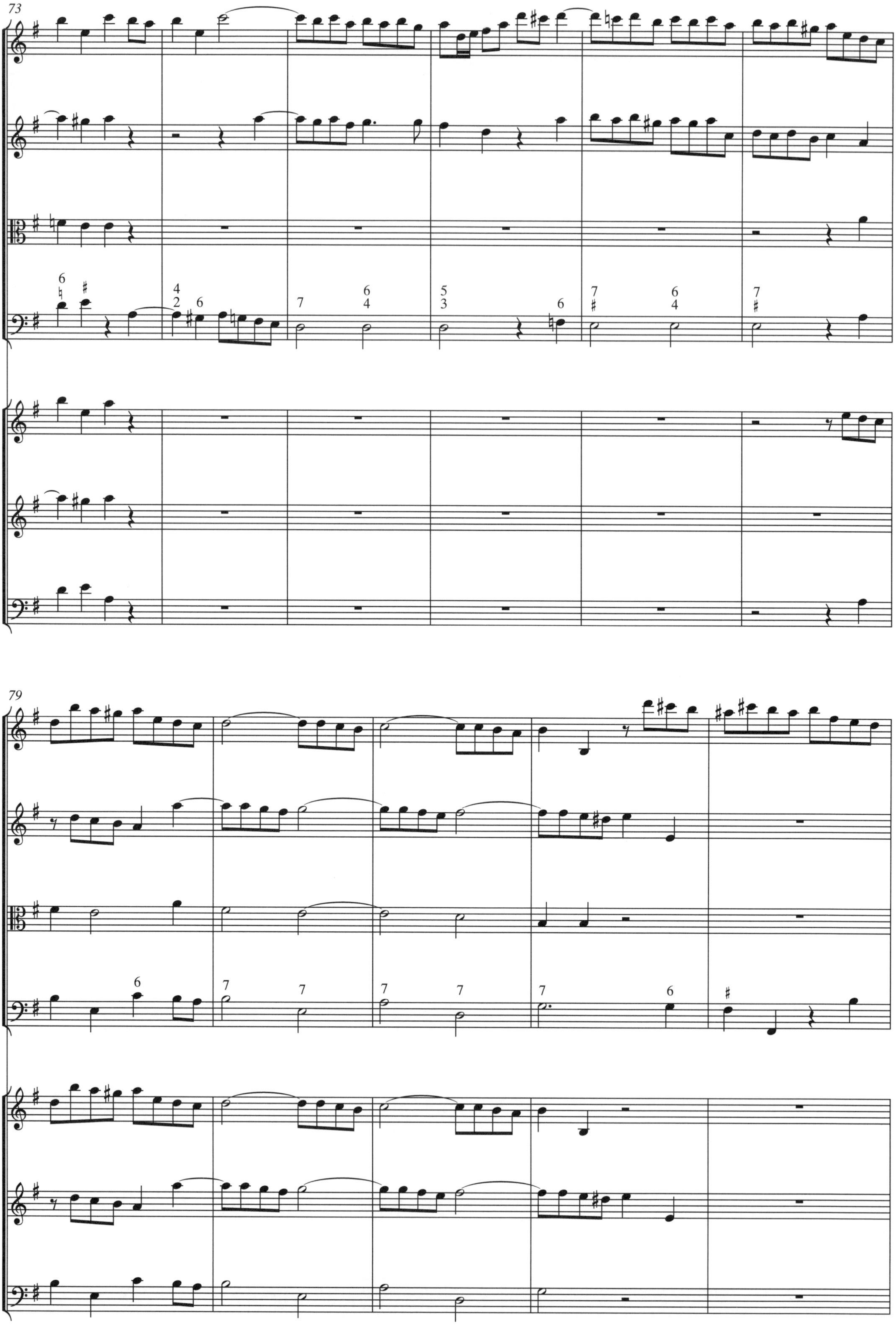
73
79

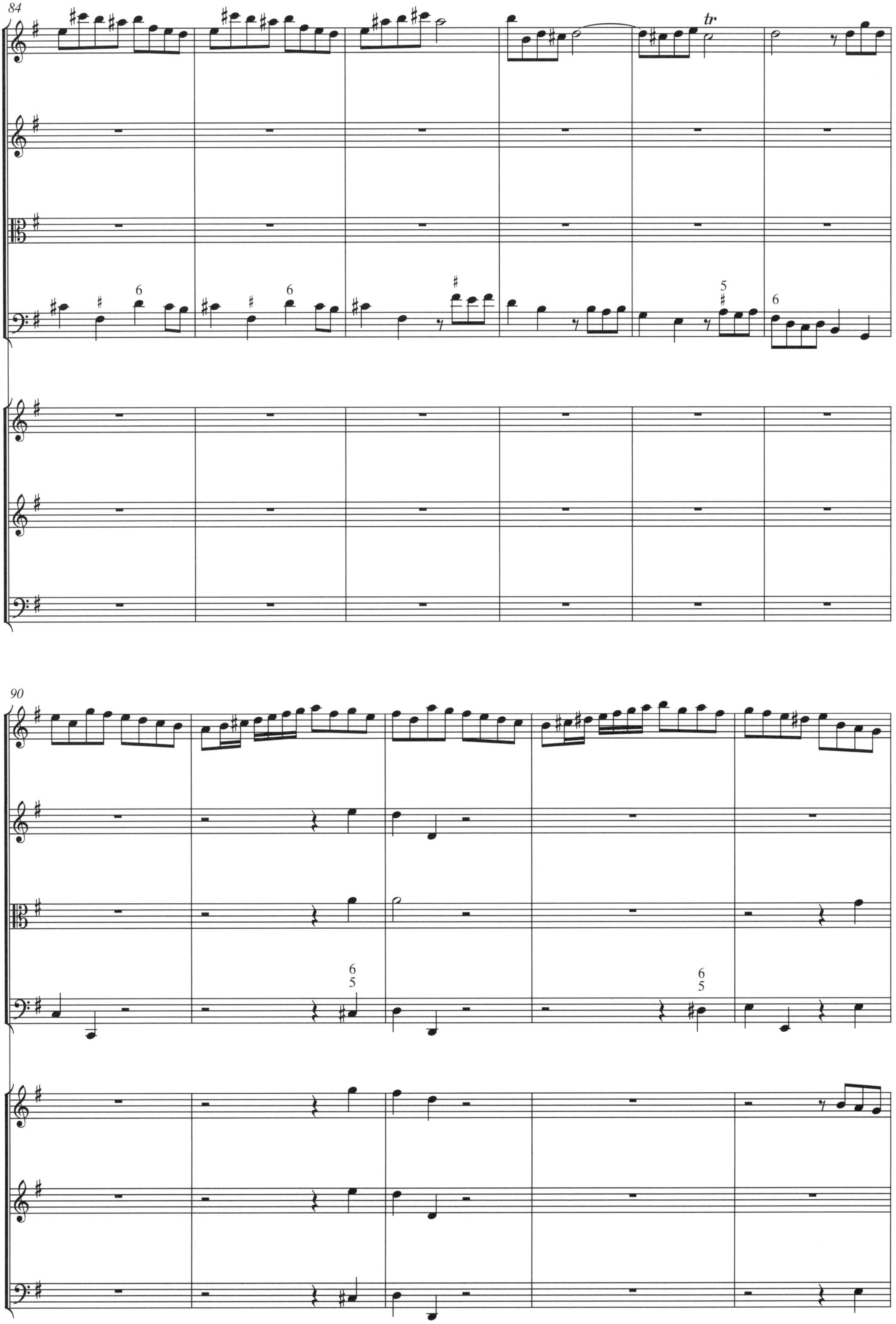
84
tr
90

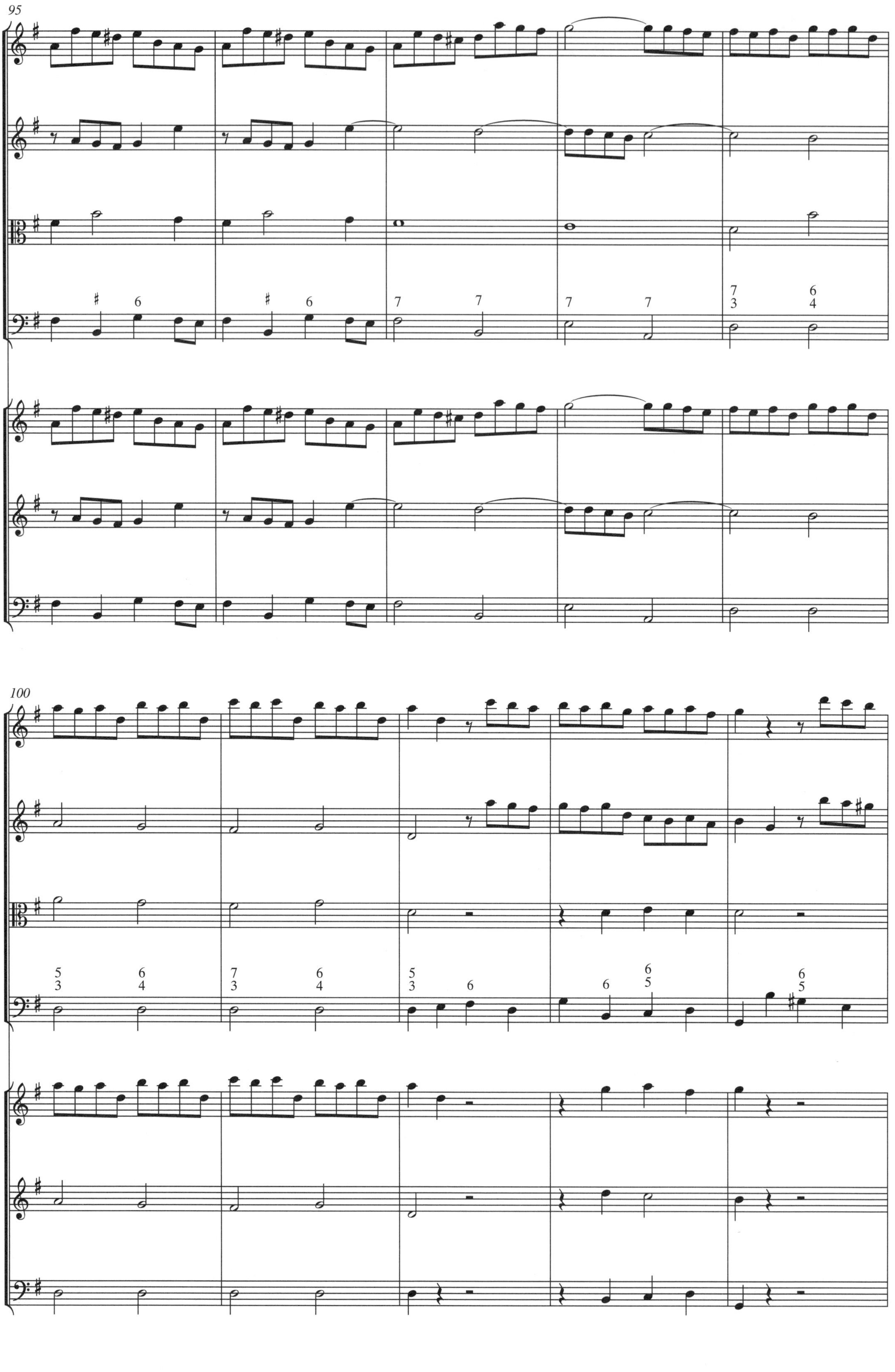
95
100

61

4. Concerto in D Major

I

From Francesco Geminiani, Sonata in D Major, Op. 1, No. 4

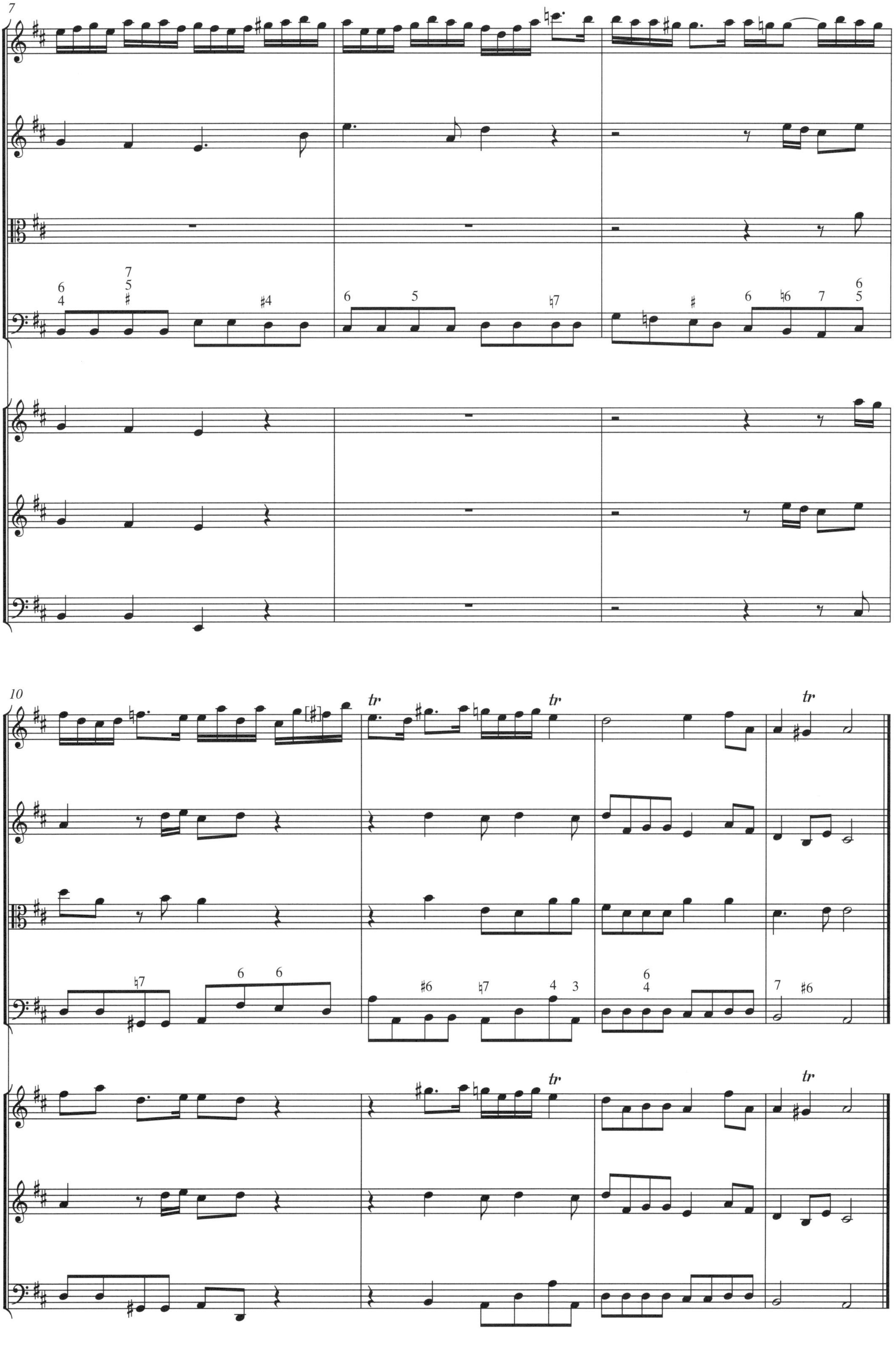
7
10

II

65

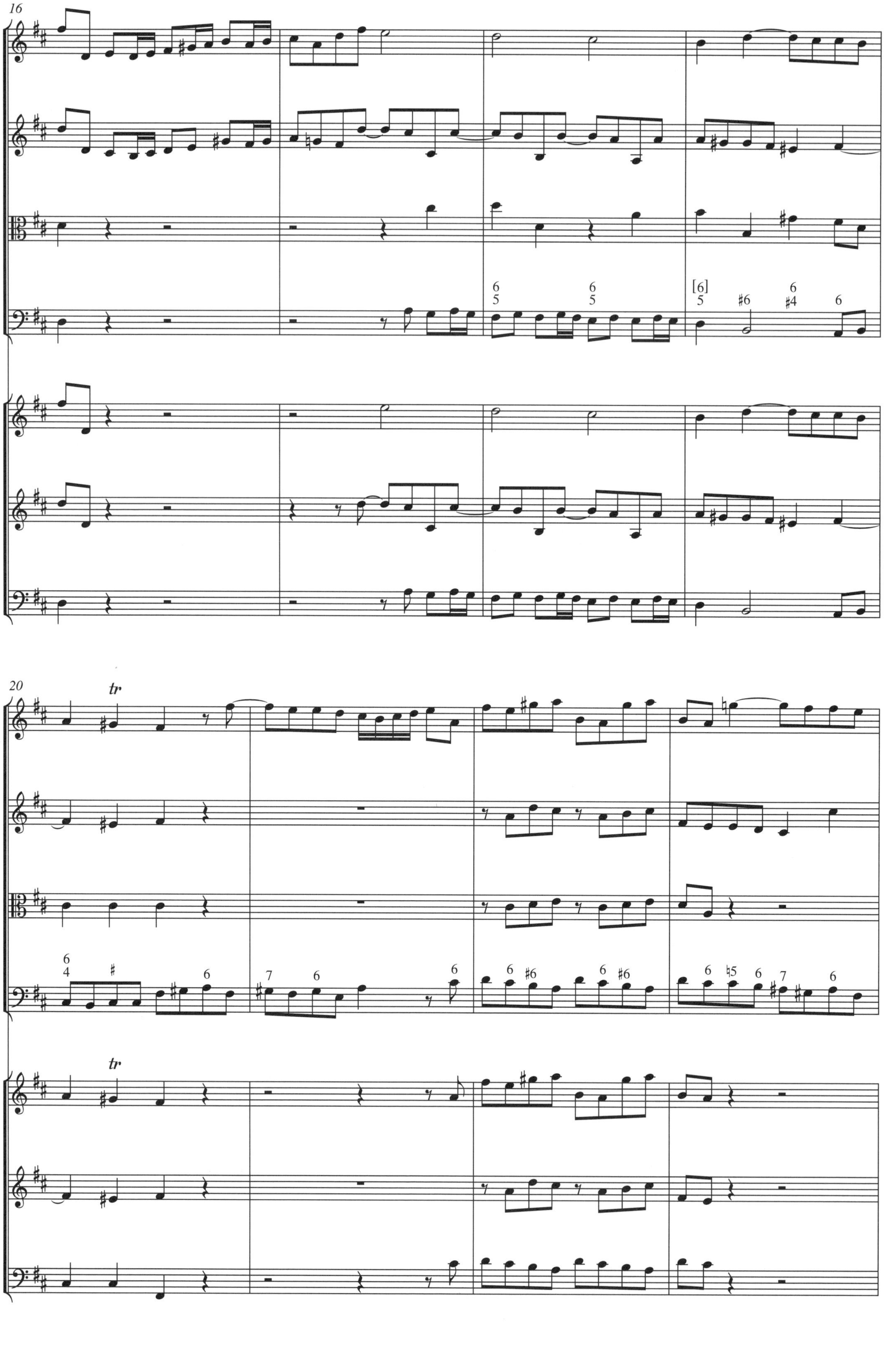
16
20
tr
tr

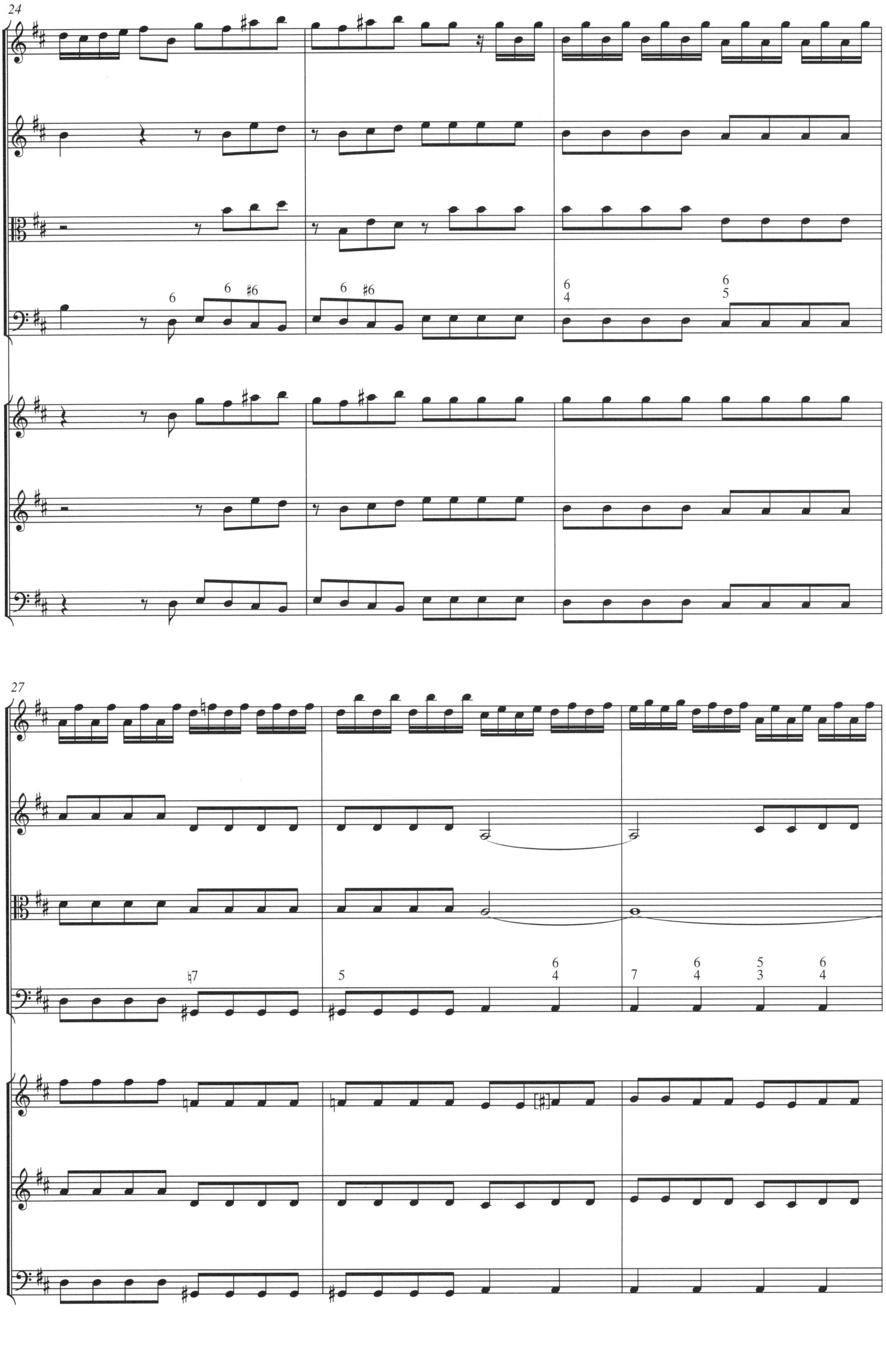

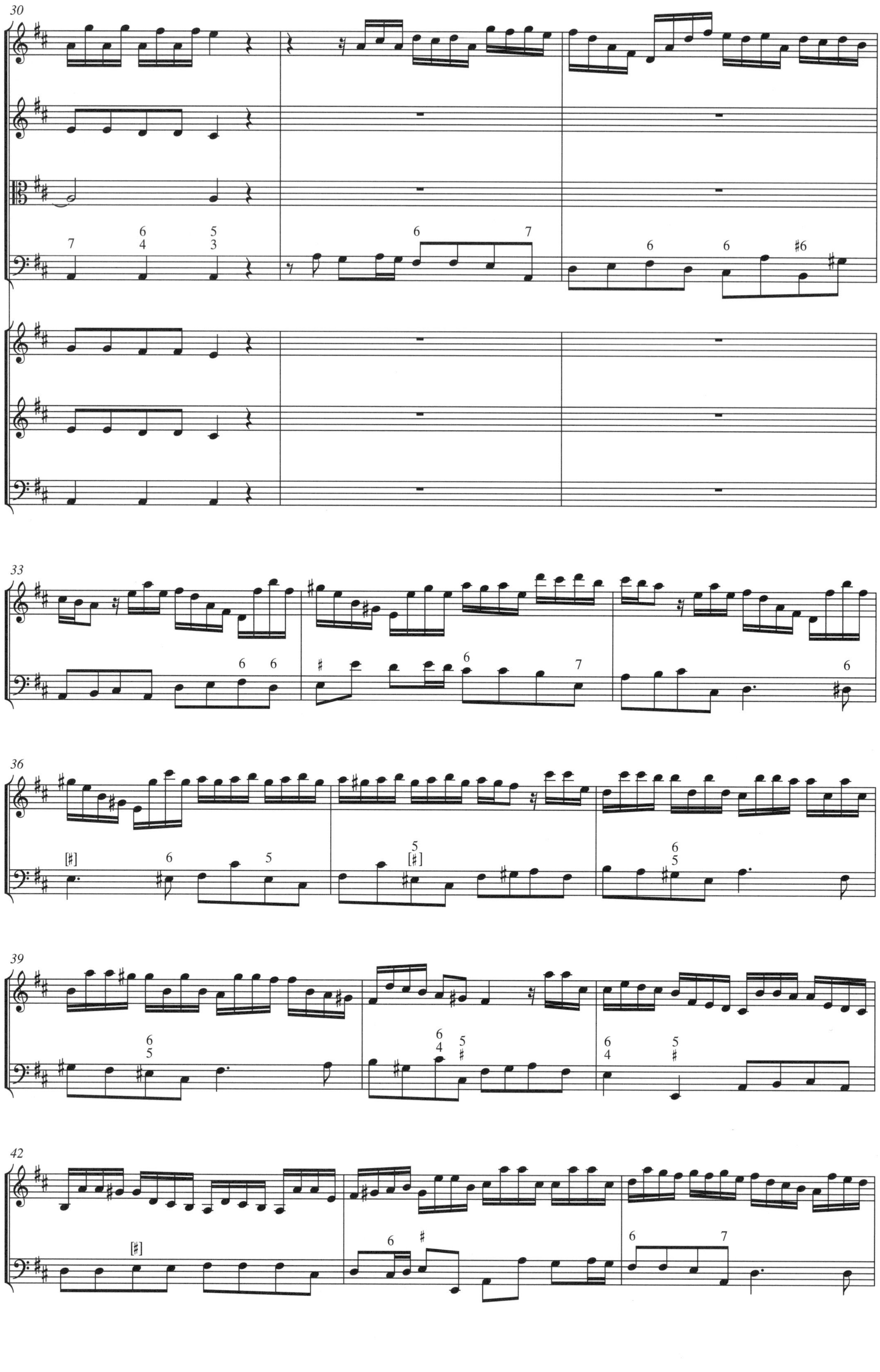
30
33
CONCERTINO
Vn. 1
B.c.
36
39
42

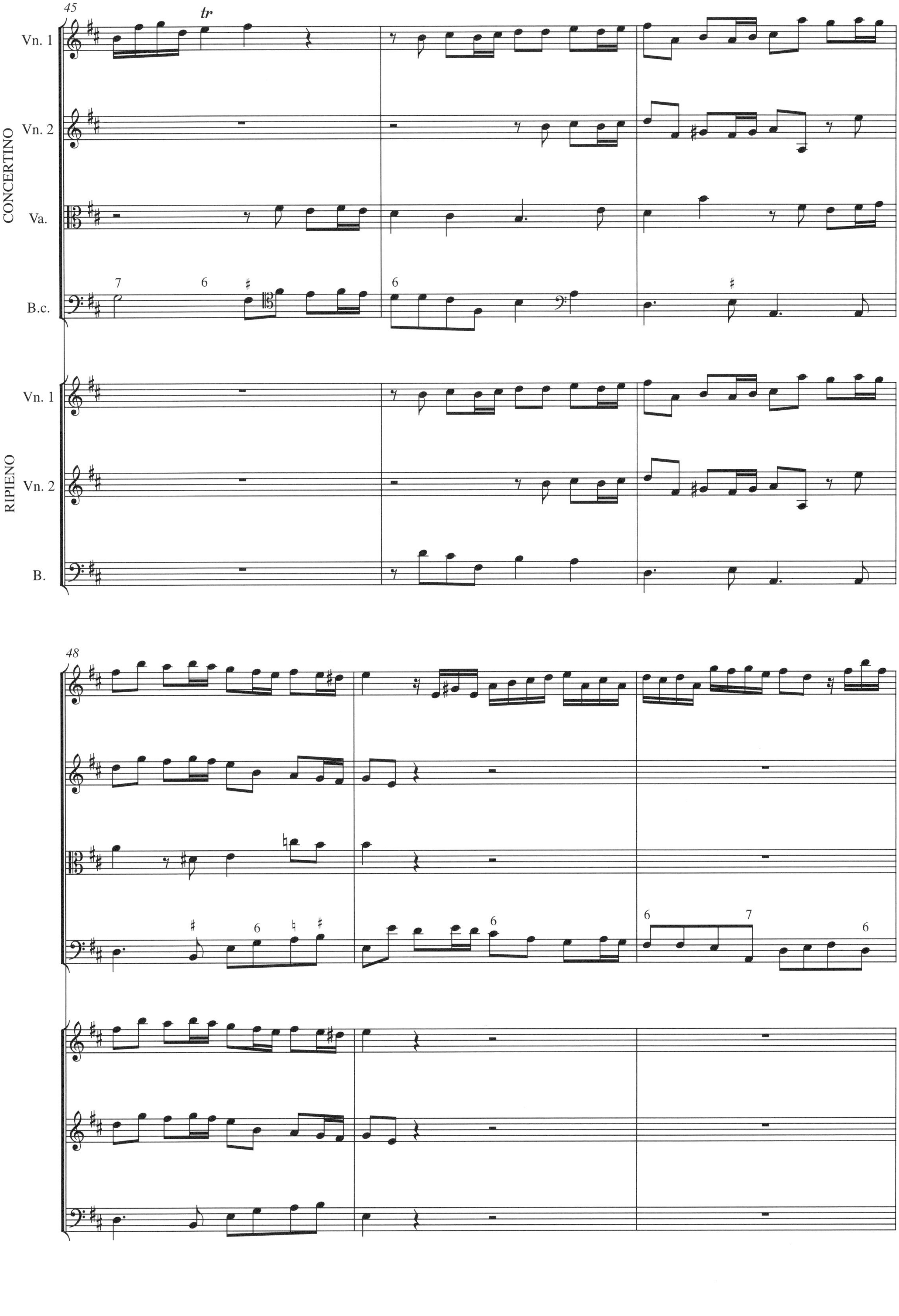
45
Vn. 1
Vn. 2
Va.
B.c.
CONCERTINO
Vn. 1
Vn. 2
B.
RIPIENO
48

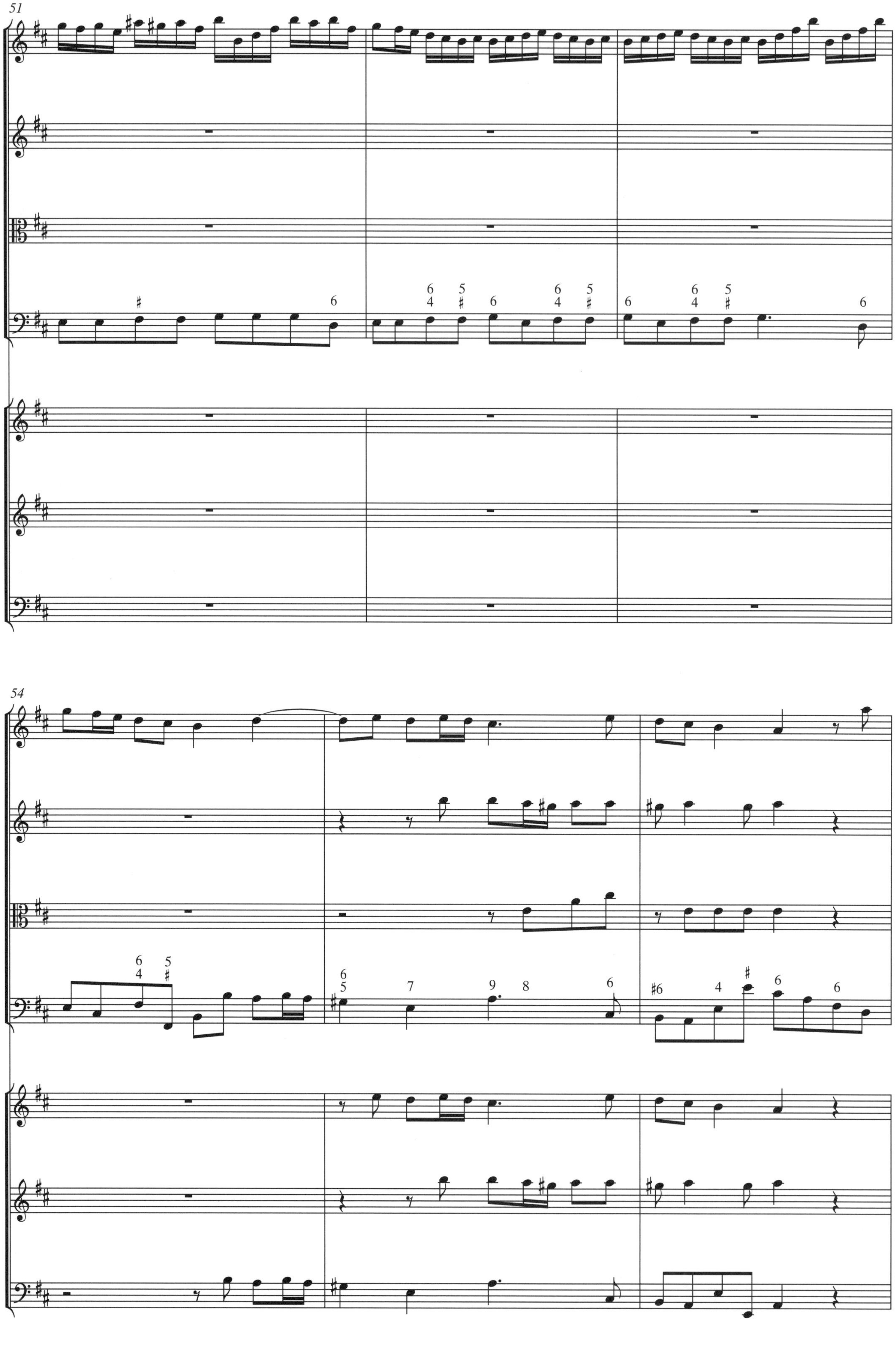
51
54

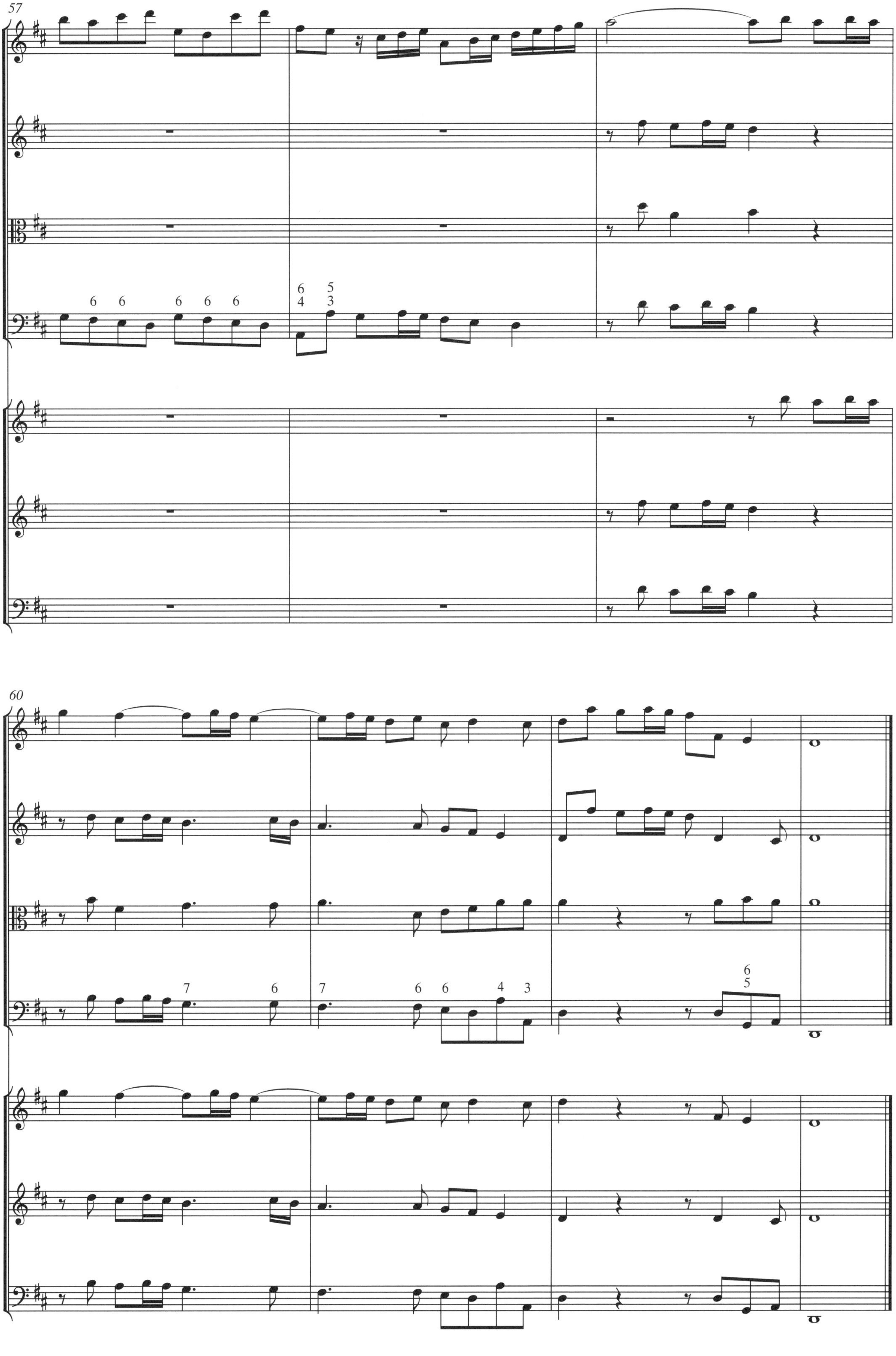
57
60

III

IV

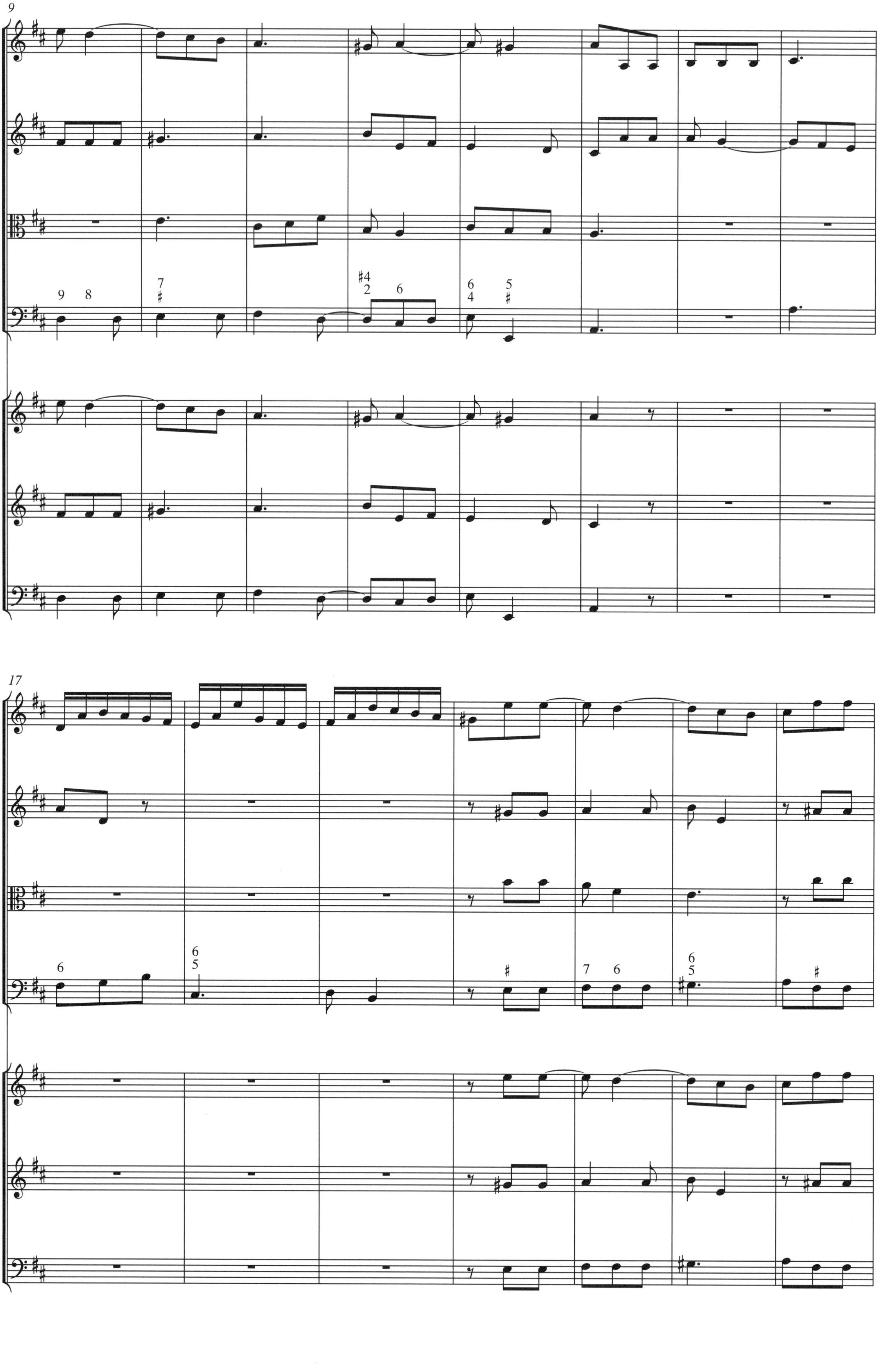
9
17

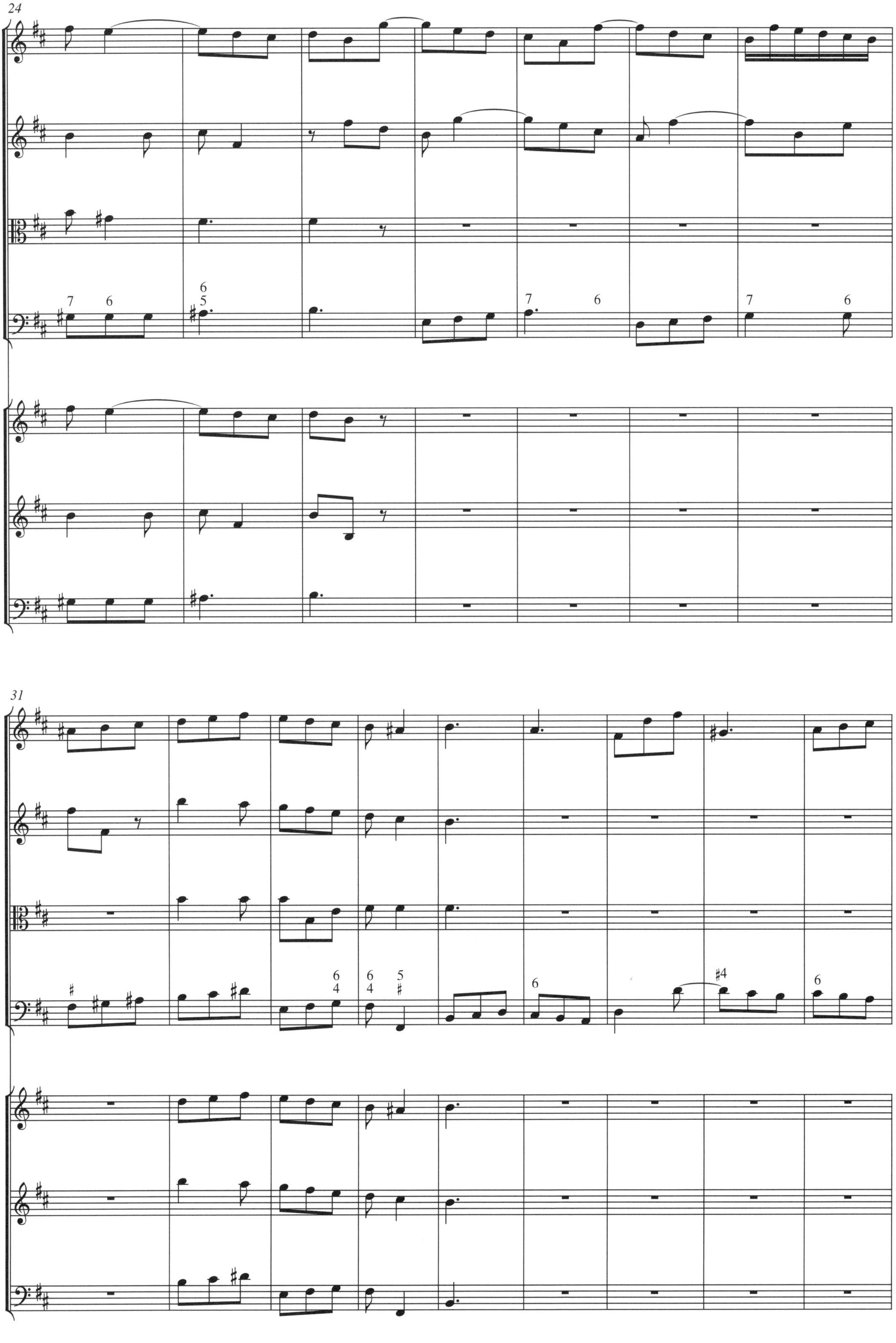
24
31

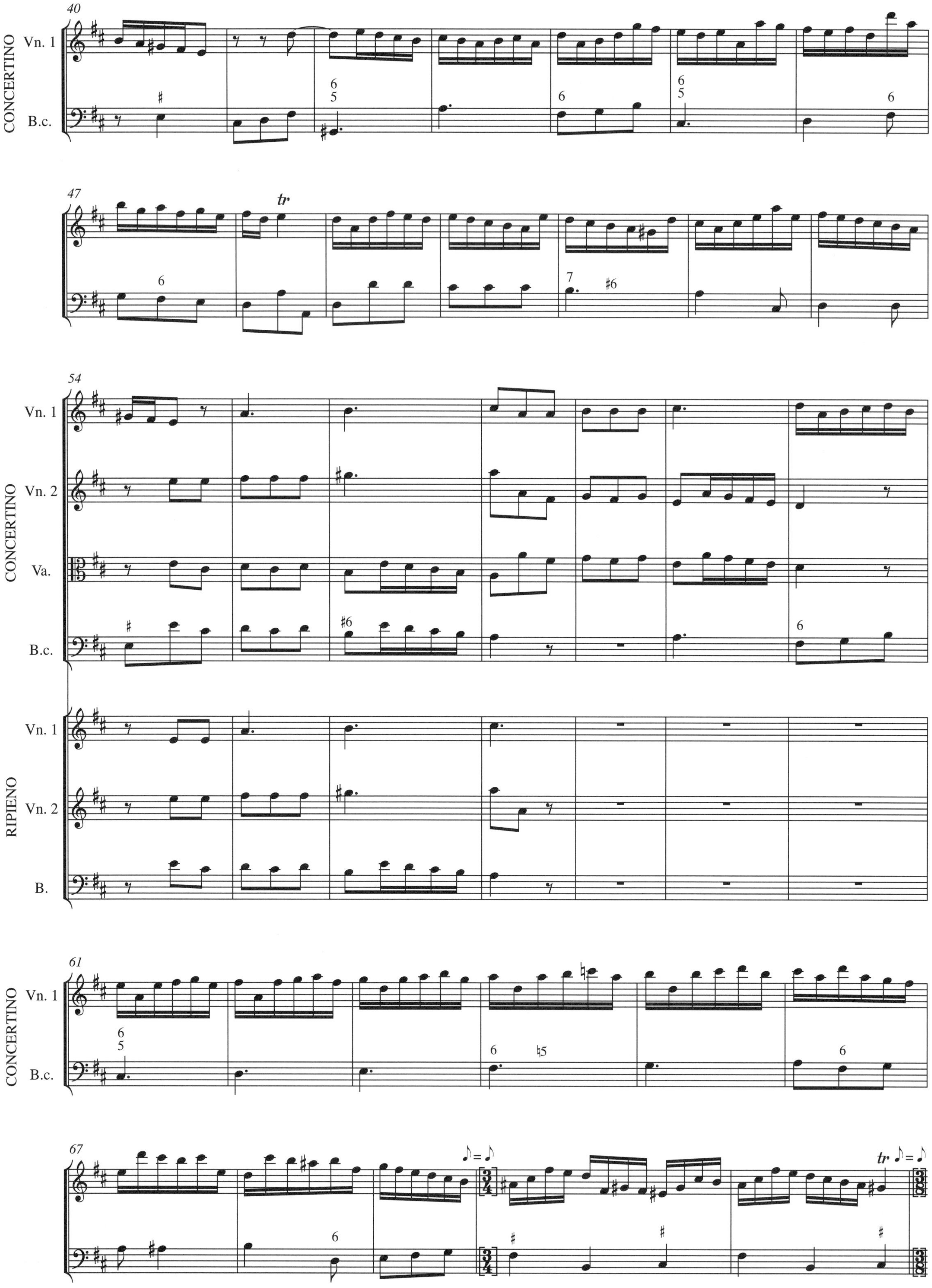

40
CONCERTINO
Vn. 1
B.c.
47
tr
54
Vn. 2
Va.
RIPIENO
B.
61
67

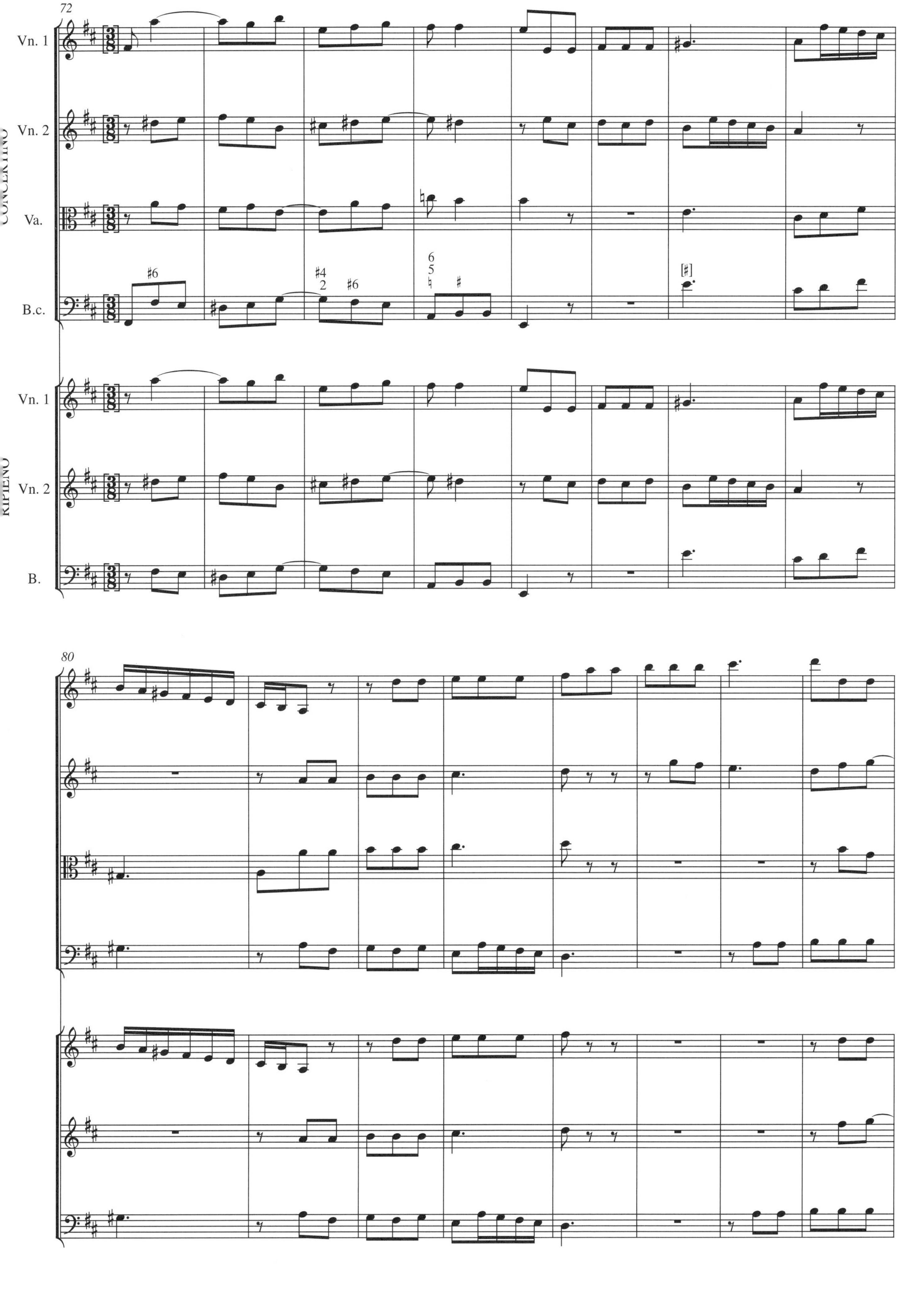
72
CONCERTINO
Vn. 1
Vn. 2
Va.
B.c.
RIPIENO
Vn. 1
Vn. 2
B.
80

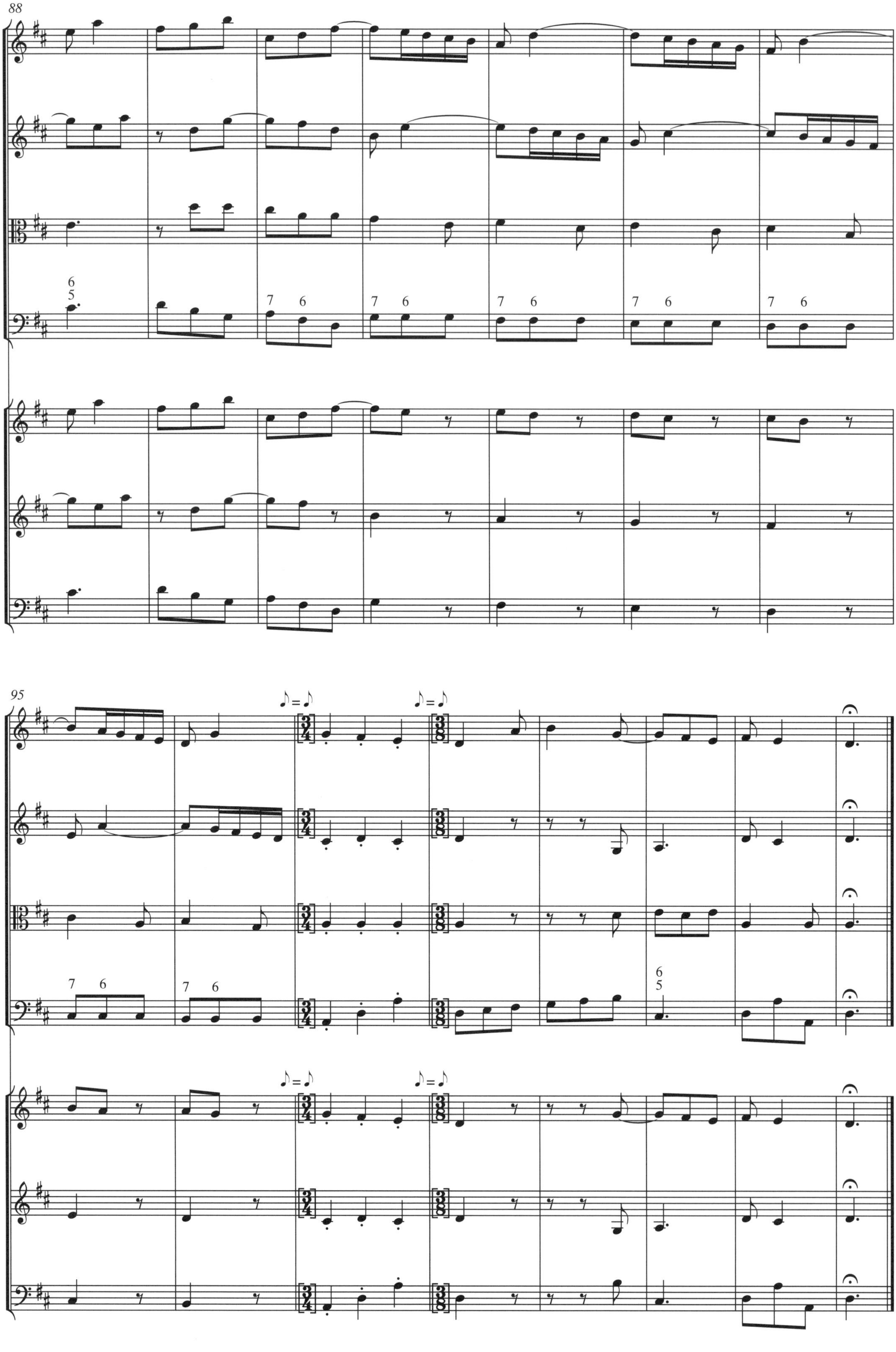
88
95

5. Concerto in B-flat Major
I

From Francesco Geminiani, Sonata in B-flat Major, Op. 1, No. 5

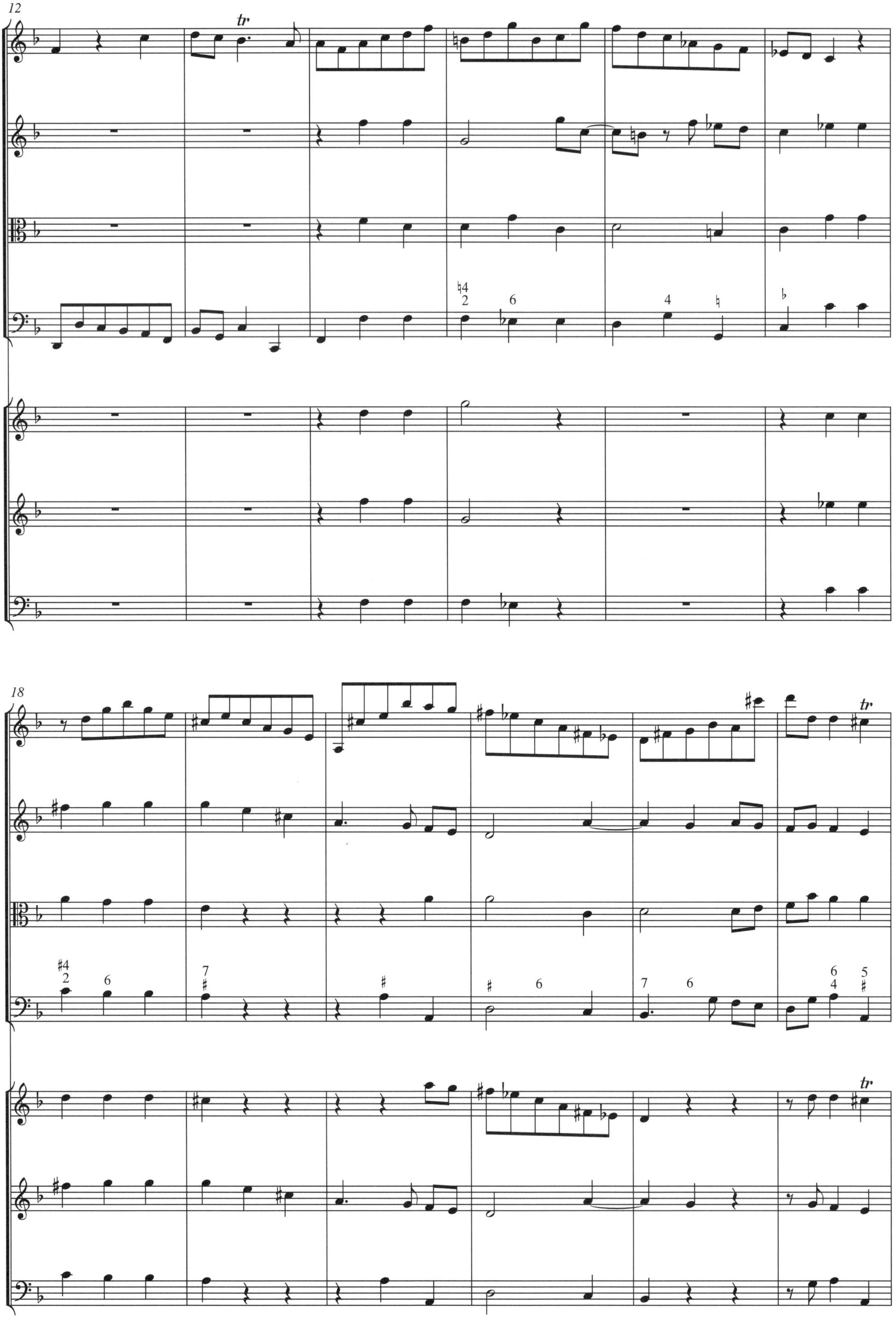
12
tr
18
tr
tr

81

II

4
Vn. 1
Vn. 2
CONCERTINO
Va.
B.c.
7
10
Vn. 1
Vn. 2
CONCERTINO
Va.
B.c.
Vn. 1
Vn. 2
RIPIENO
B.

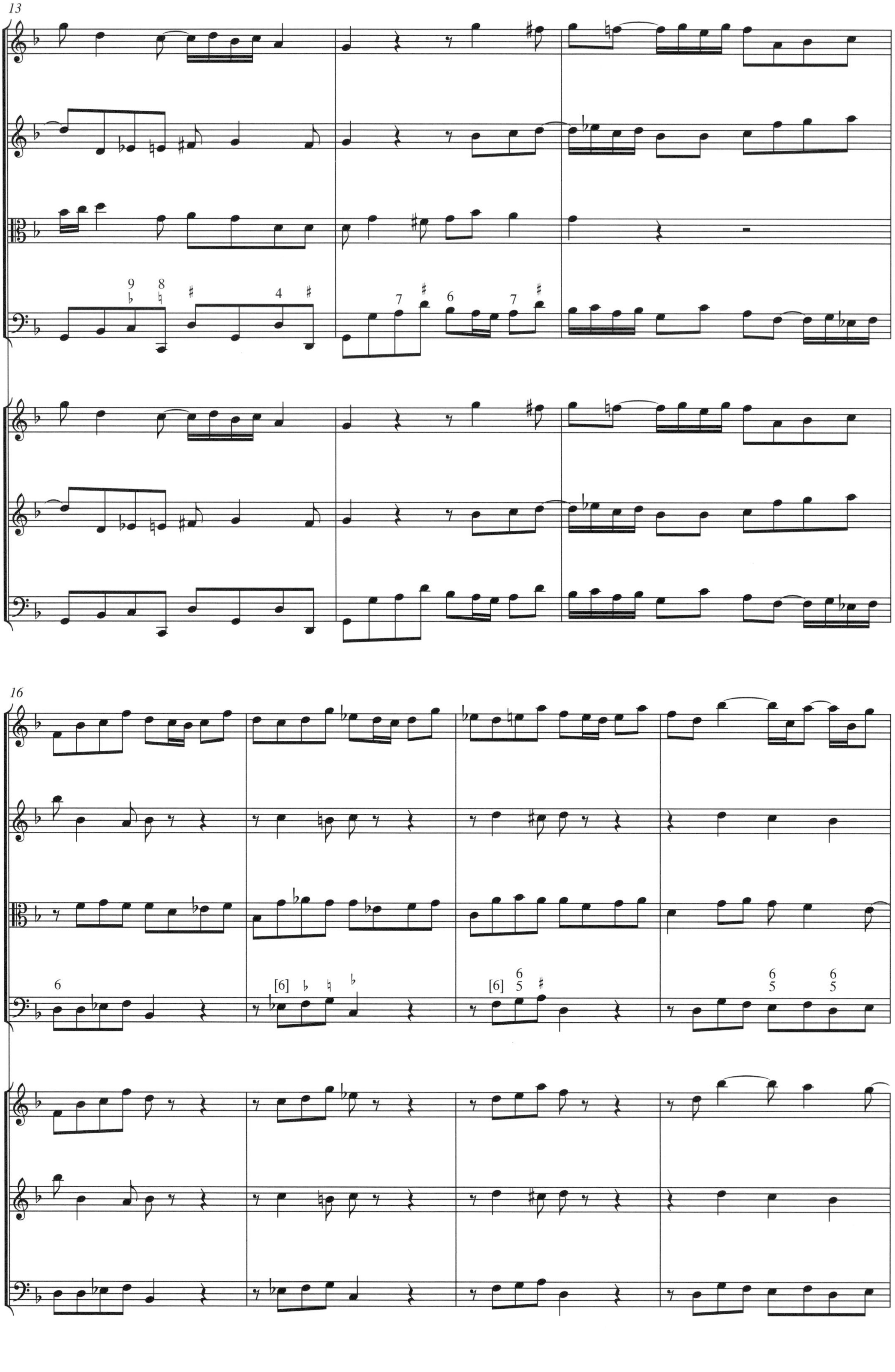
13
16

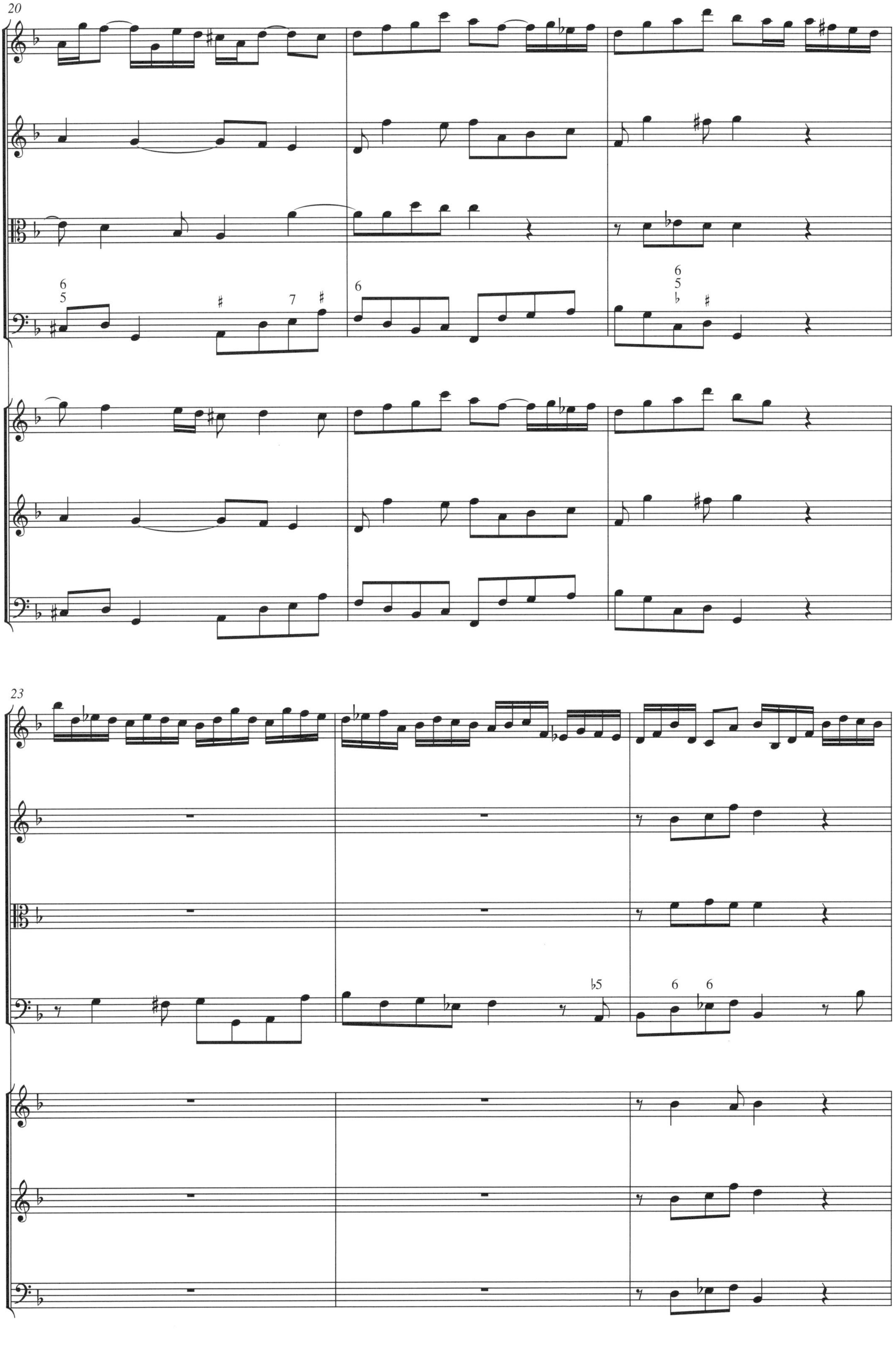
20
6
5
♯
7
♯
6
6
5
♭
♯
23
♭5
6
6

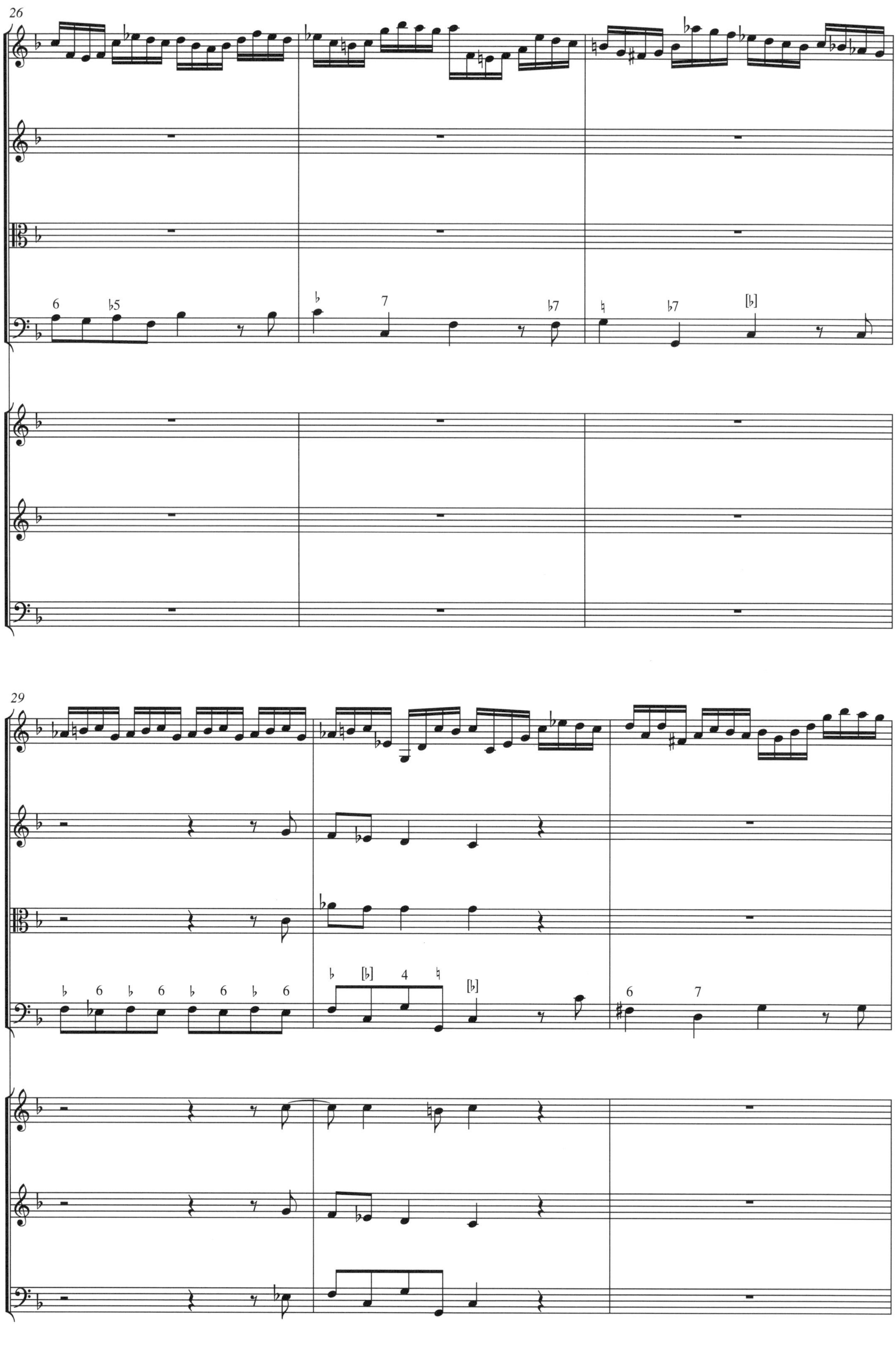
26
29

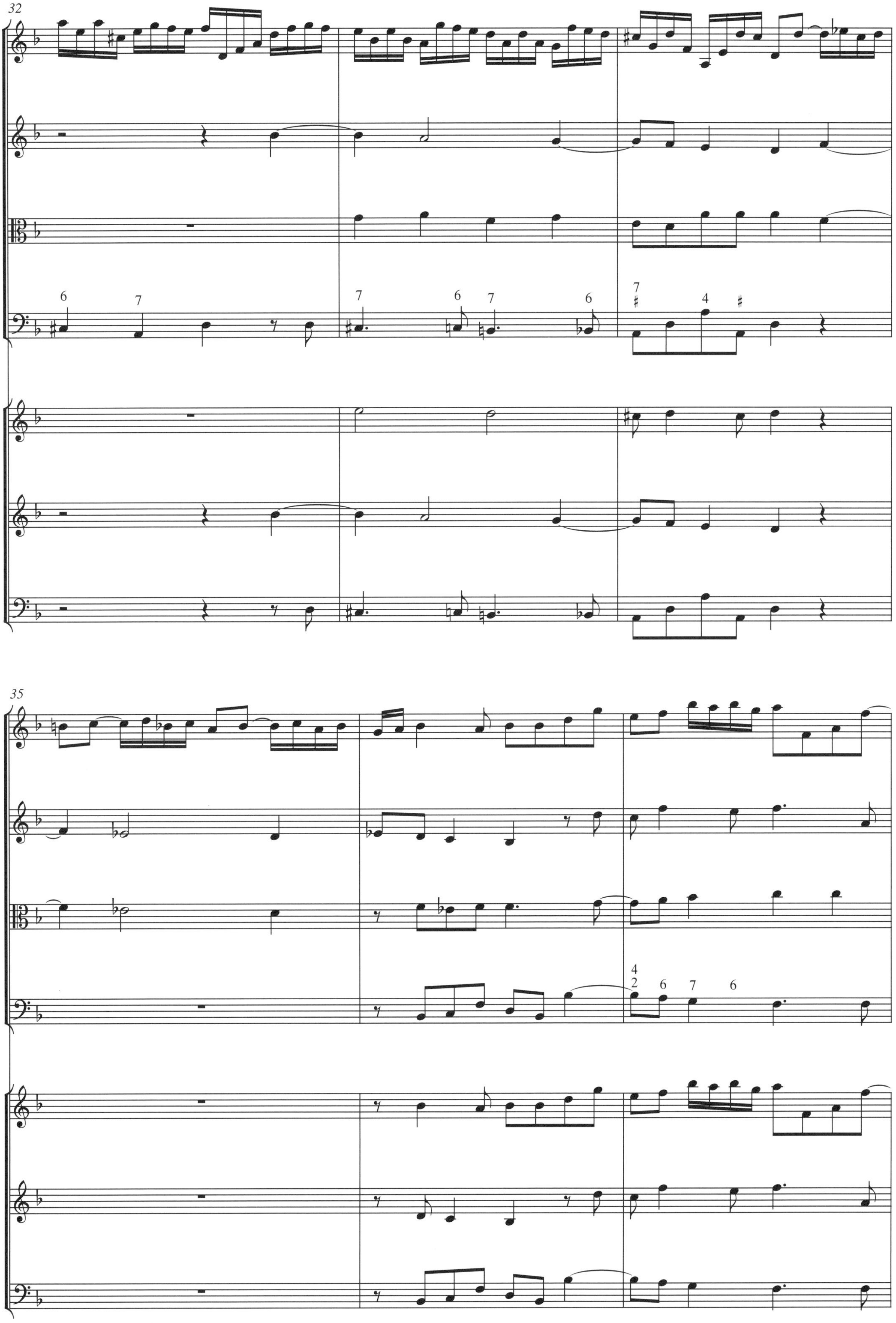
32
35

88

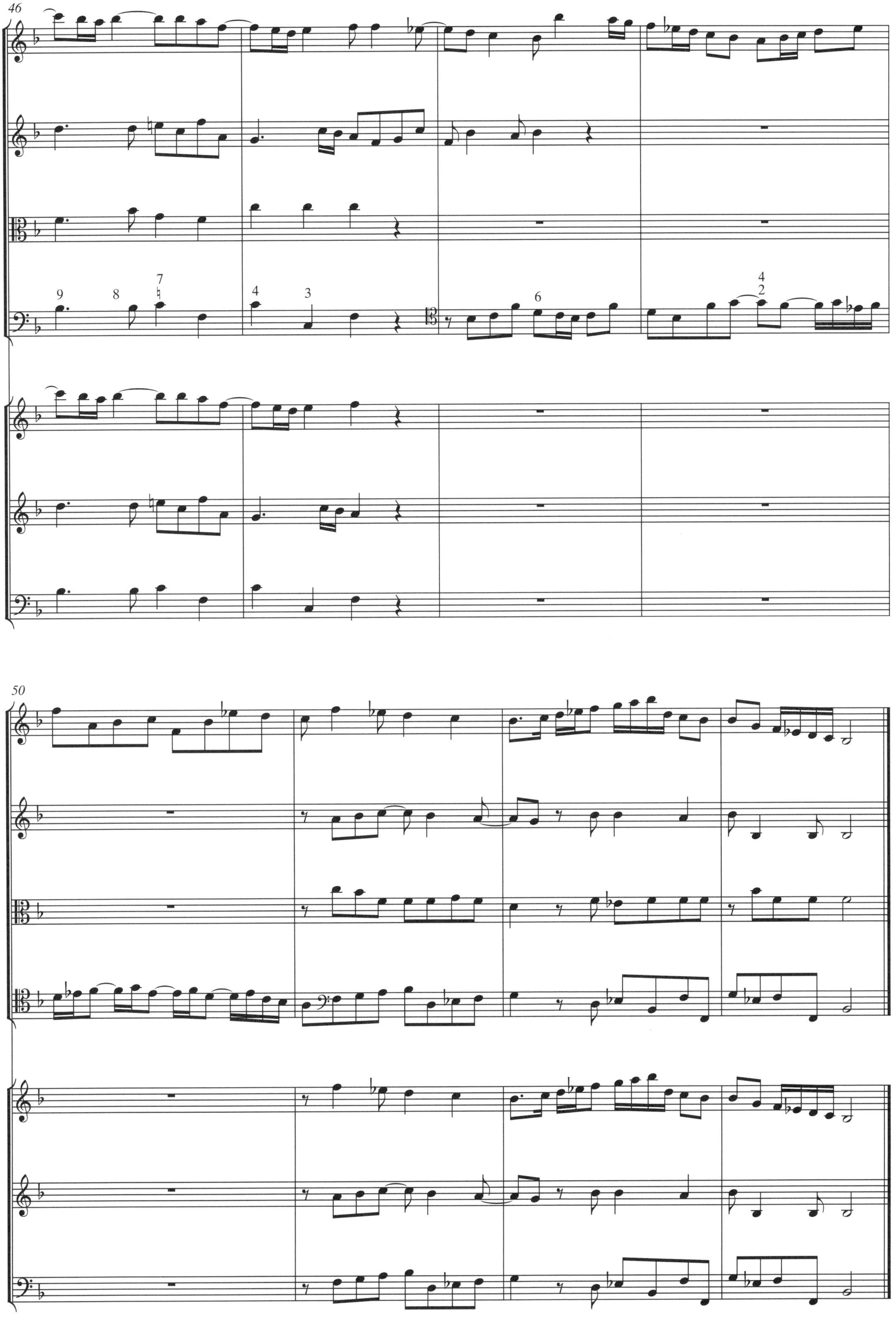
46
50

III

IV

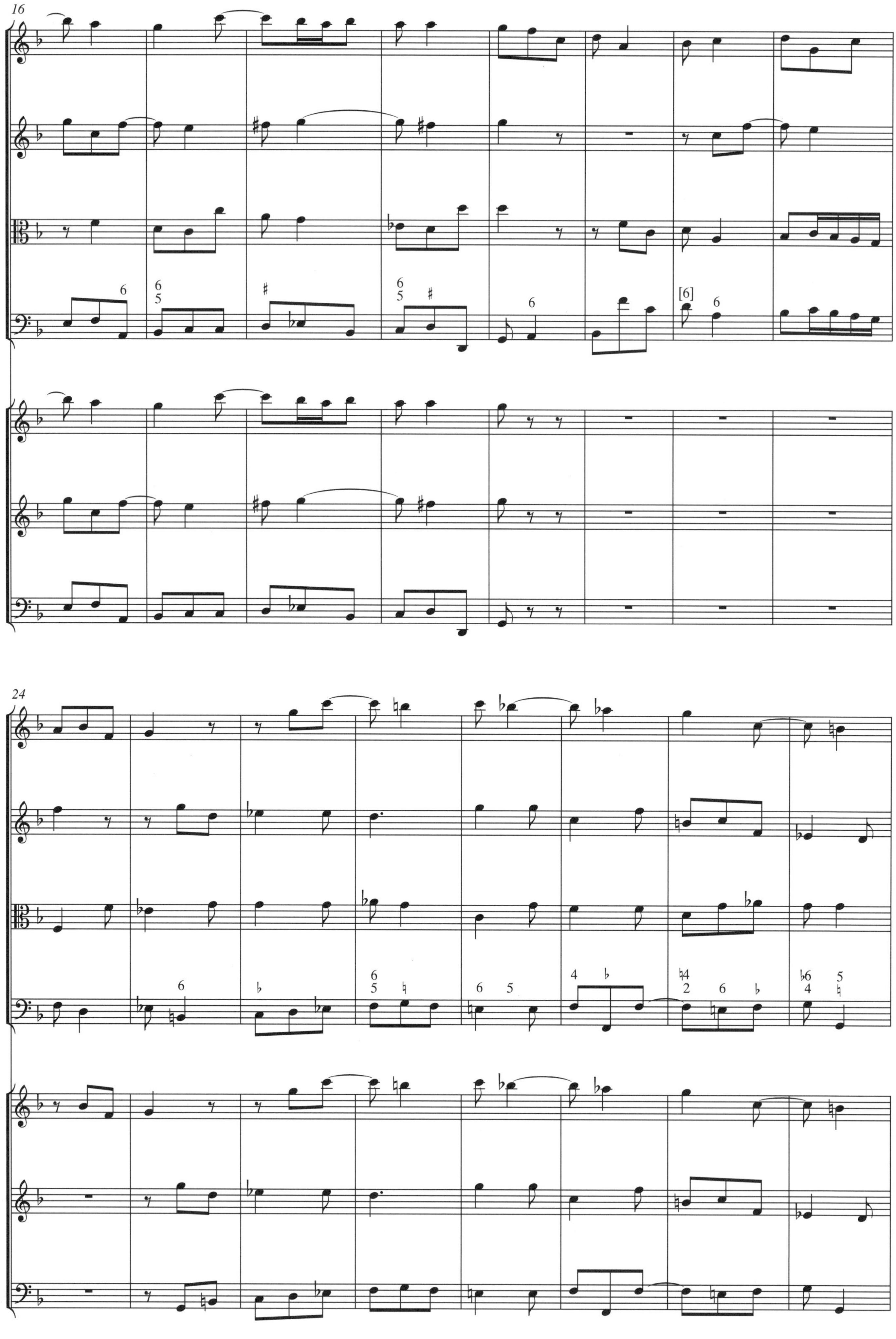
16
24

93

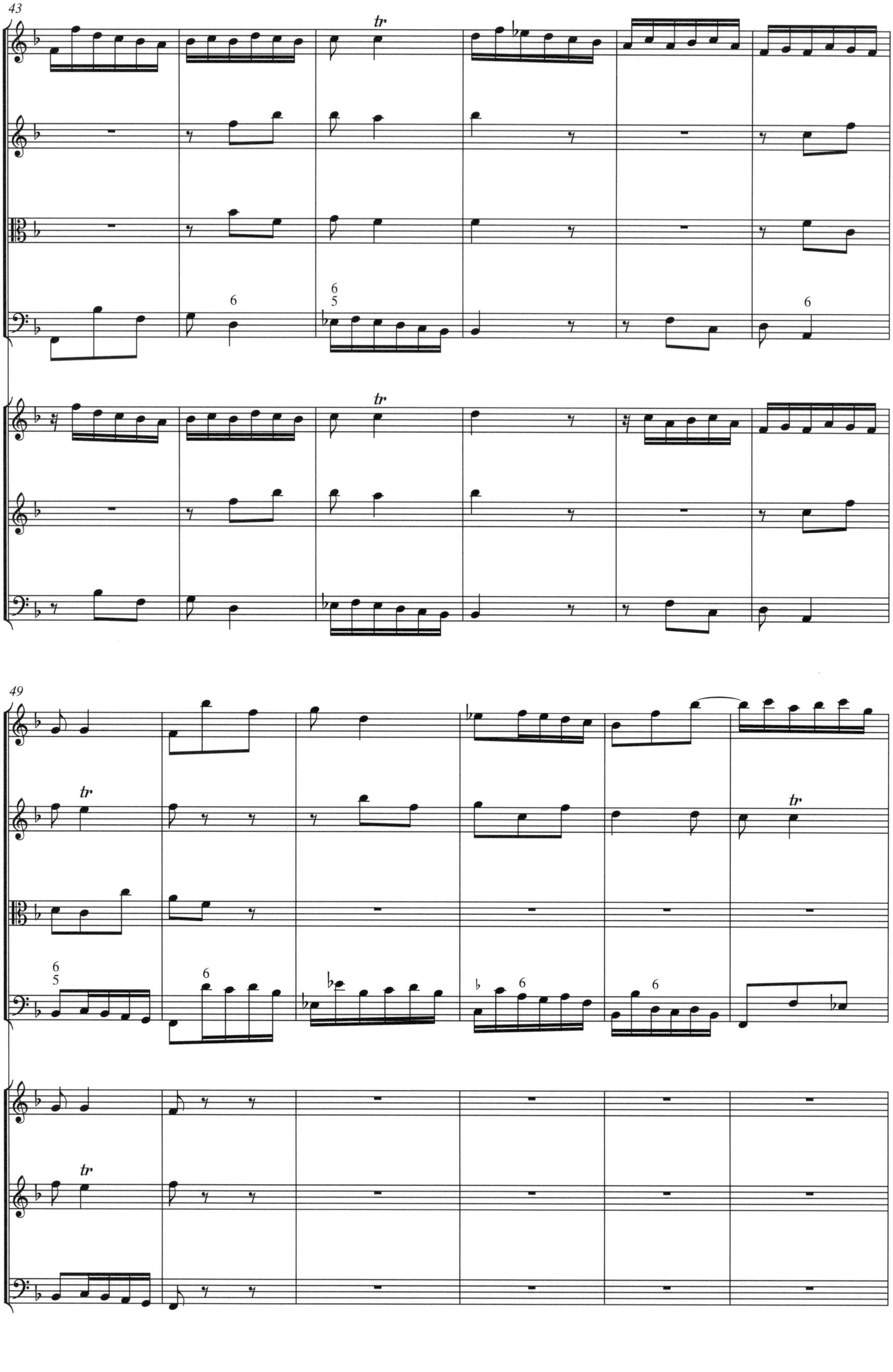
43
49

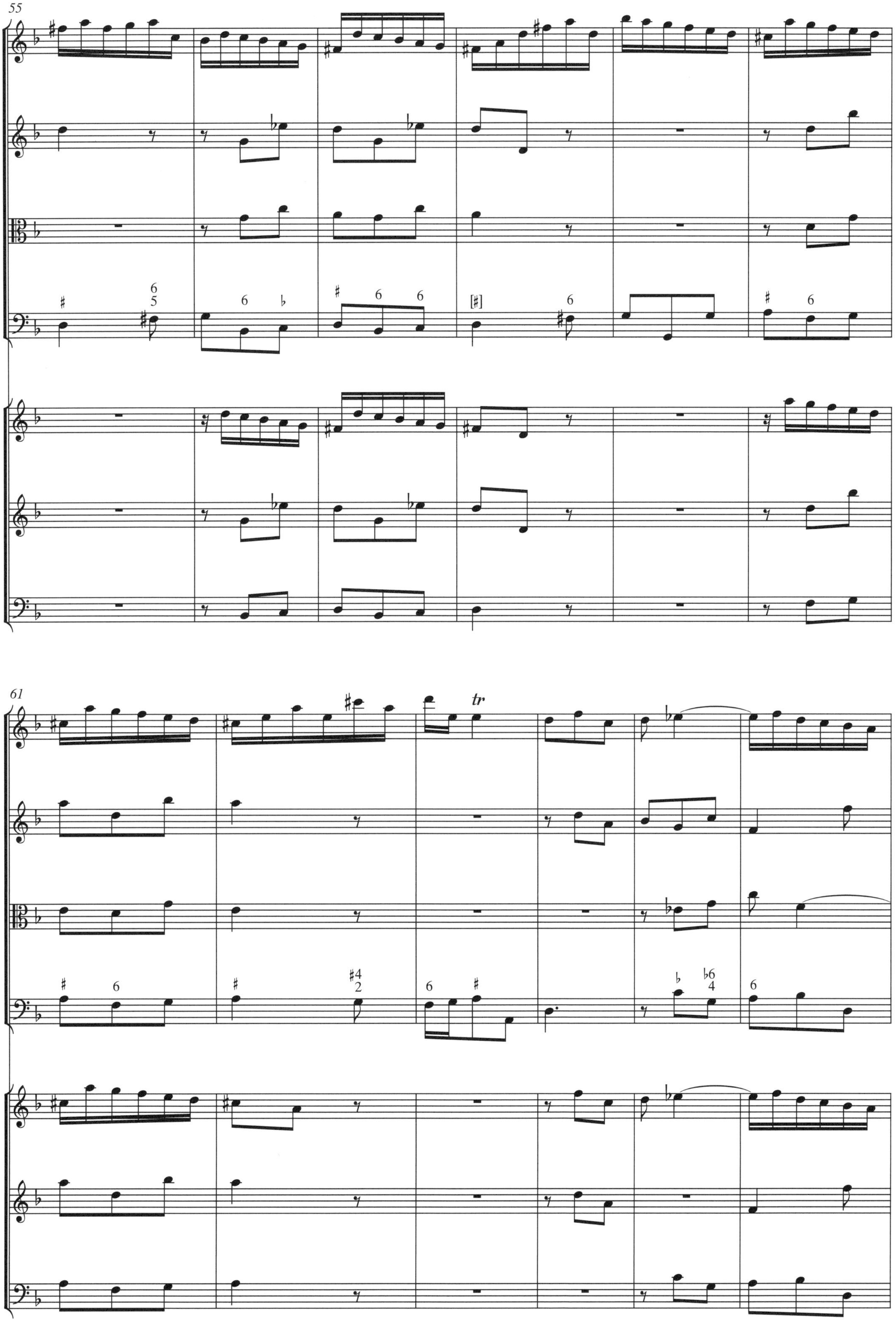

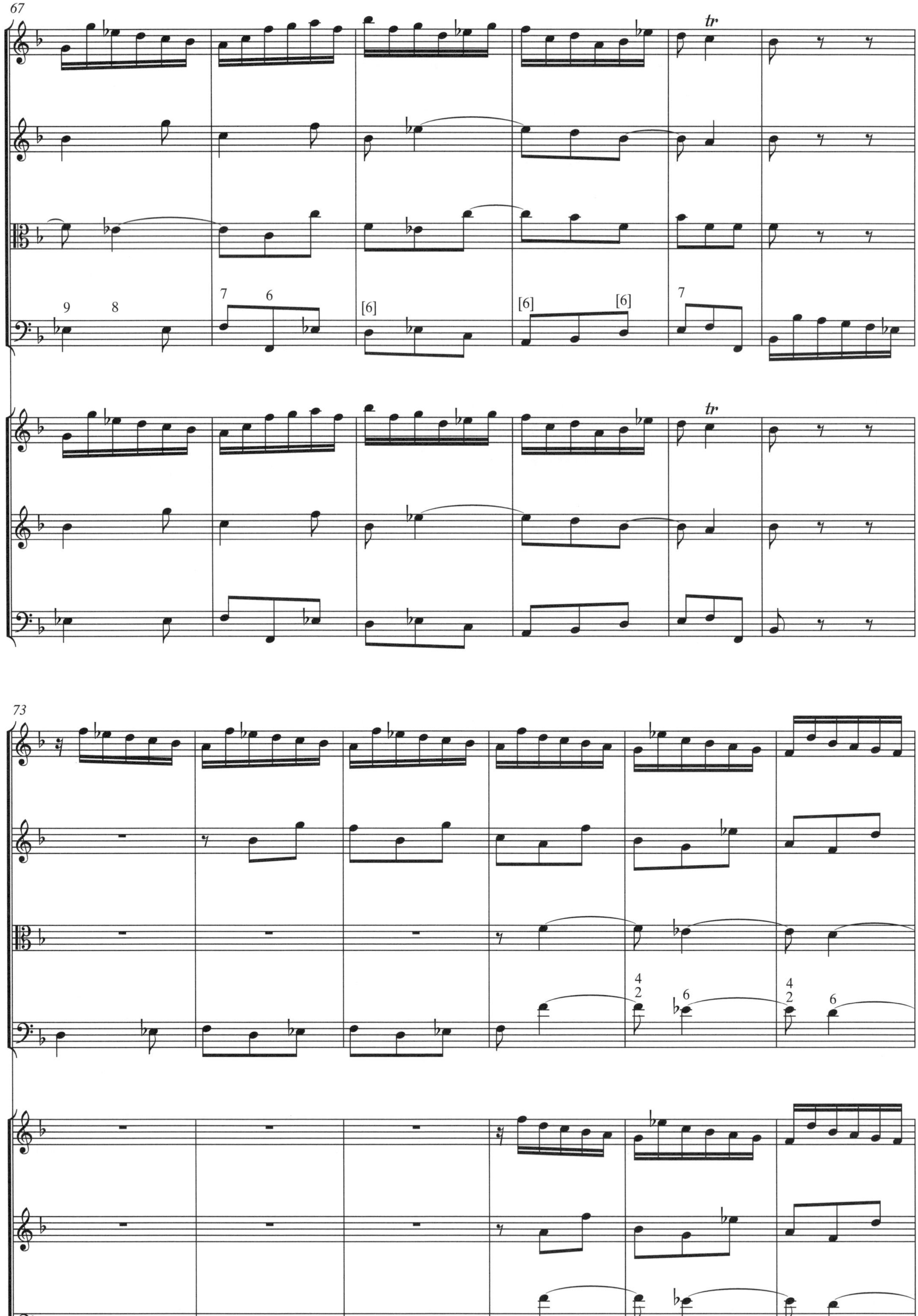
67
73

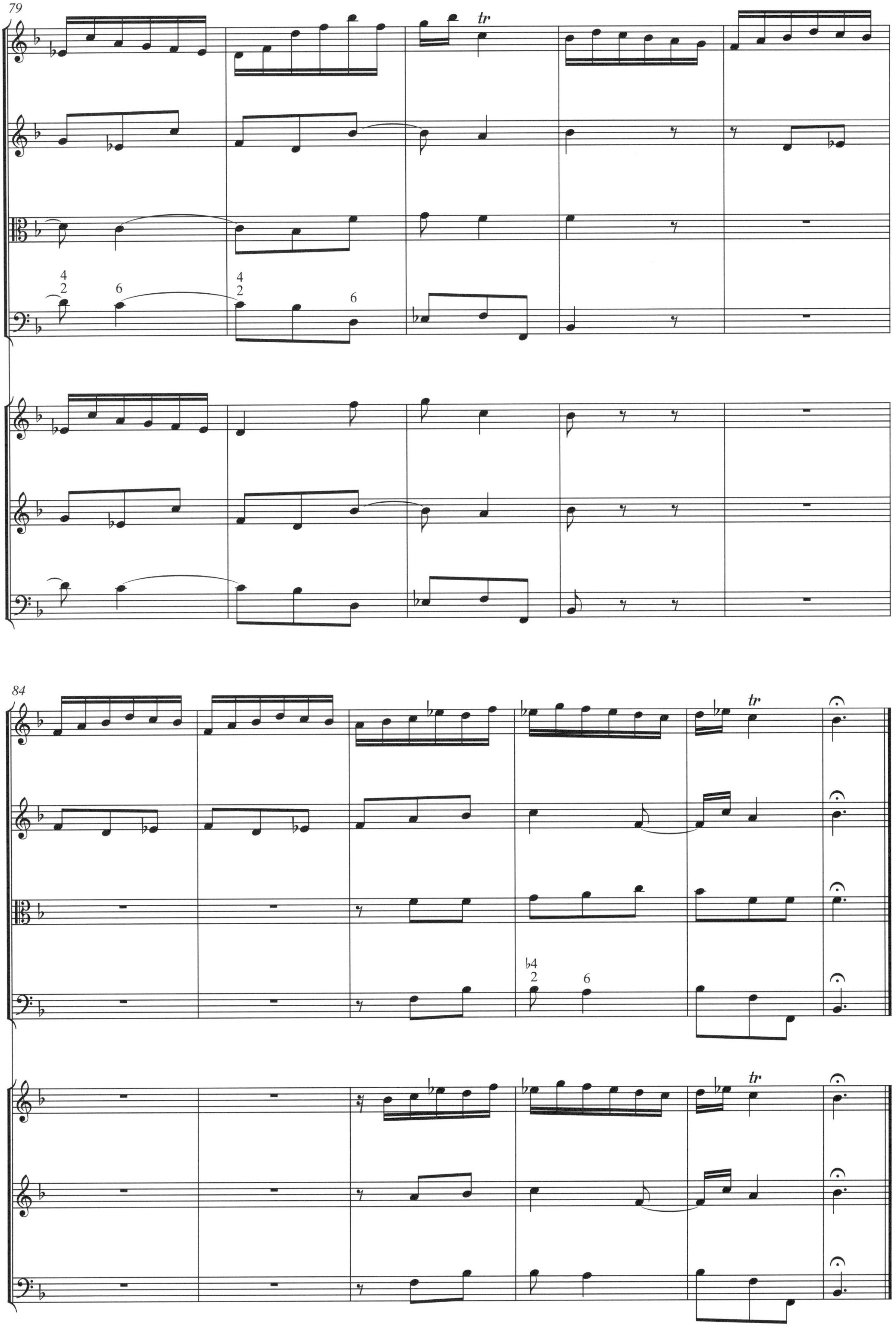
79
tr
4
2
6
4
2
6
84
tr
♭4
2
6
tr

6. Concerto in G minor
I

From Francesco Geminiani, Sonata in G Minor, Op. 1, No. 6

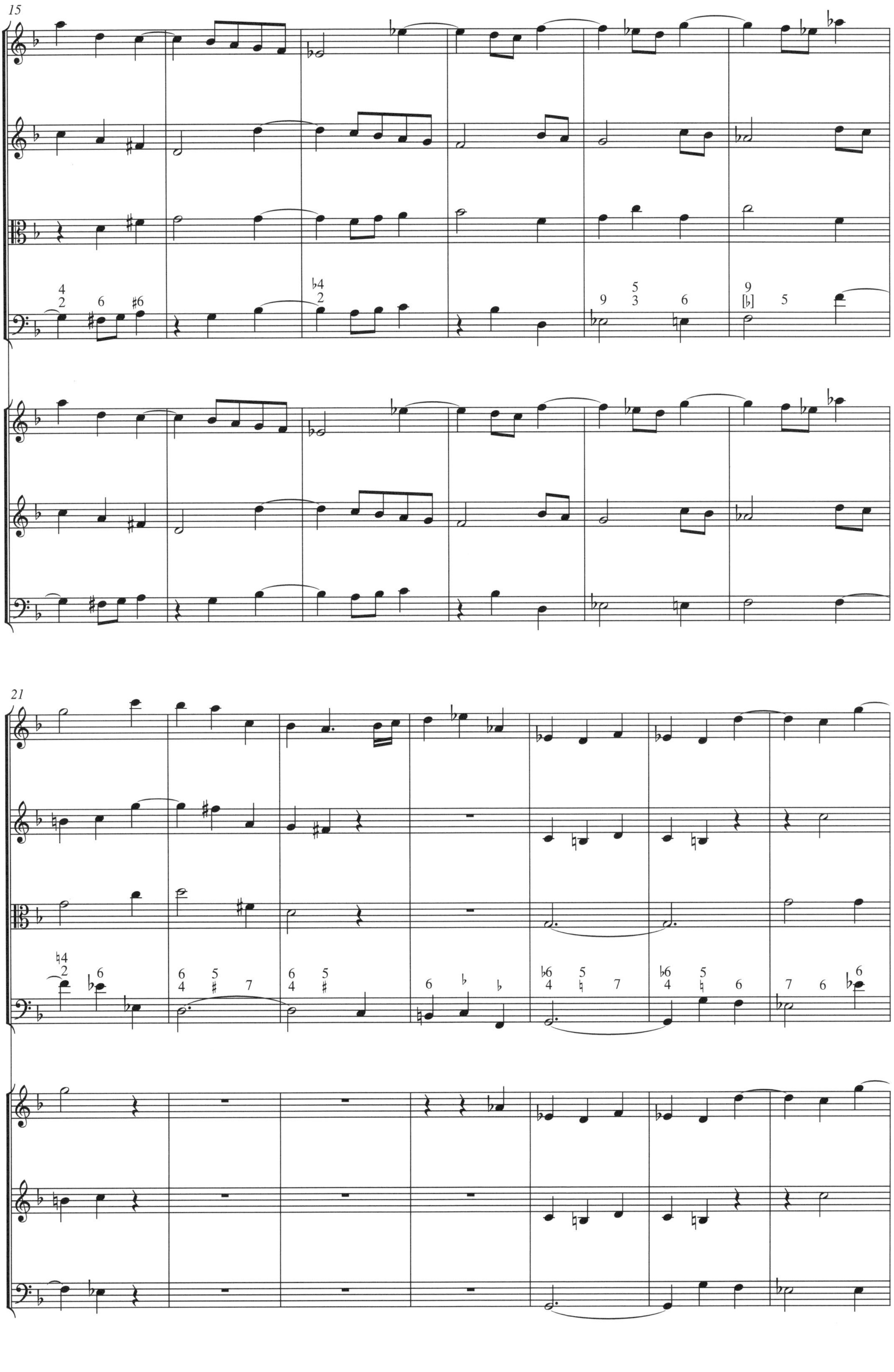
15
21

100

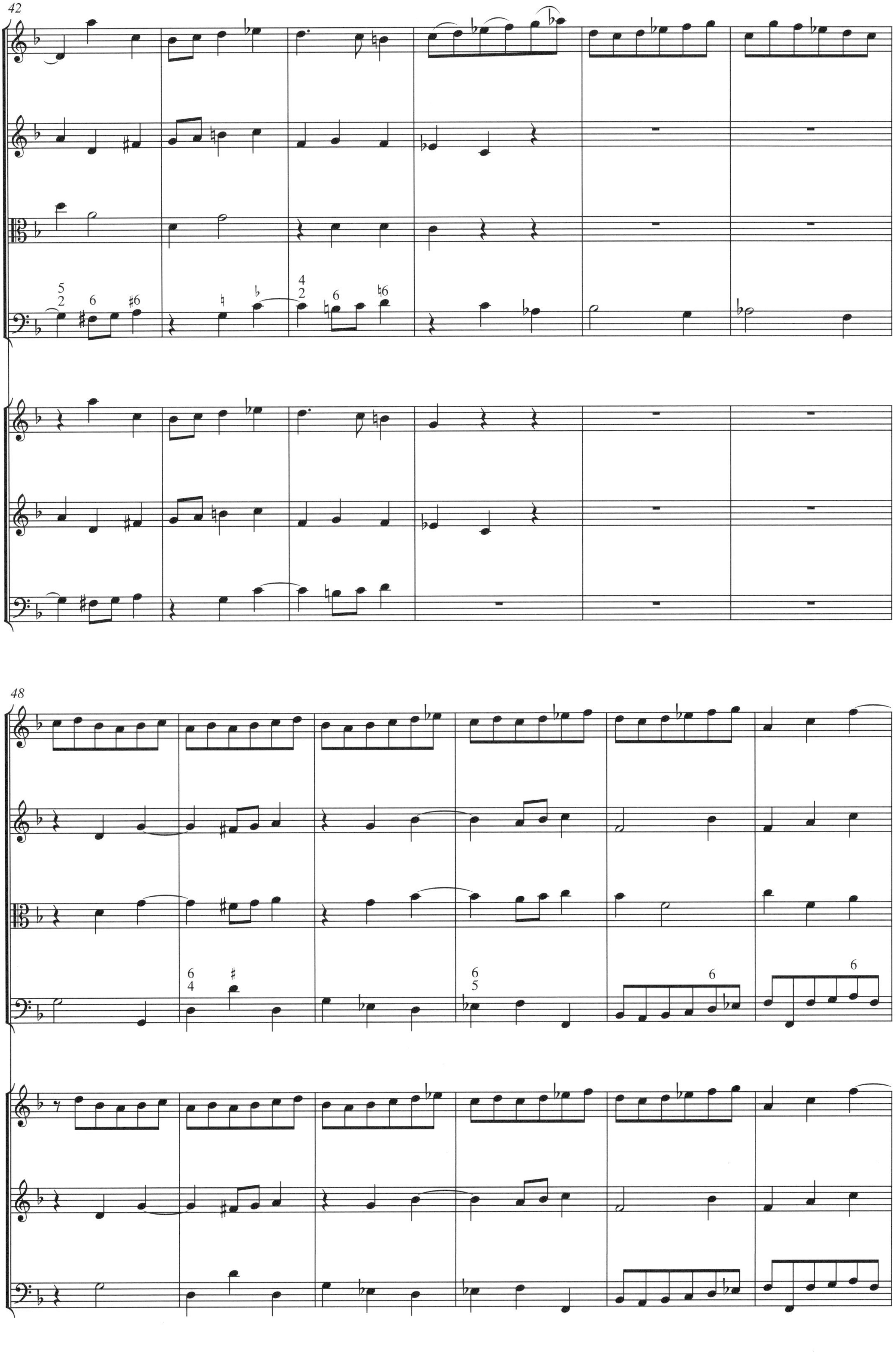
42
48

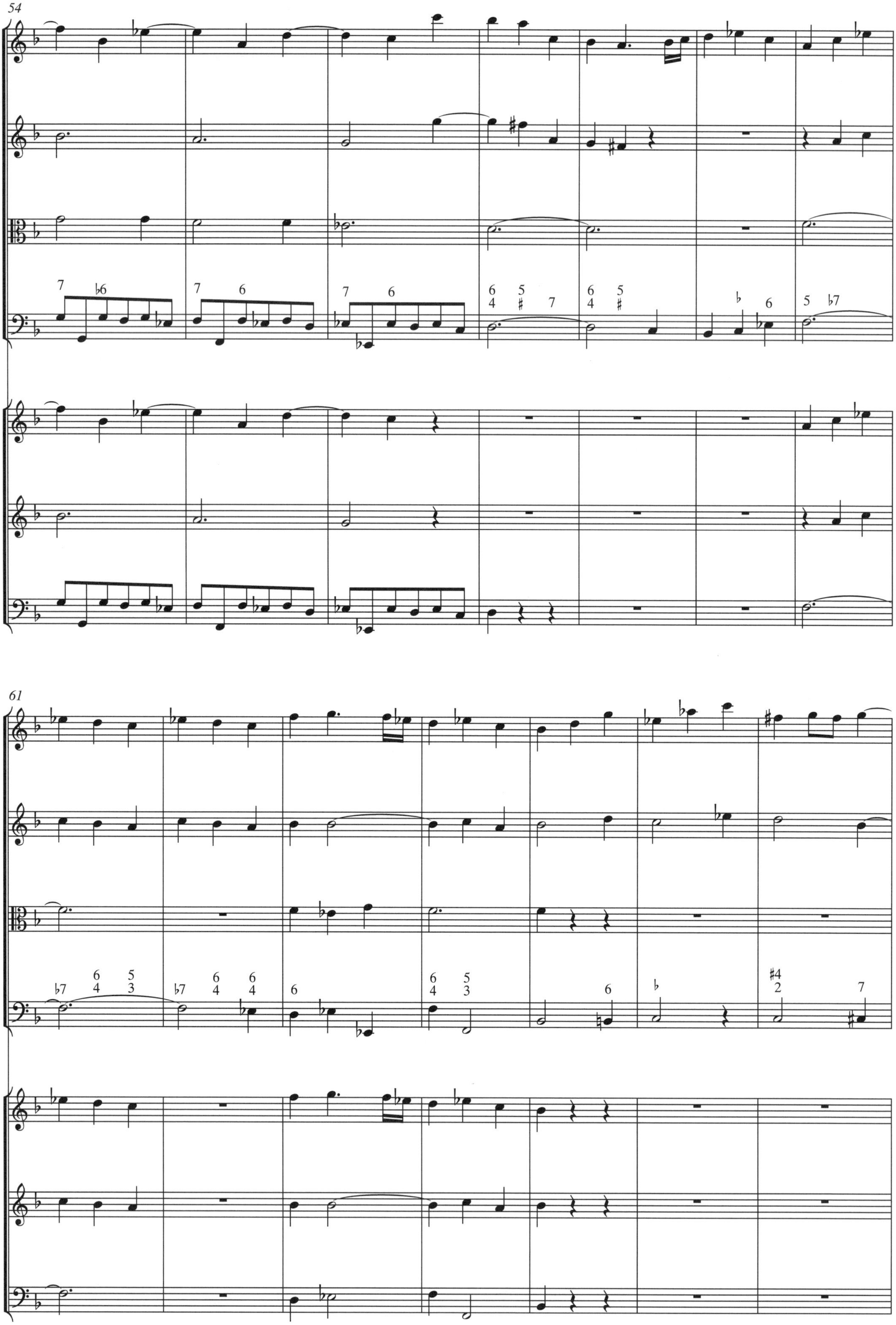

II

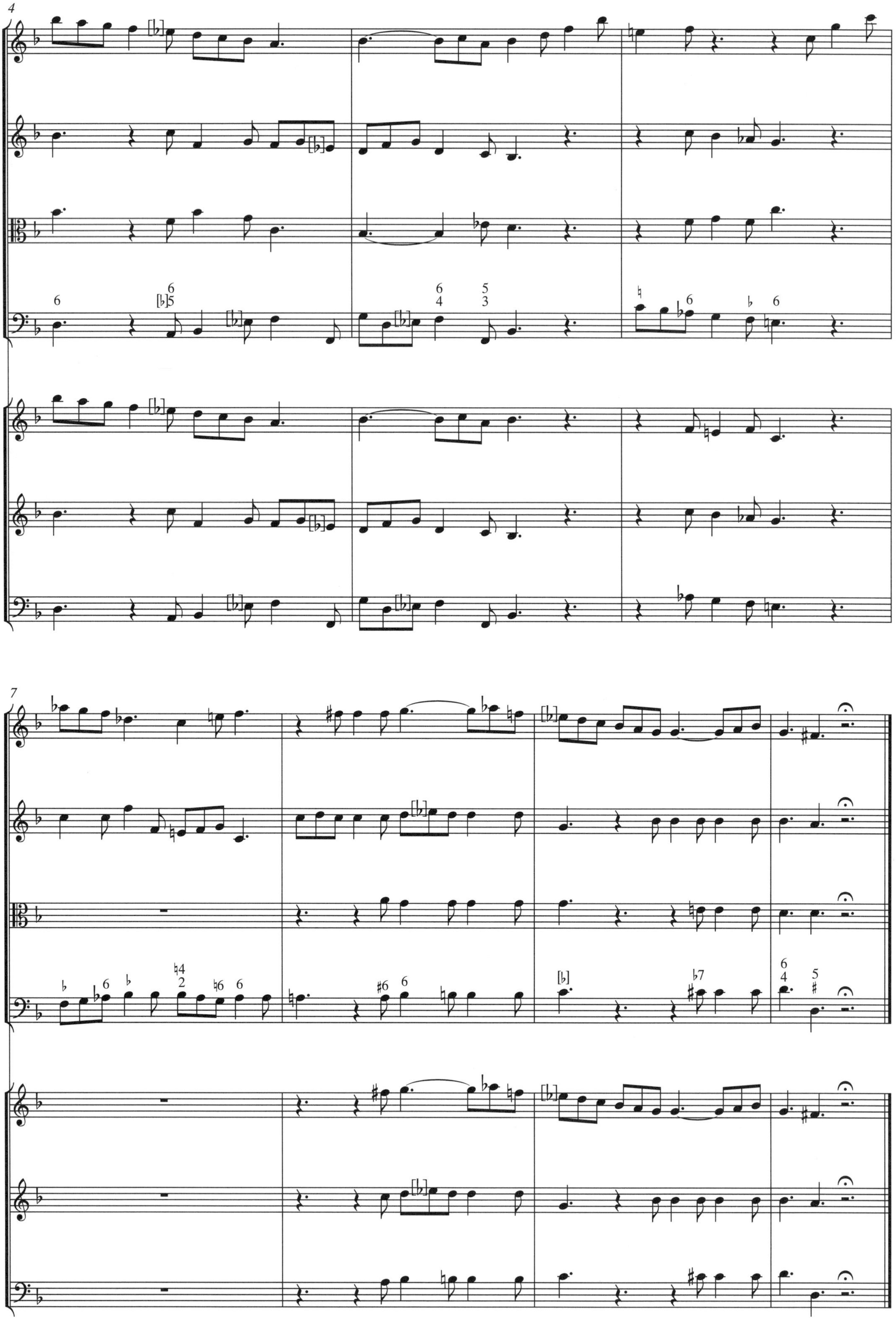

III

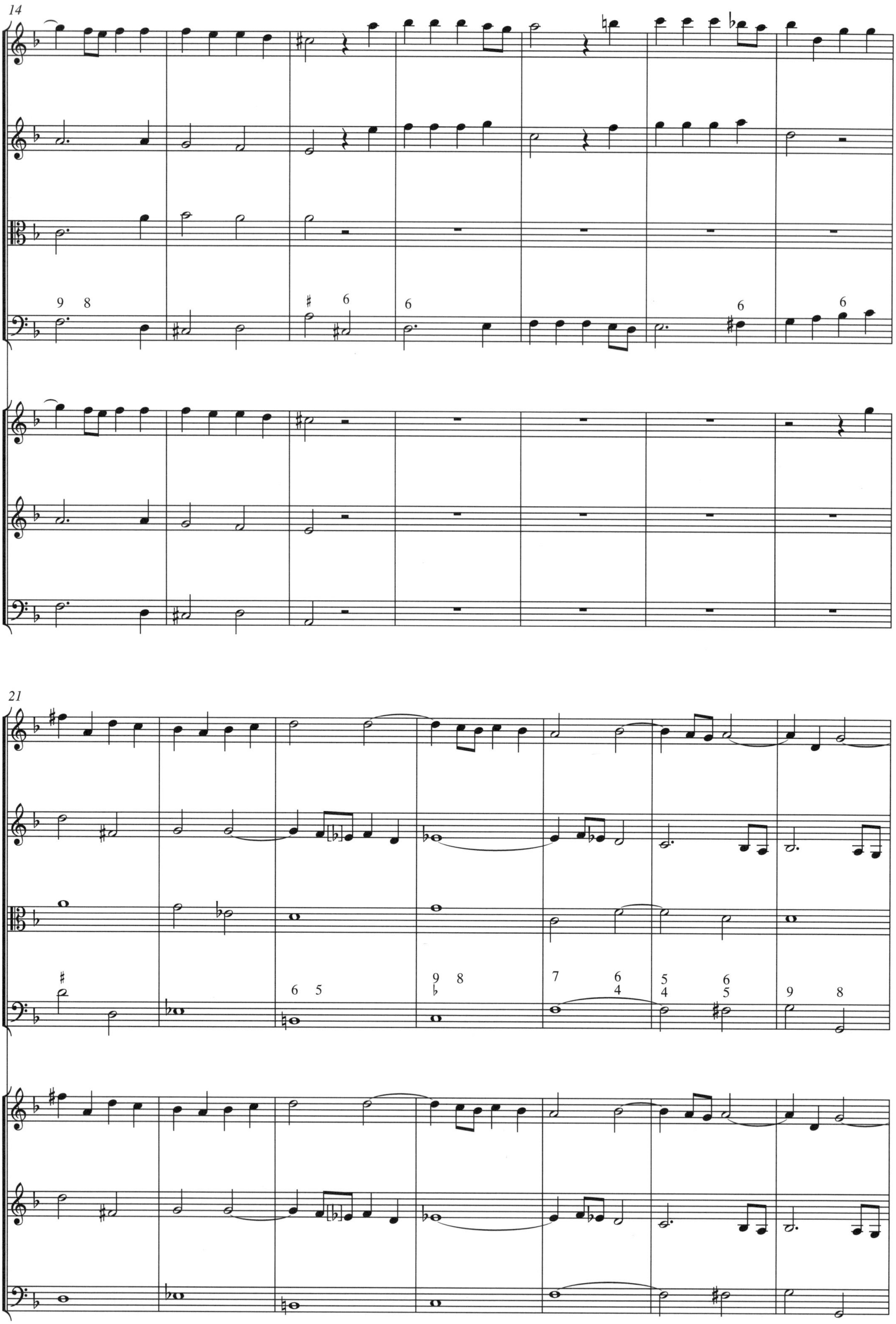

107

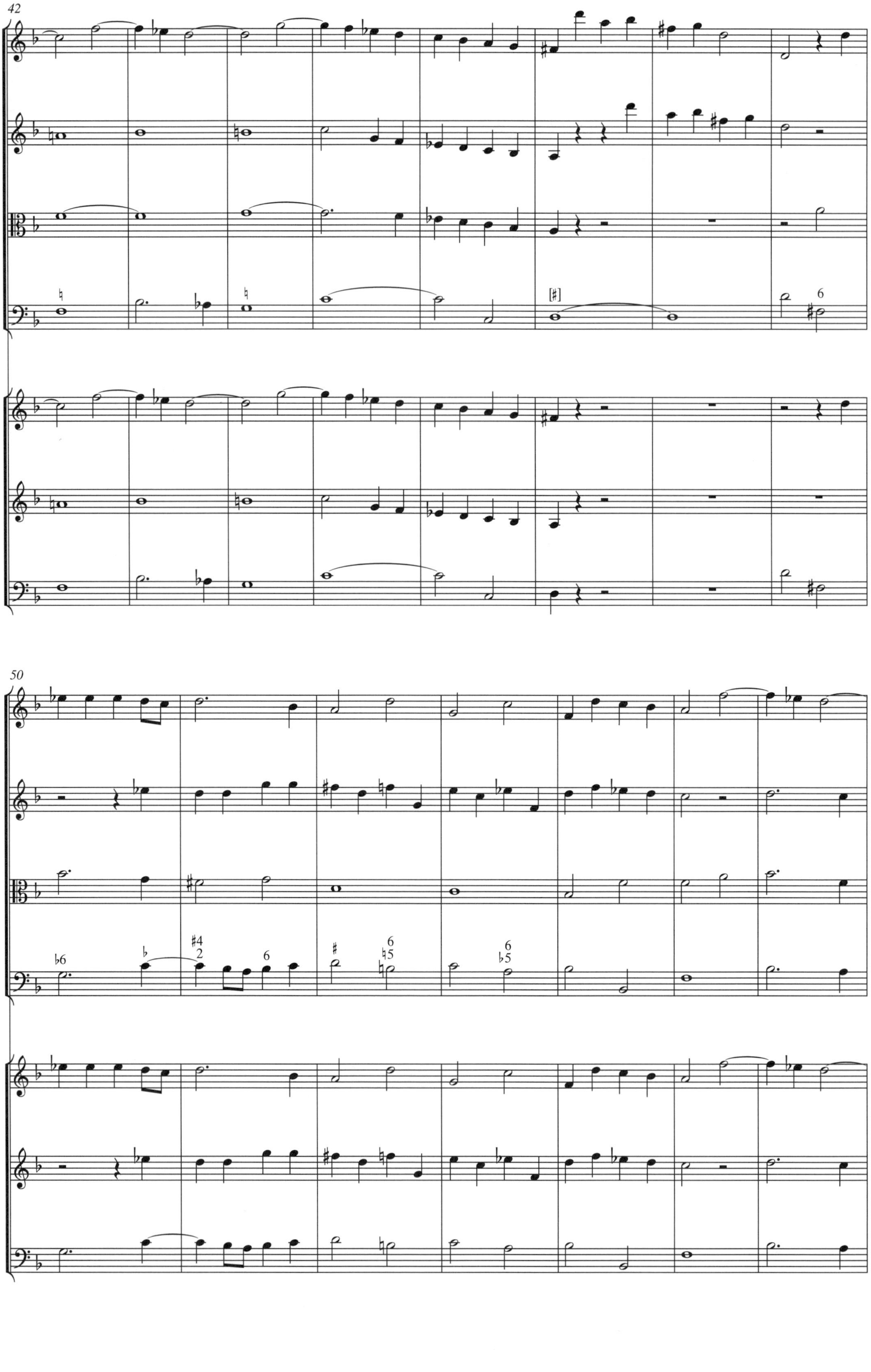
42
50

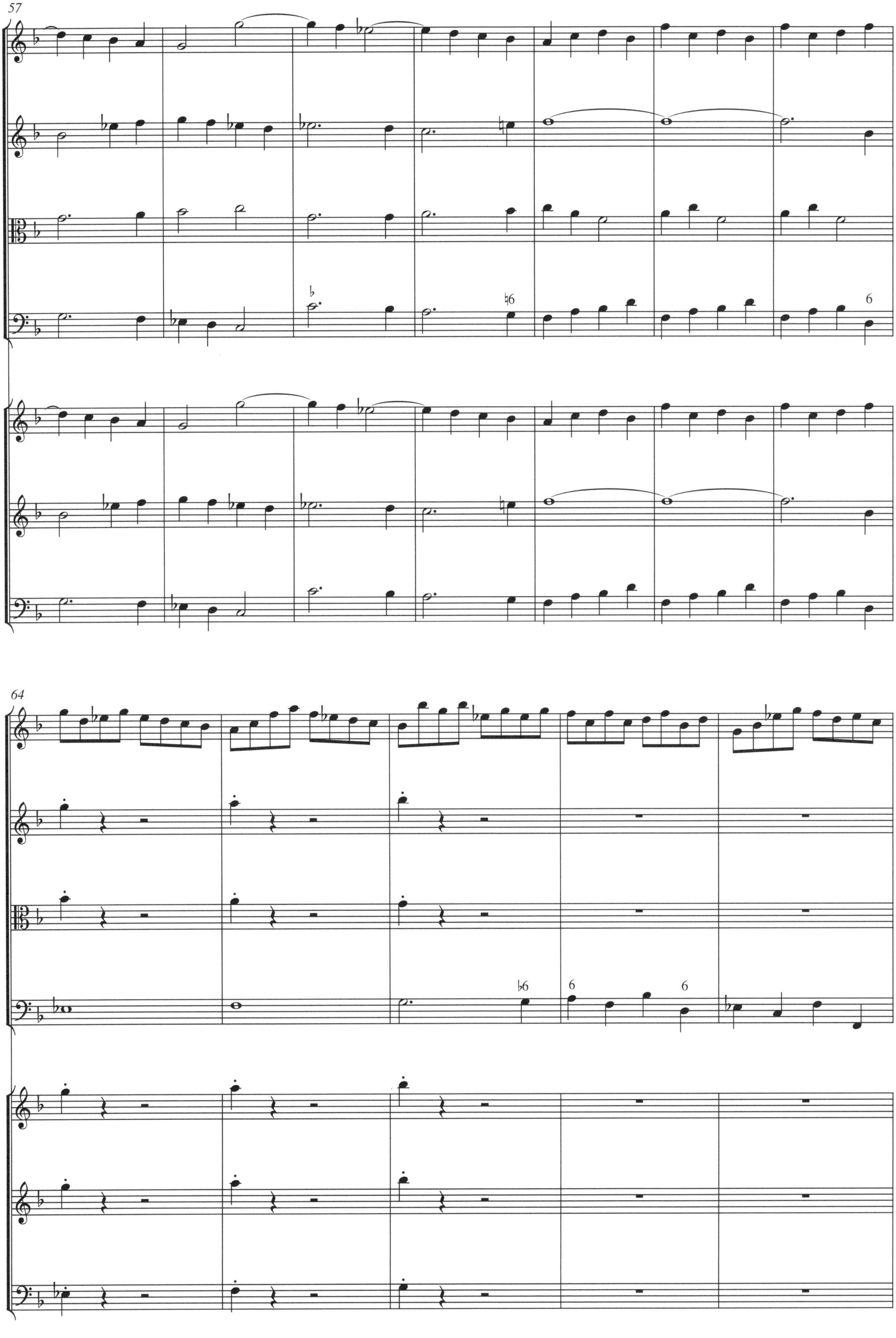
57
64

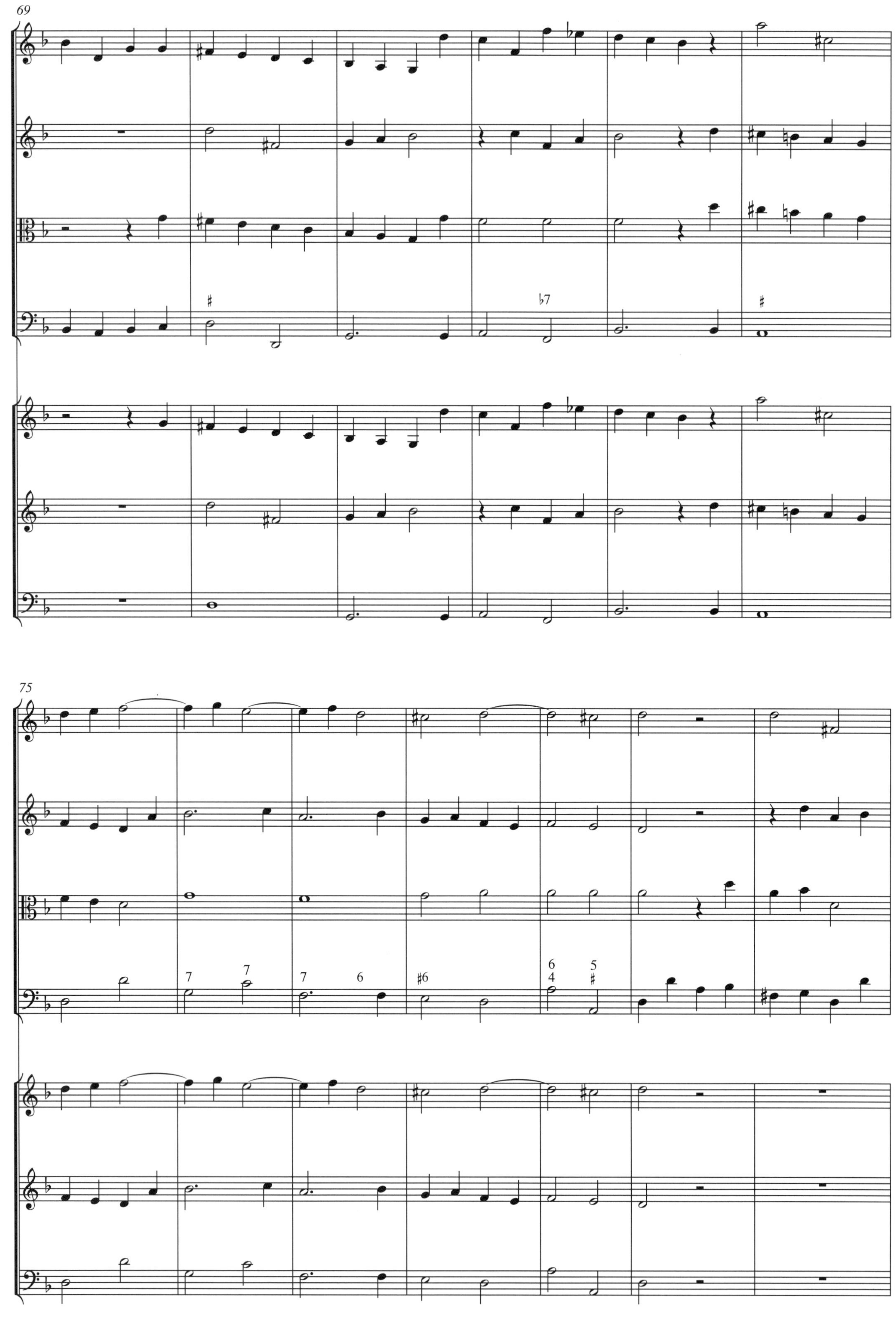
69
75

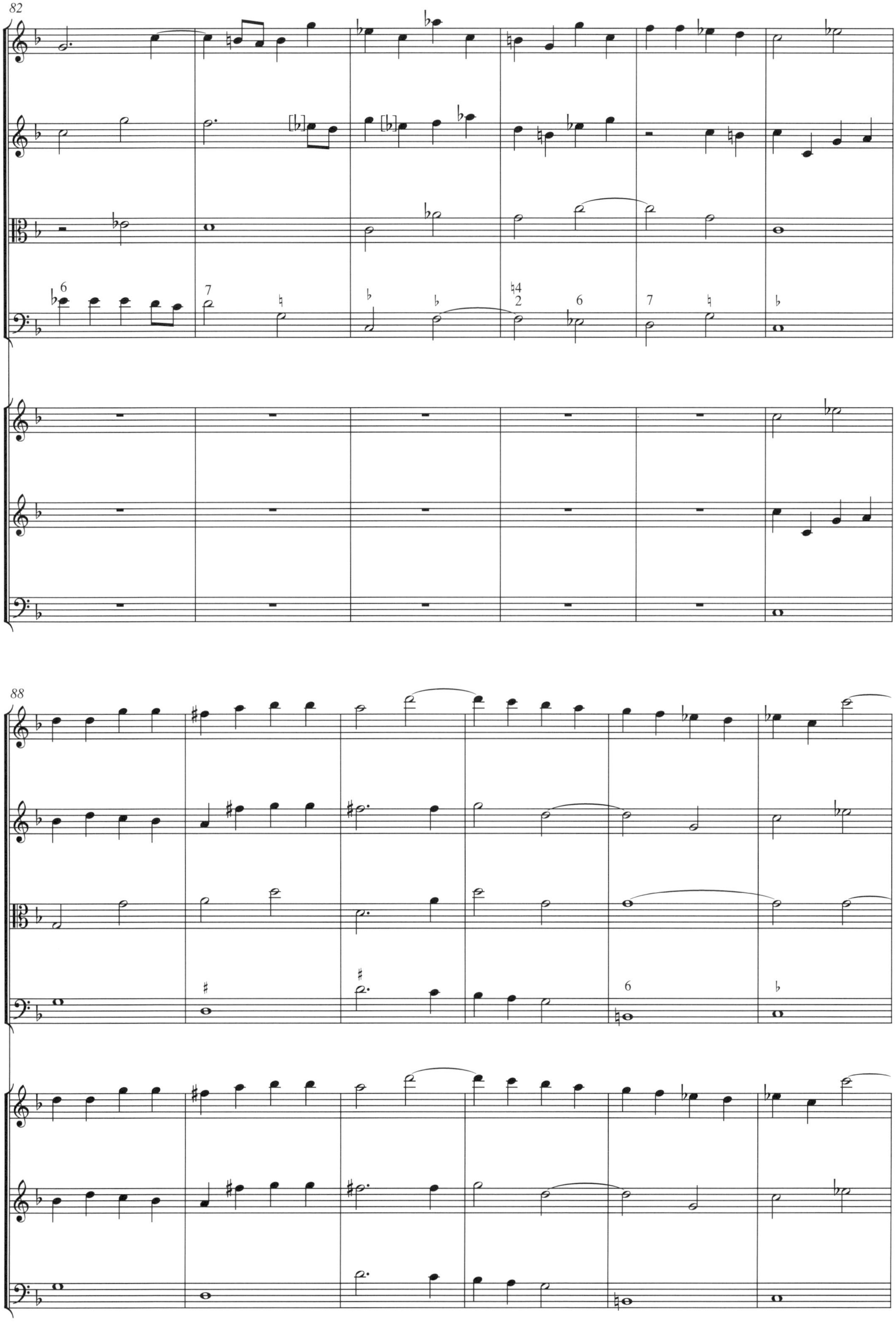

112

tasto solo

IV

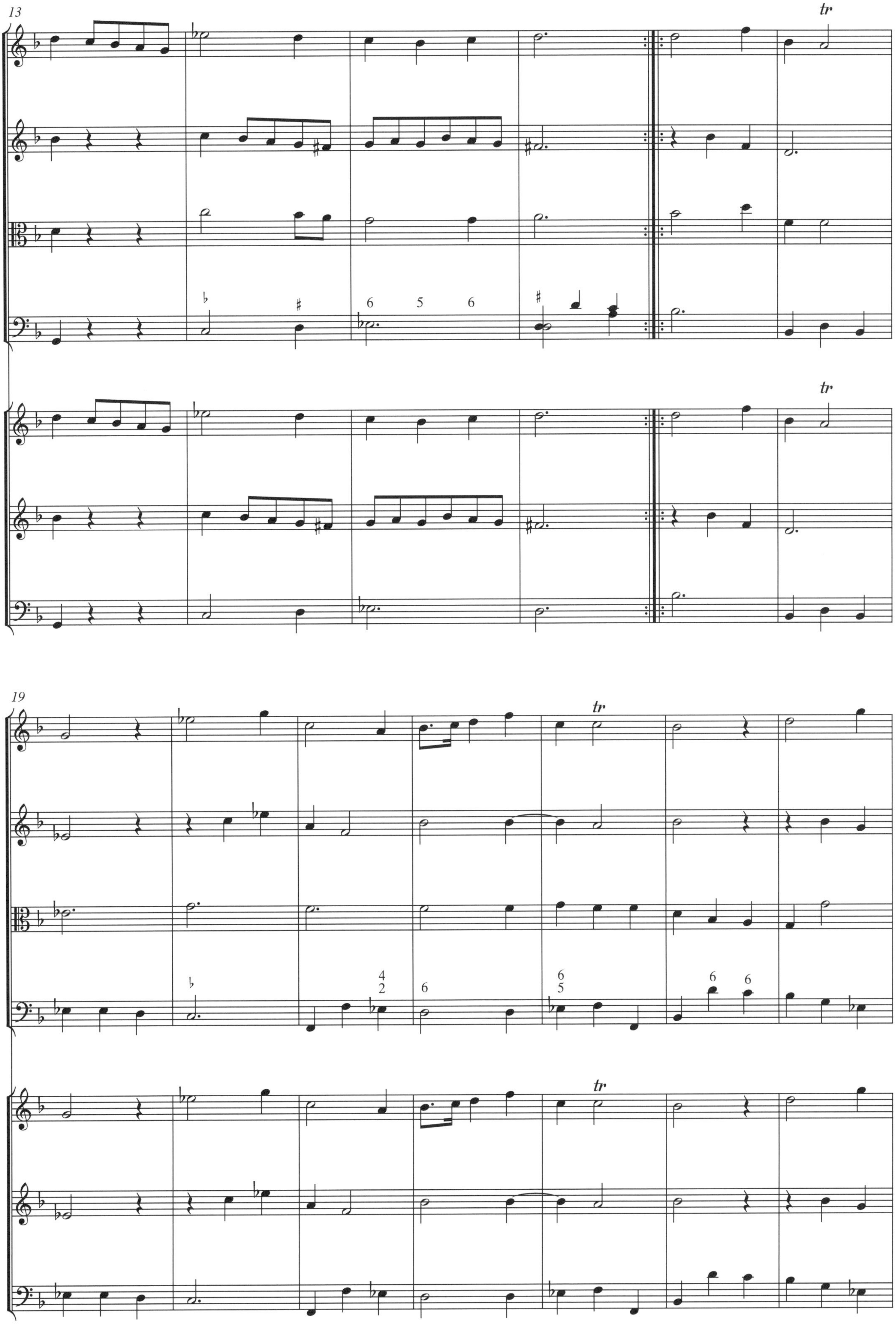
13
tr
tr
19
tr
tr

26
tr
tr
♯4 2
6
6
6
♯
♯4 2
♮6
6
♭
6 4
5 ♯
tr
tr

[Fine]

33
[Variation 1]
Harpsichord
38
44
1.
2.
50

117

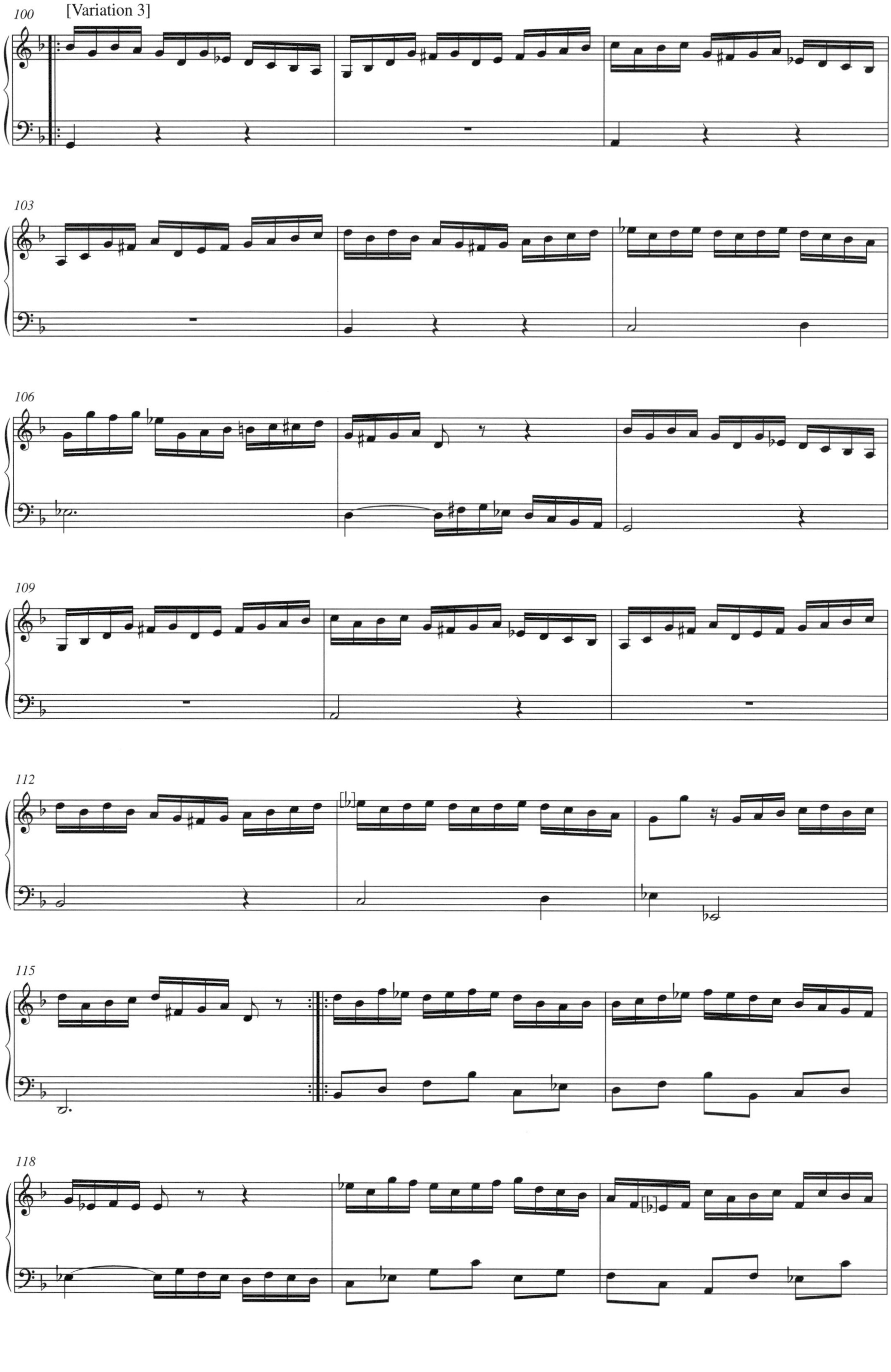
100
[Variation 3]
103
106
109
112
115
118

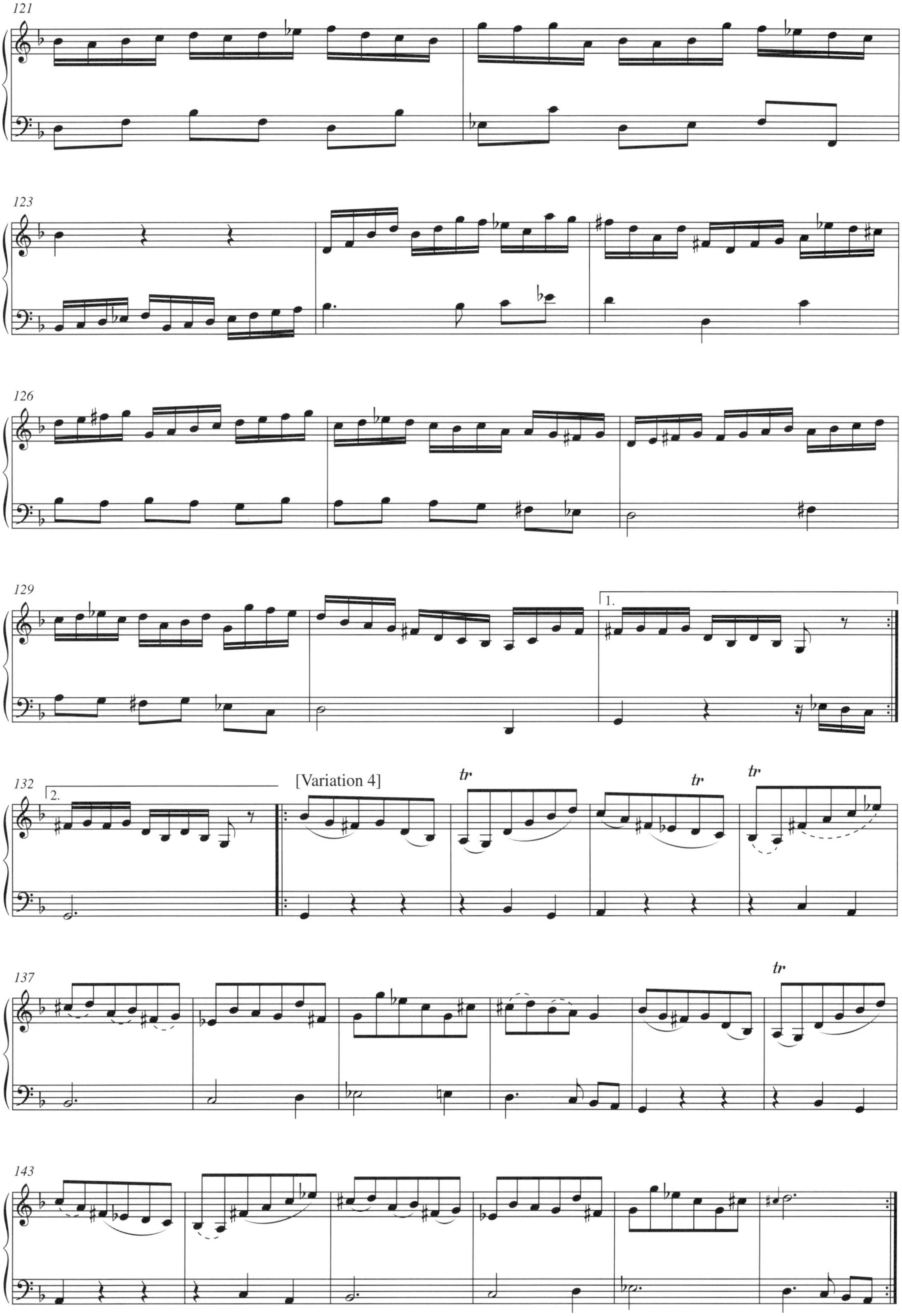
121
123
126
129
1.
132
2.
[Variation 4]
tr
tr
tr
137
tr
143

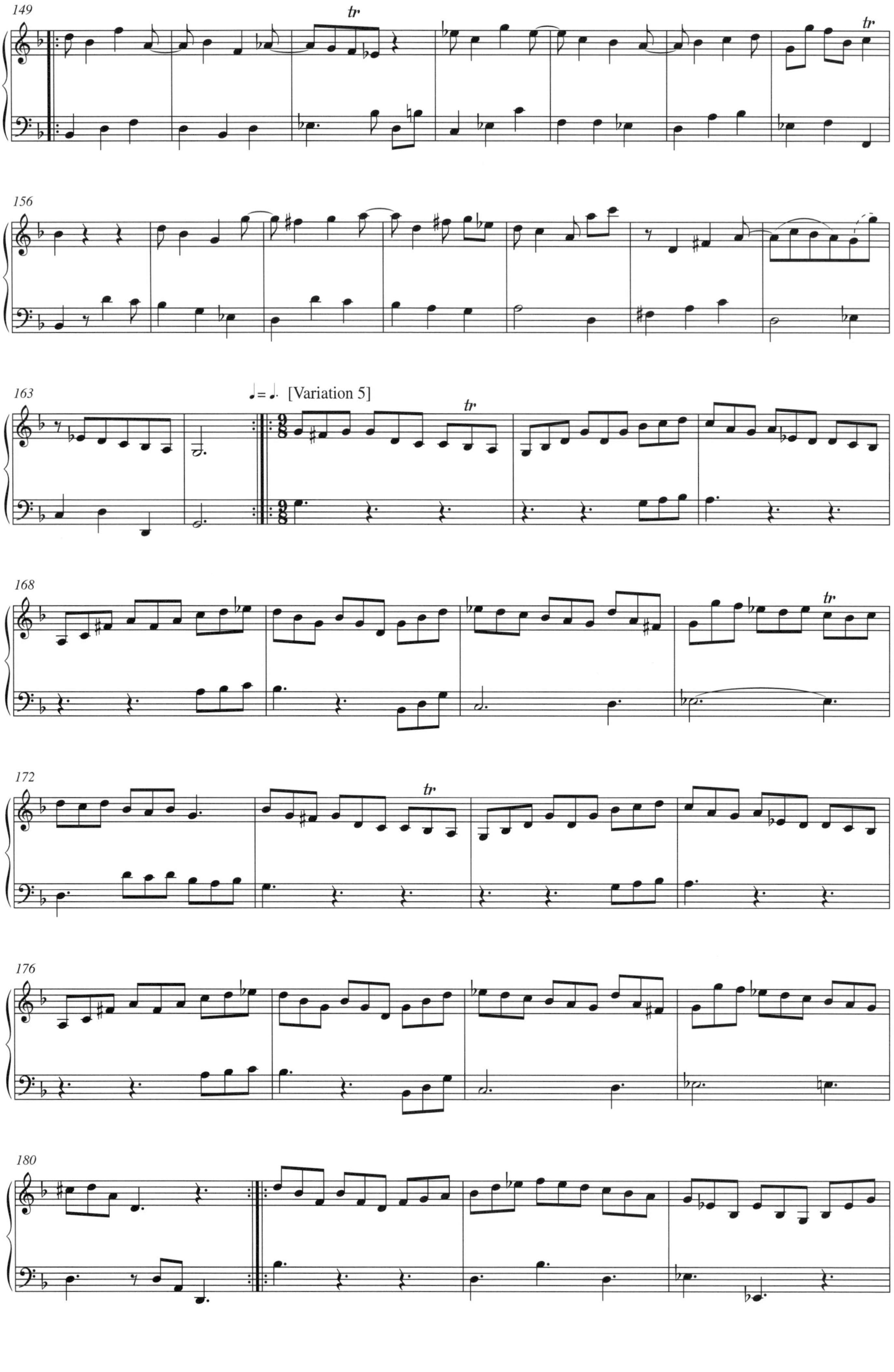
149
tr
tr
156
163
[Variation 5]
tr
168
tr
172
tr
176
180

121

Da Capo il Minuet

7. Concerto in C Minor

I

From Franceso Geminiani, Sonata in C Minor, Op. 1, No. 7

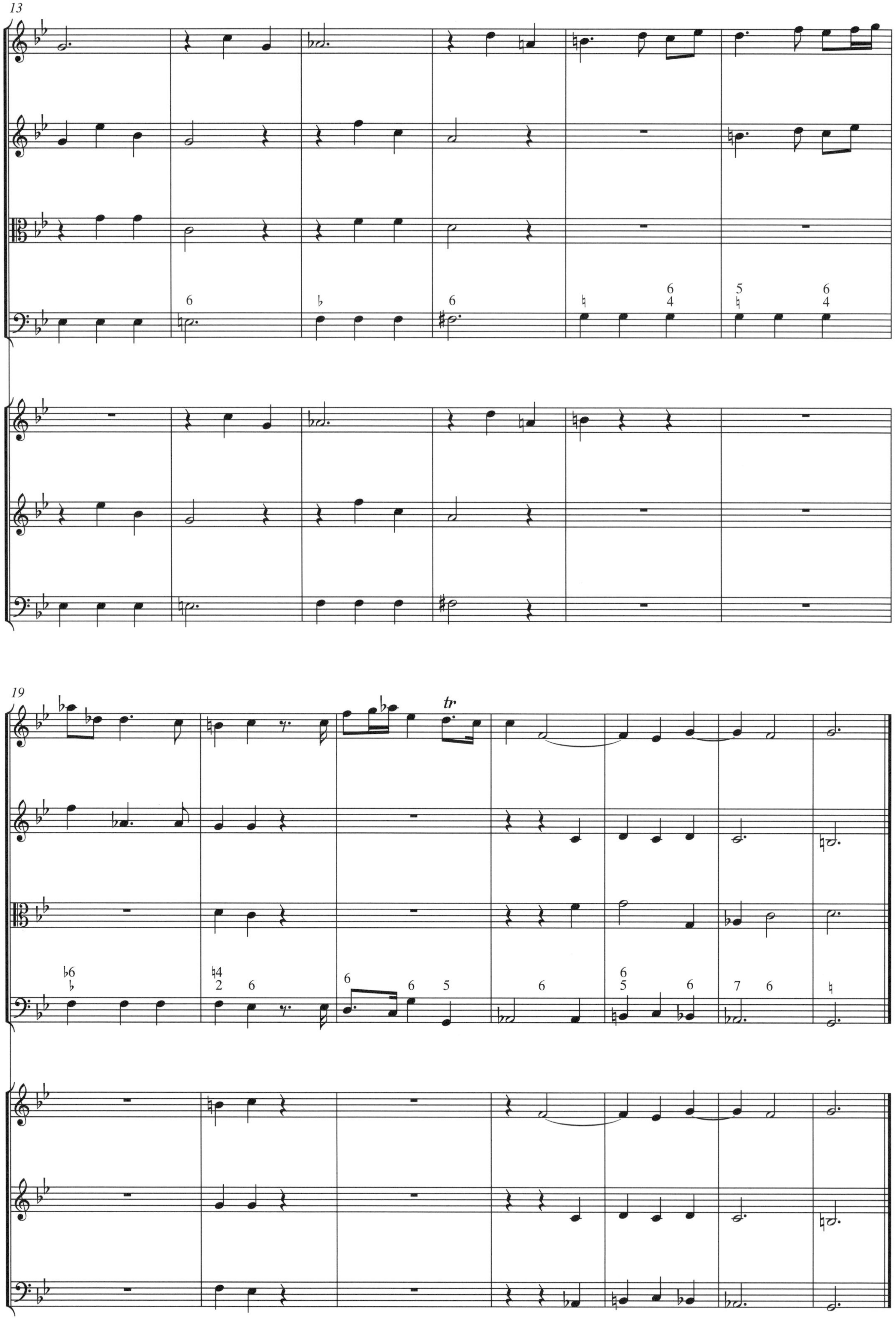
13
19
tr

II

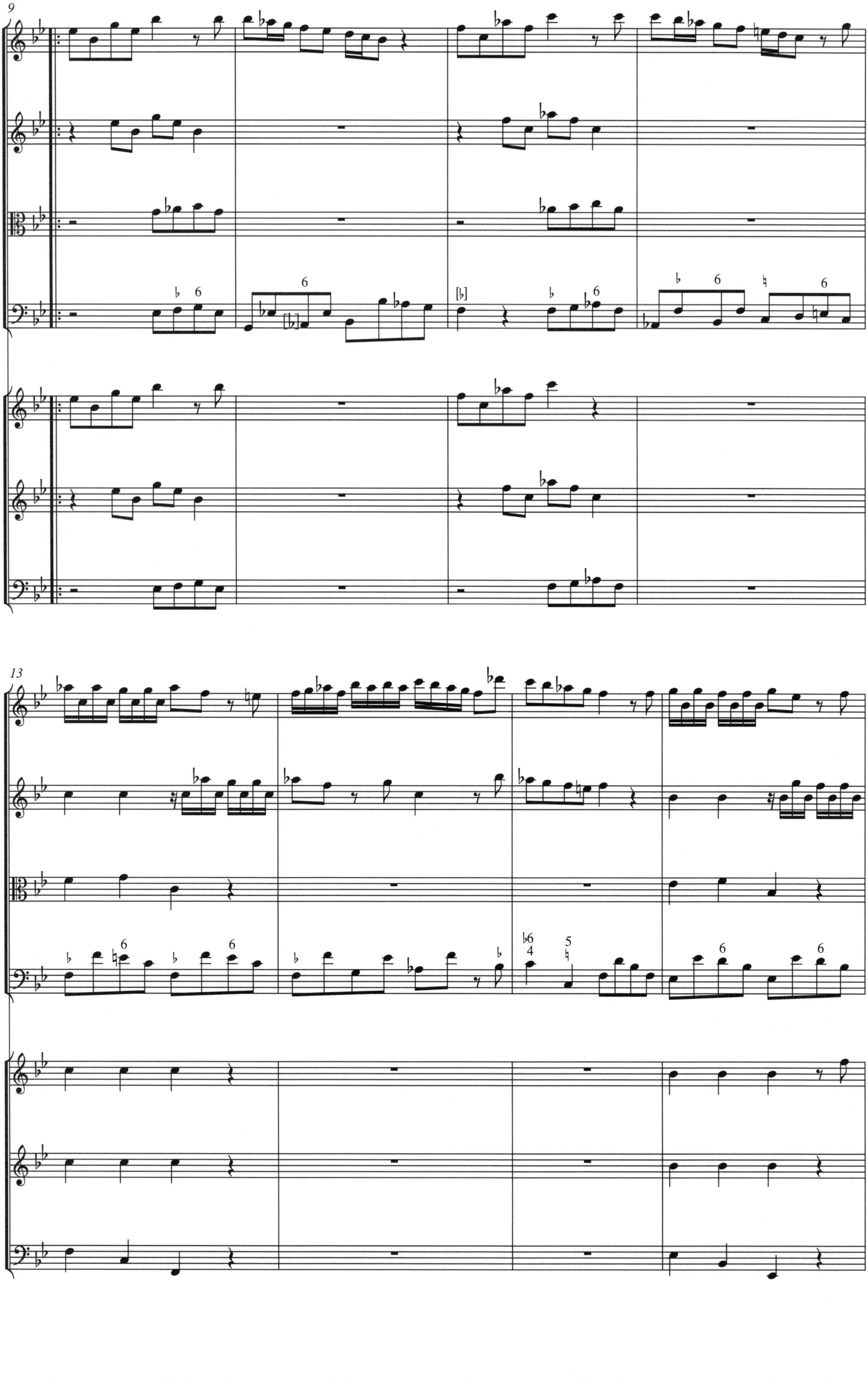
9
13

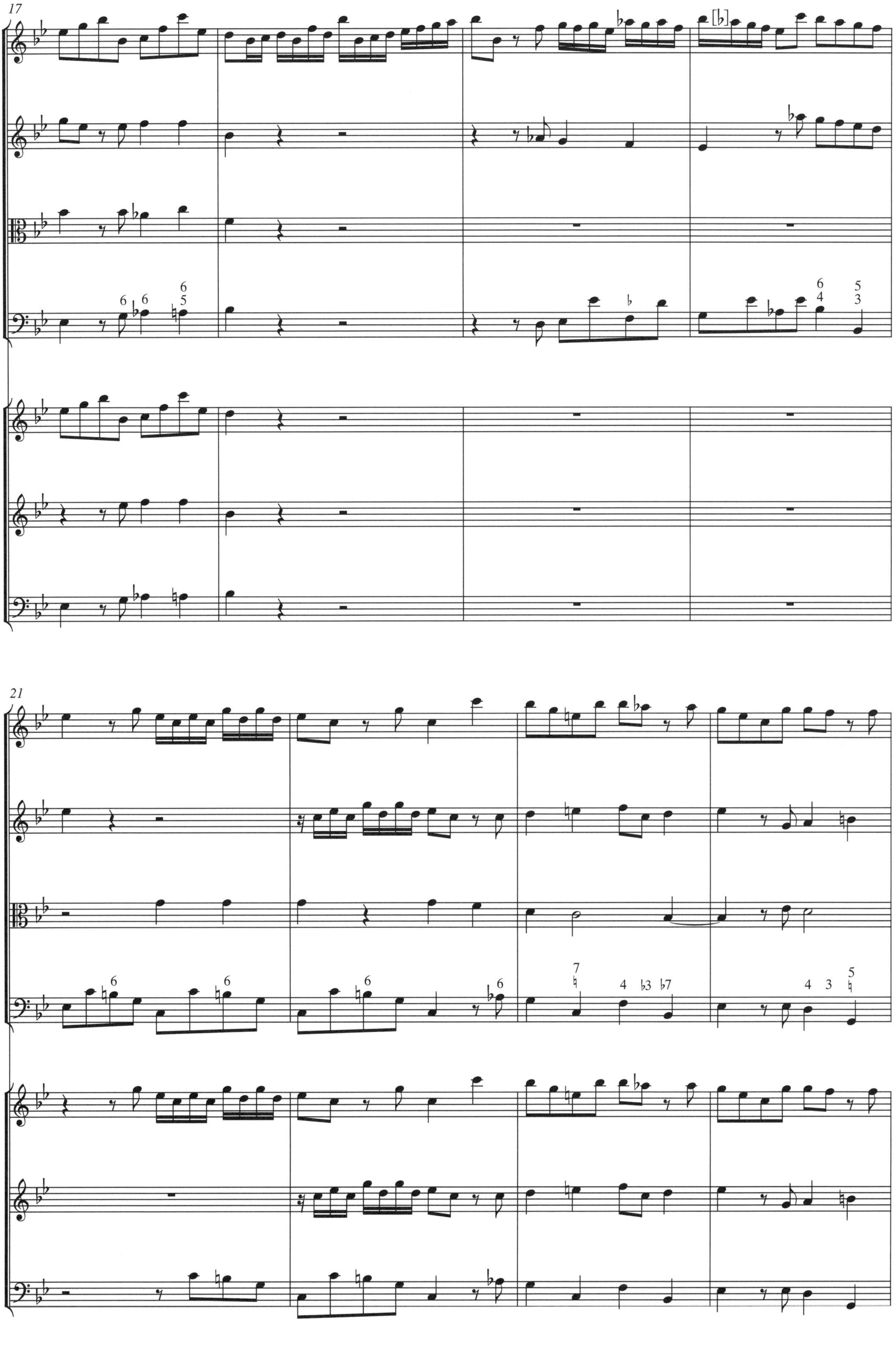
17
21

III

IV

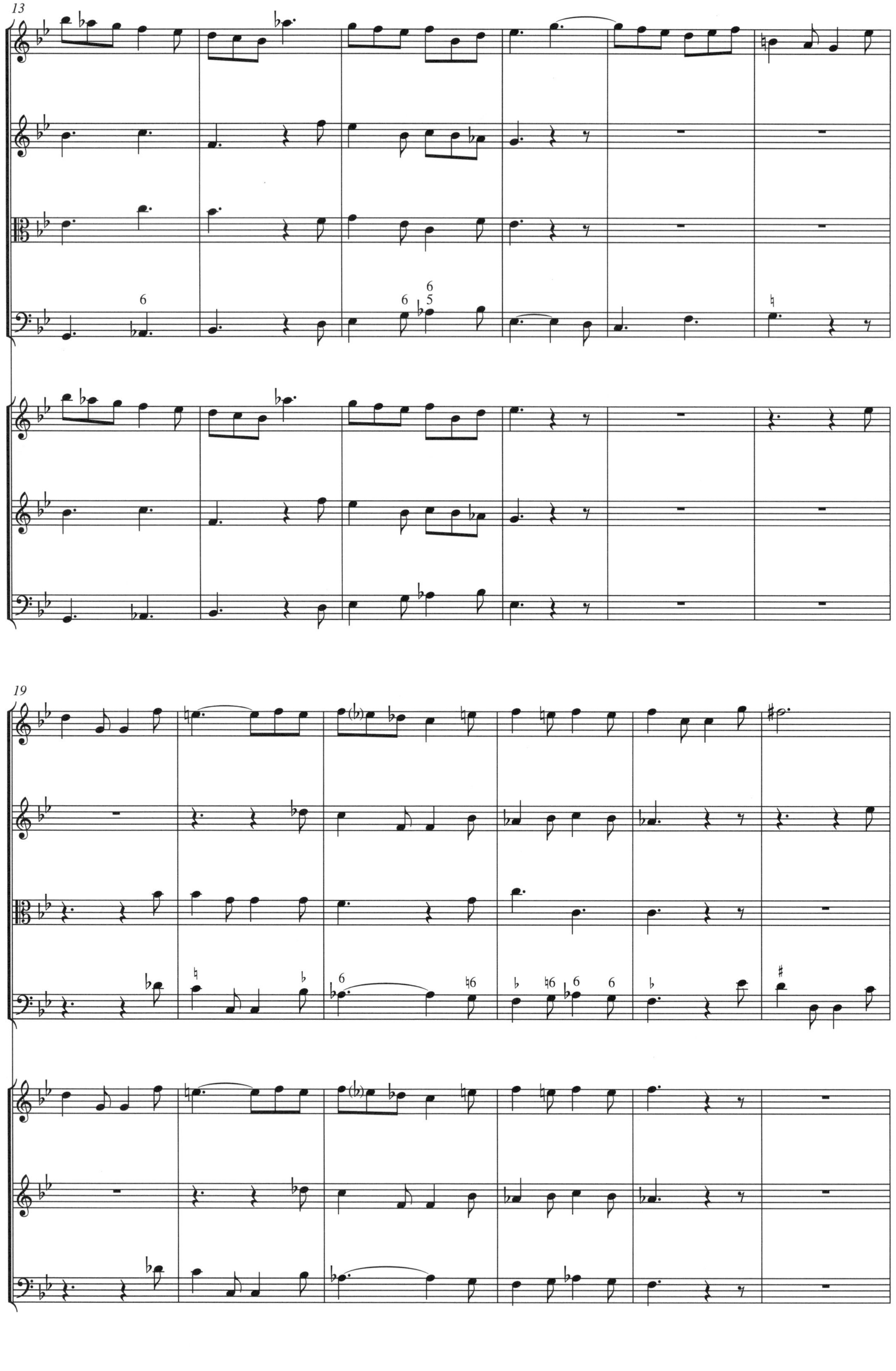
13
19

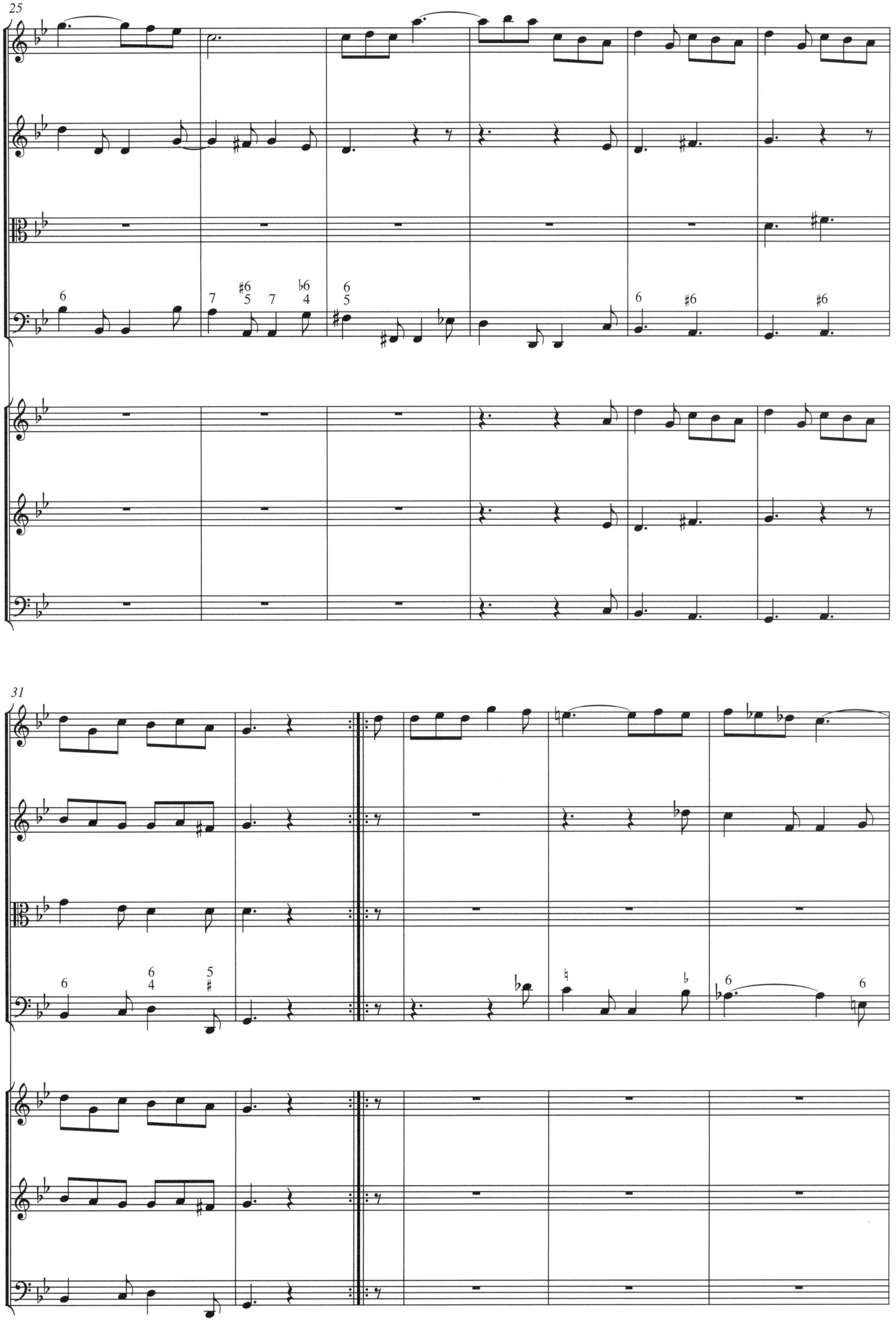
25
31

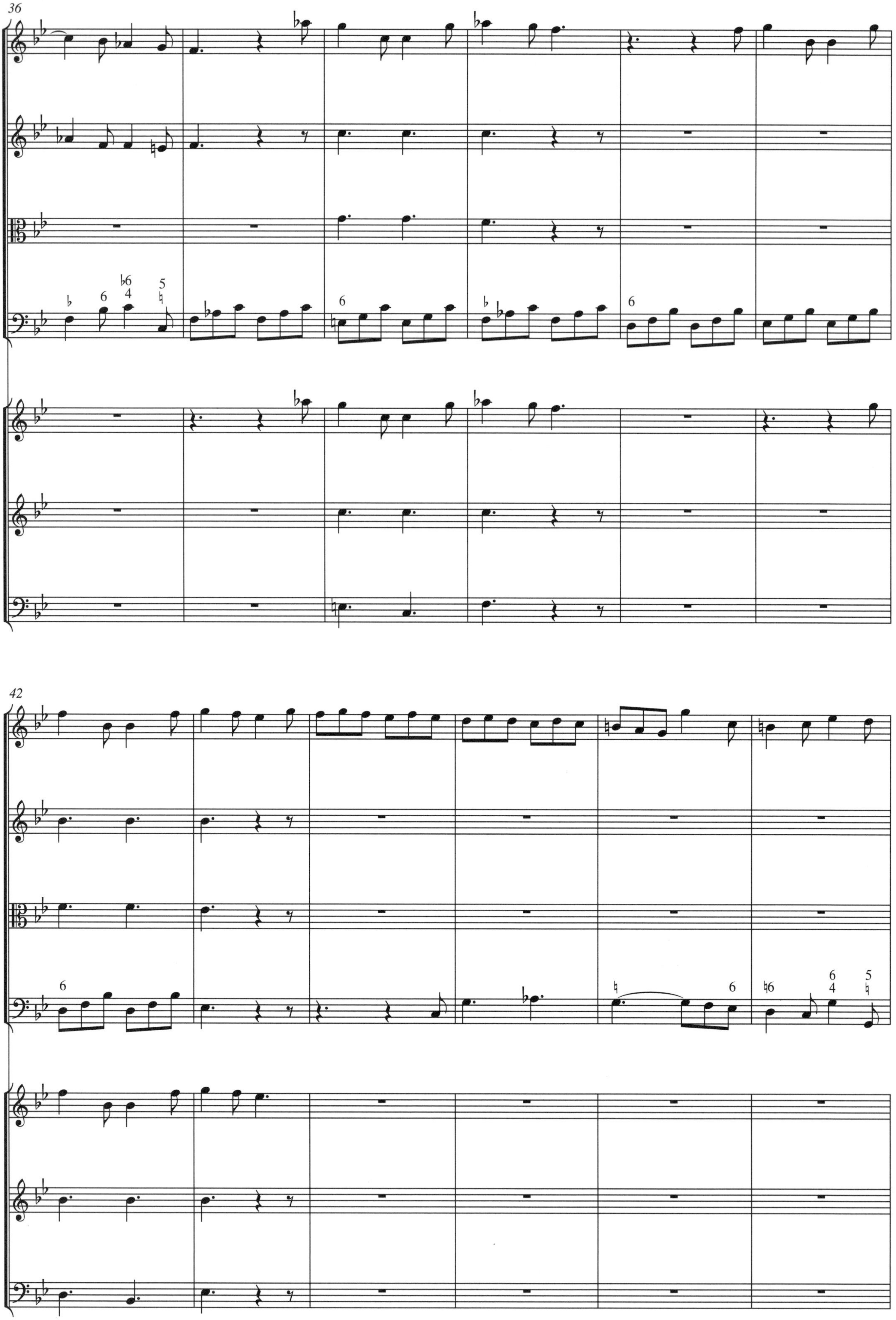
36
42

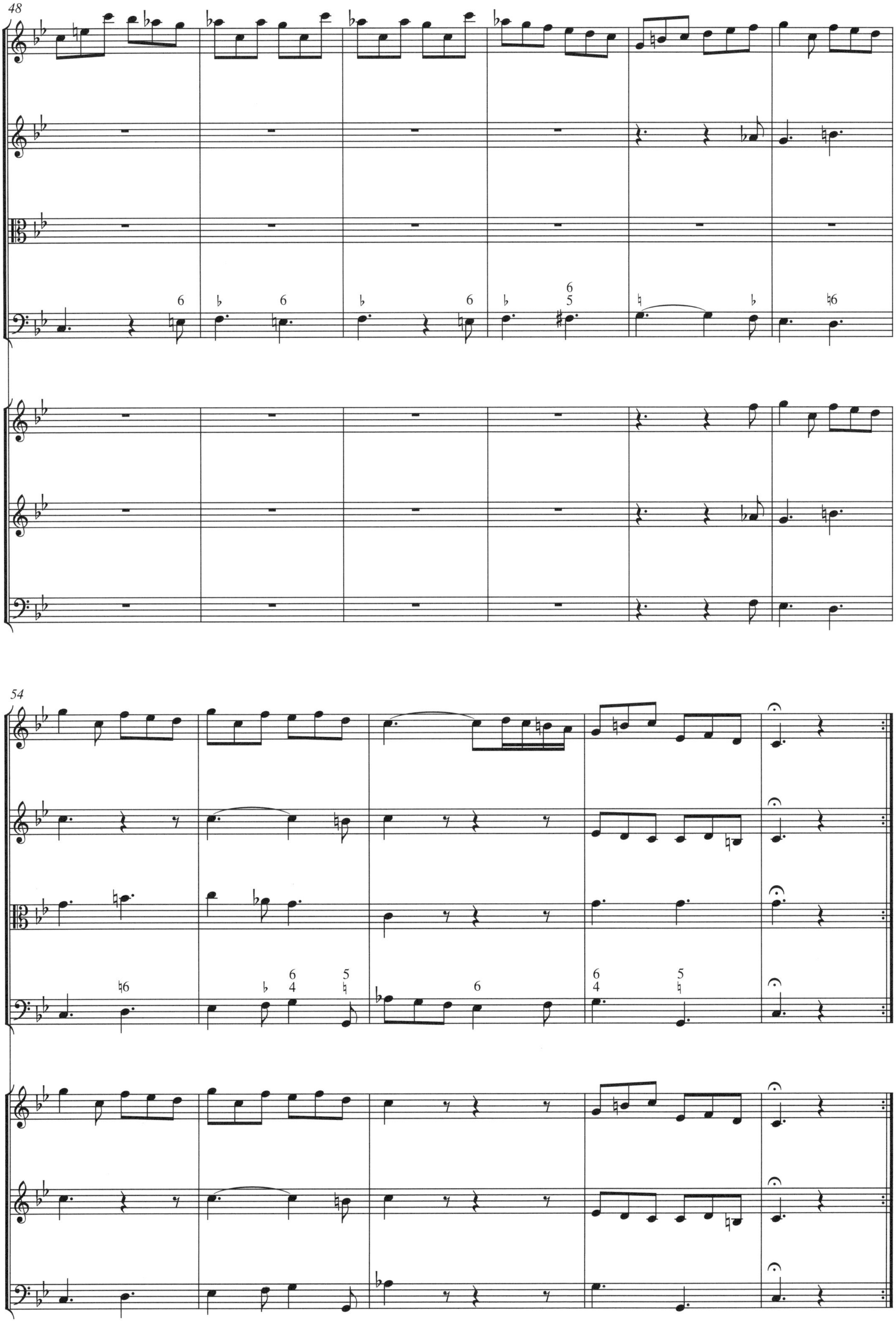
48
54

8. Concerto in B Minor
I

From Francesco Geminiani, Sonata in B Minor, Op. 1, No. 8

135

II

137

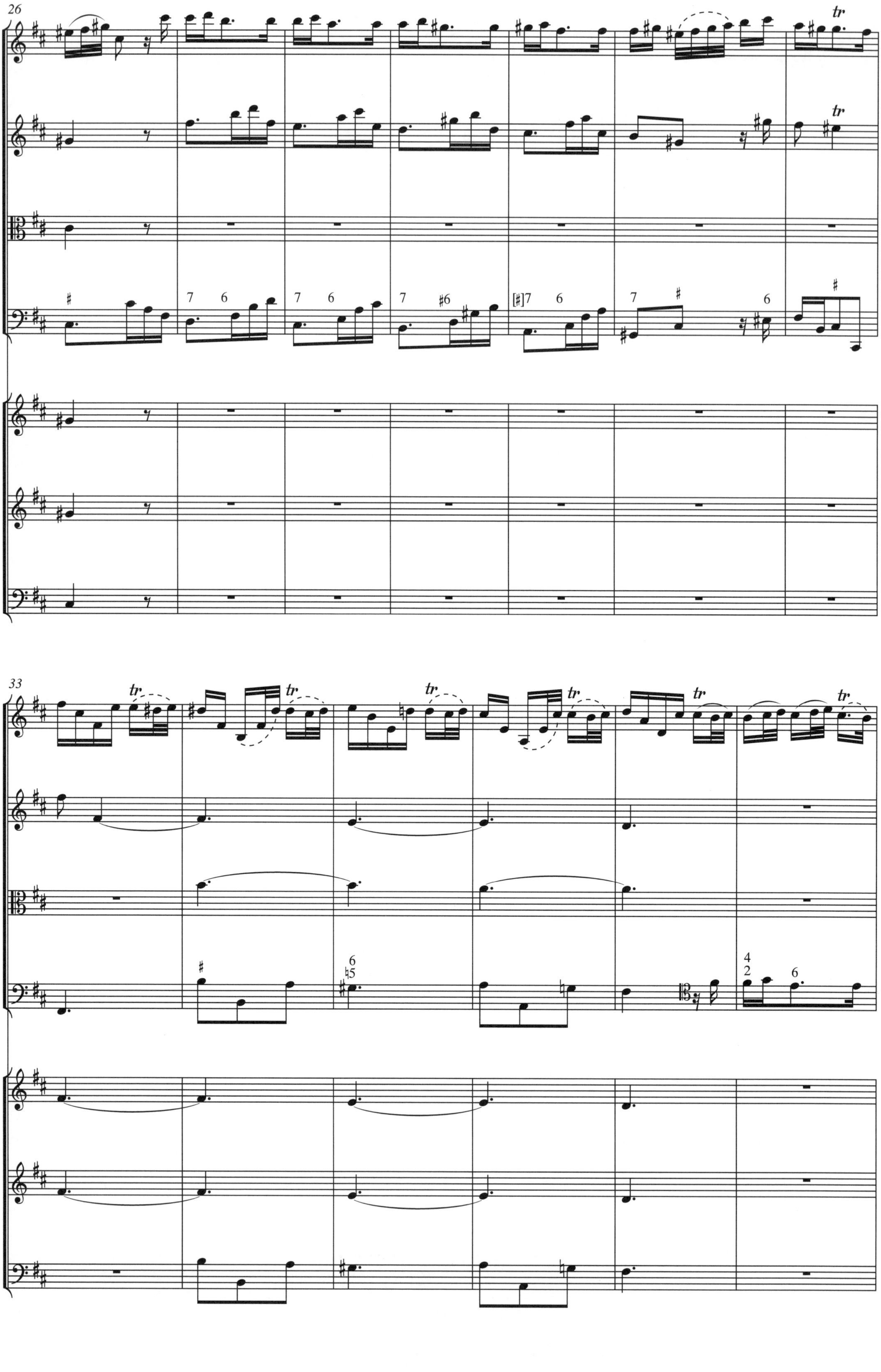
26
tr
tr
7 6 7 6 7 ♯6 [♯]7 6 7 ♯ 6 ♯
33
tr tr tr tr tr tr
♯ 6 ♮5 4 2 6

139

III

141

IV

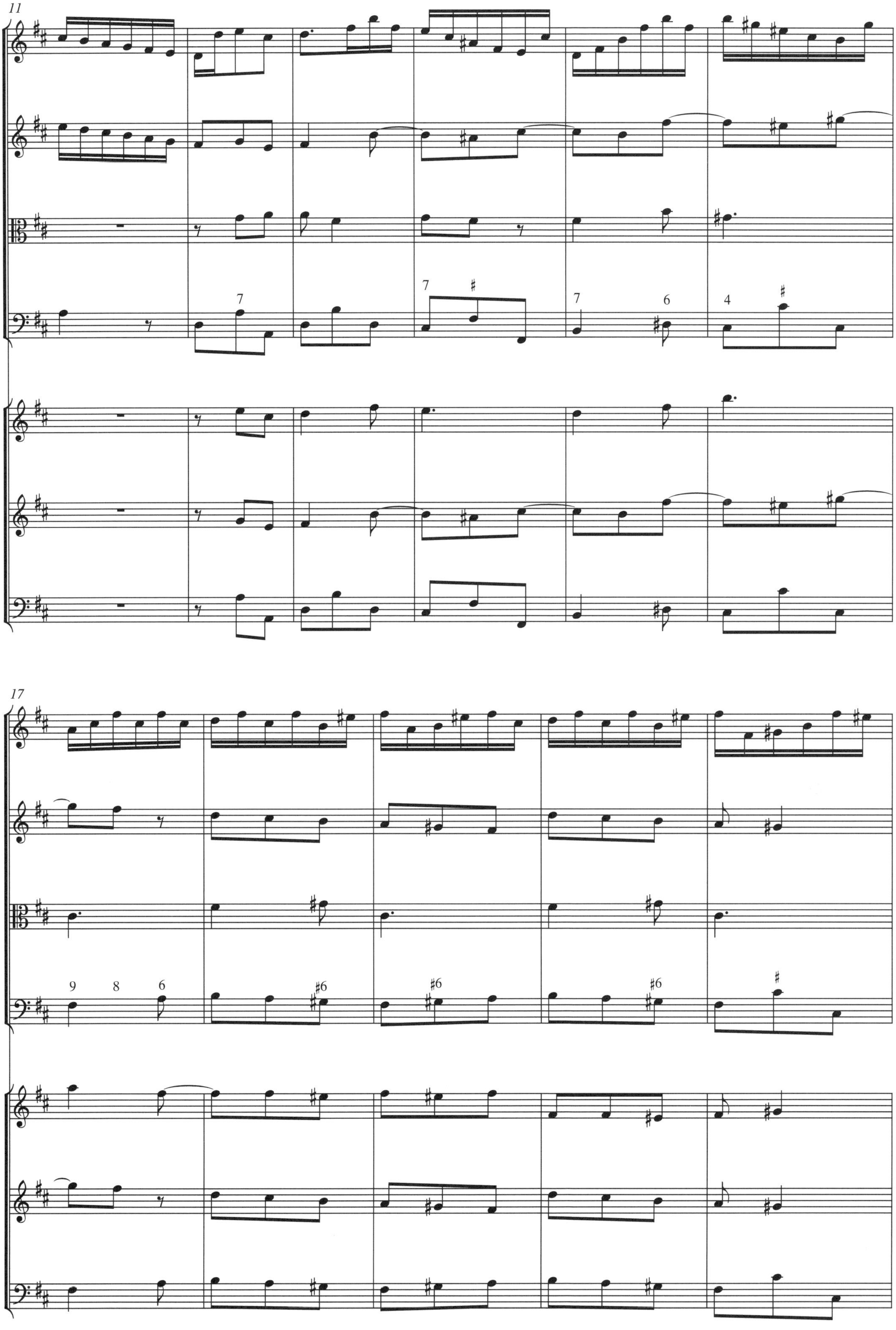
11
17

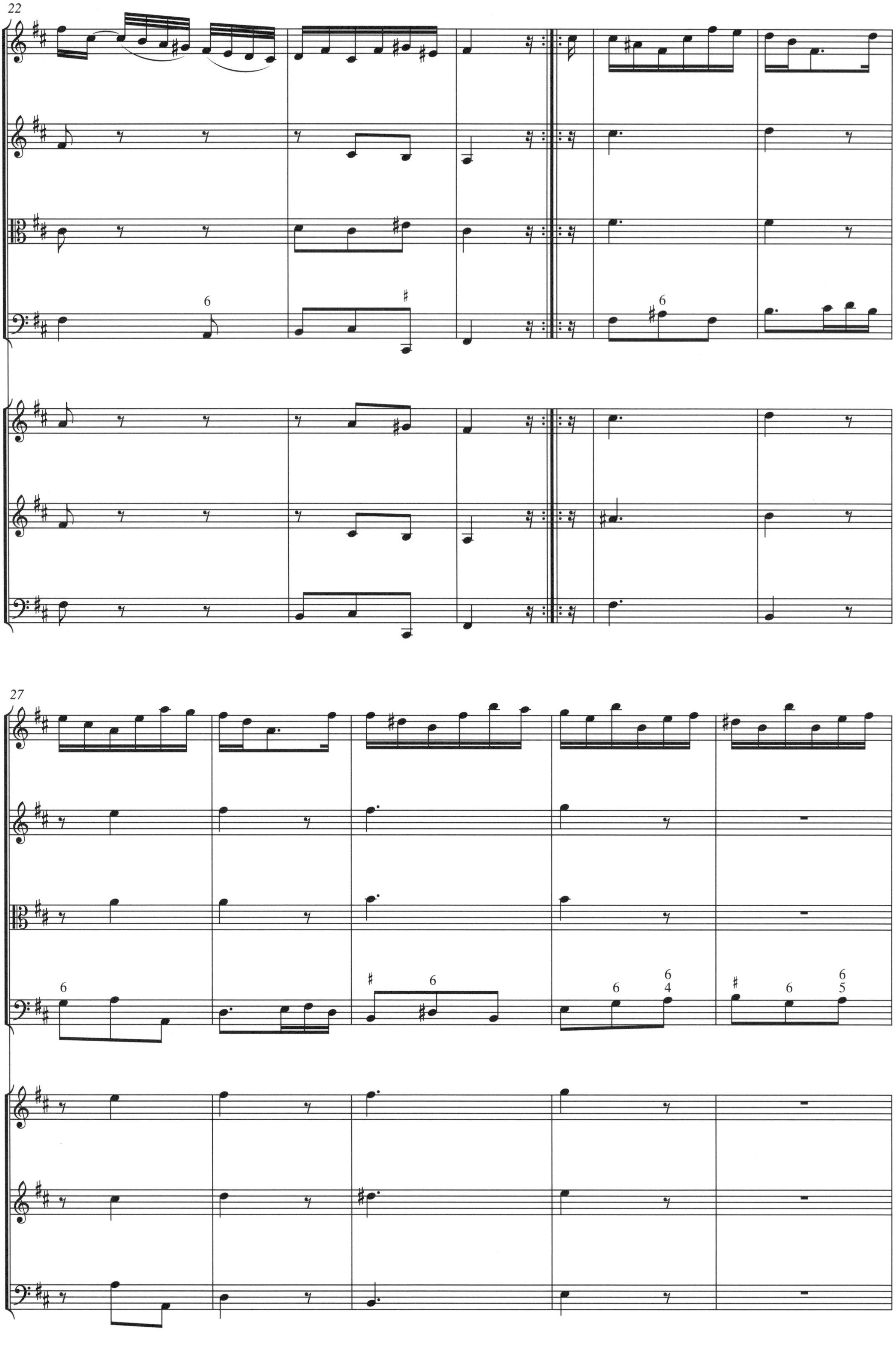
22
27

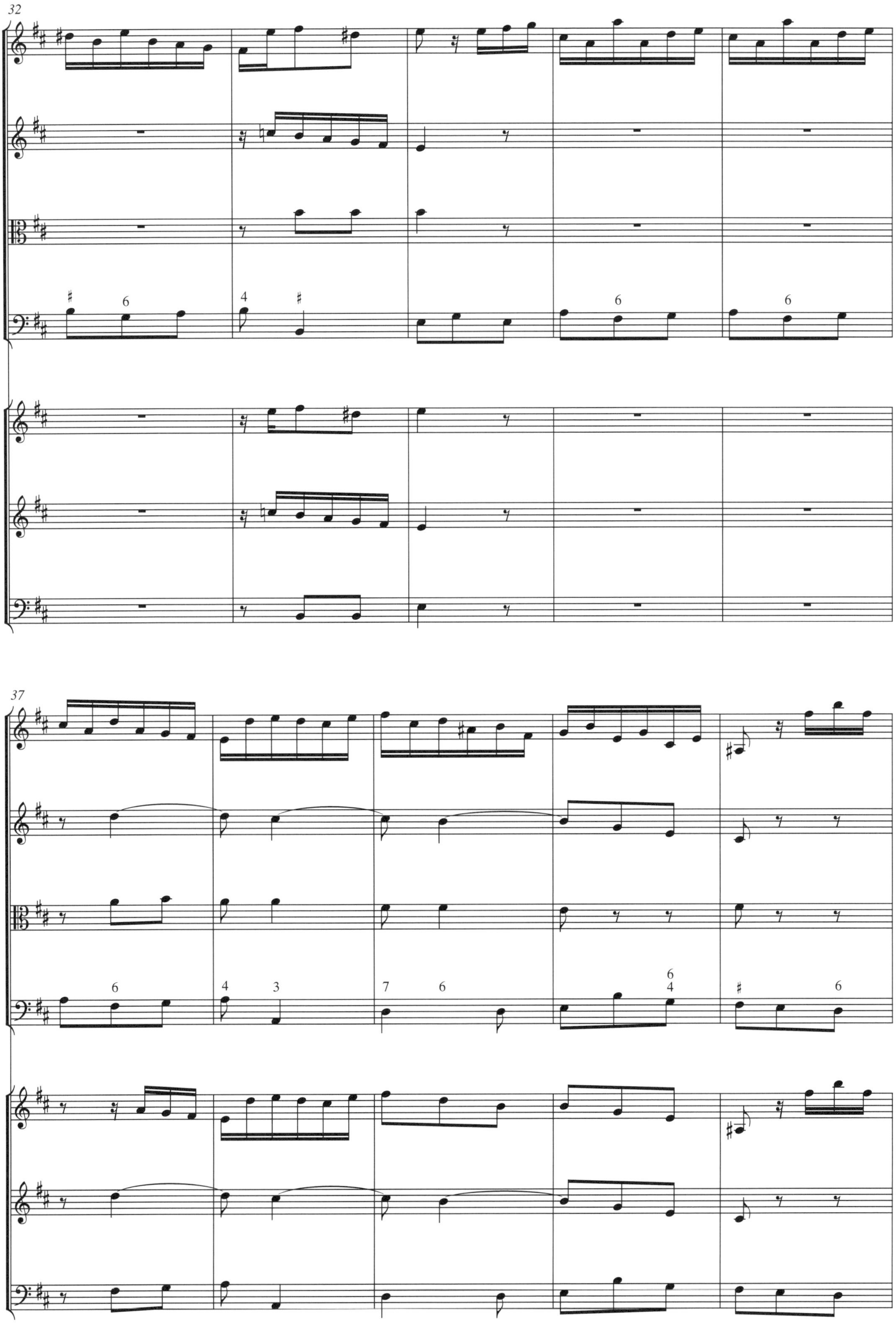
32
37

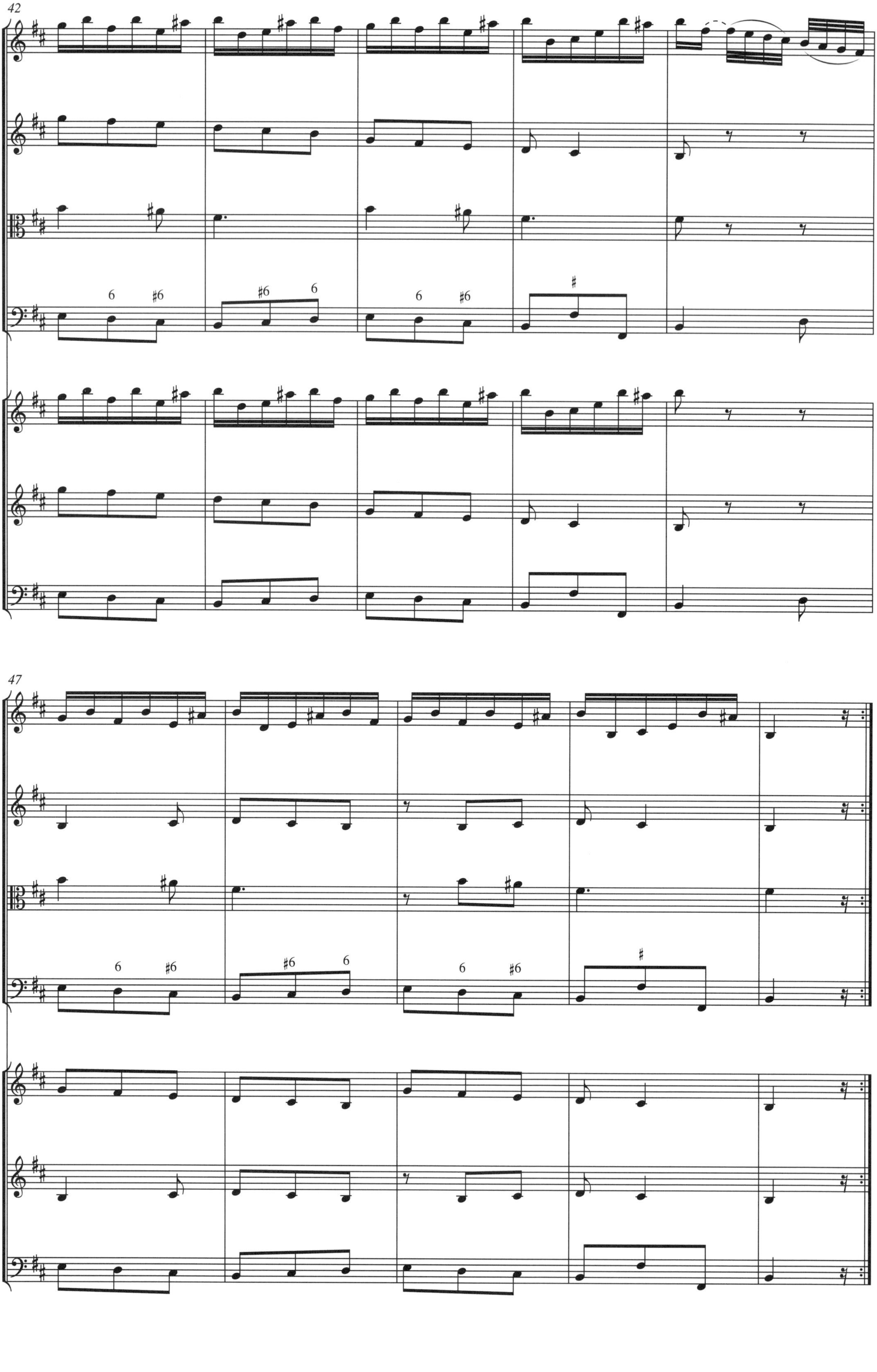

9. Concerto in F Major
I

From Francesco Geminiani, Sonata in F Major, Op. 1, No. 9

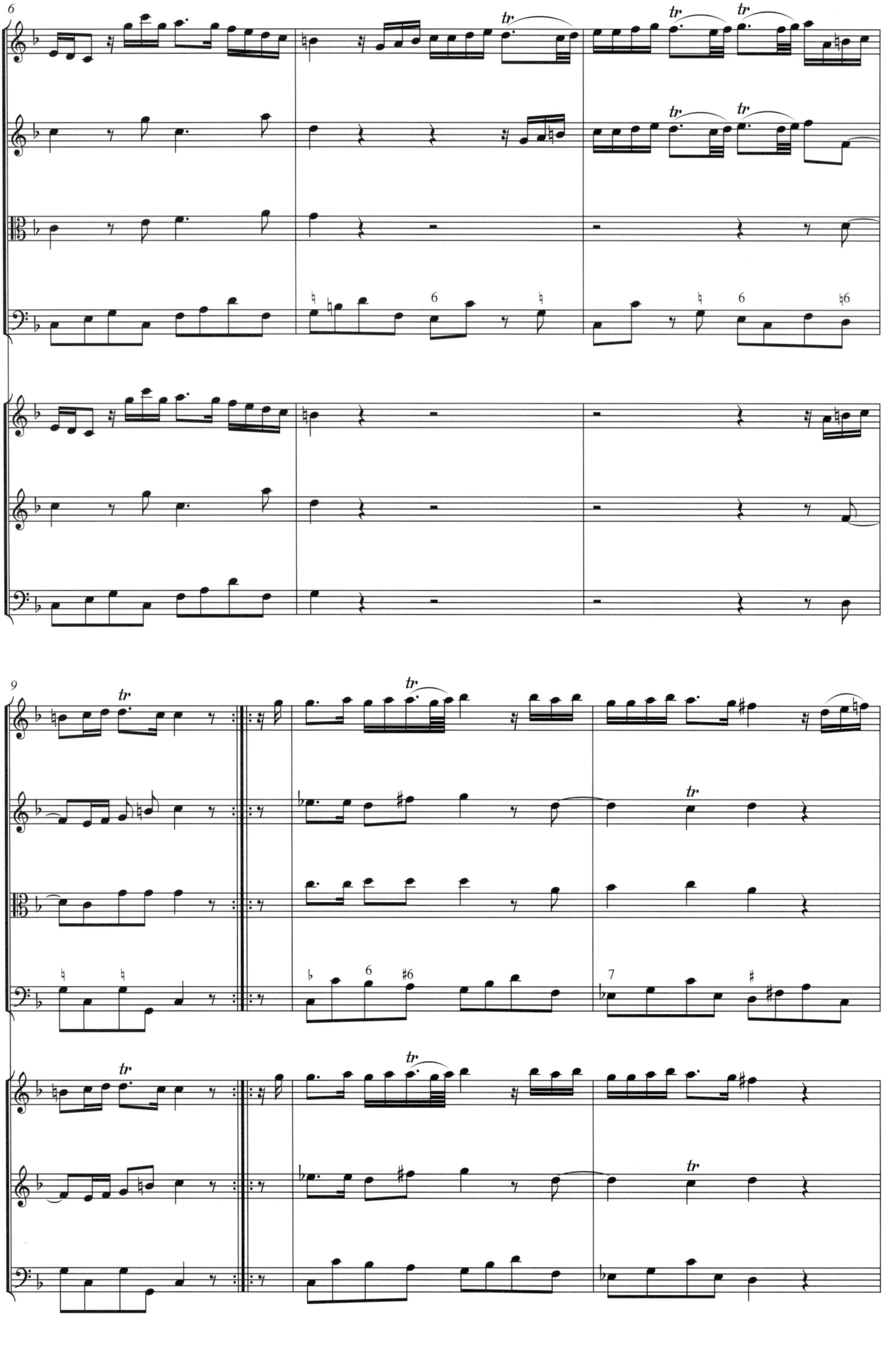

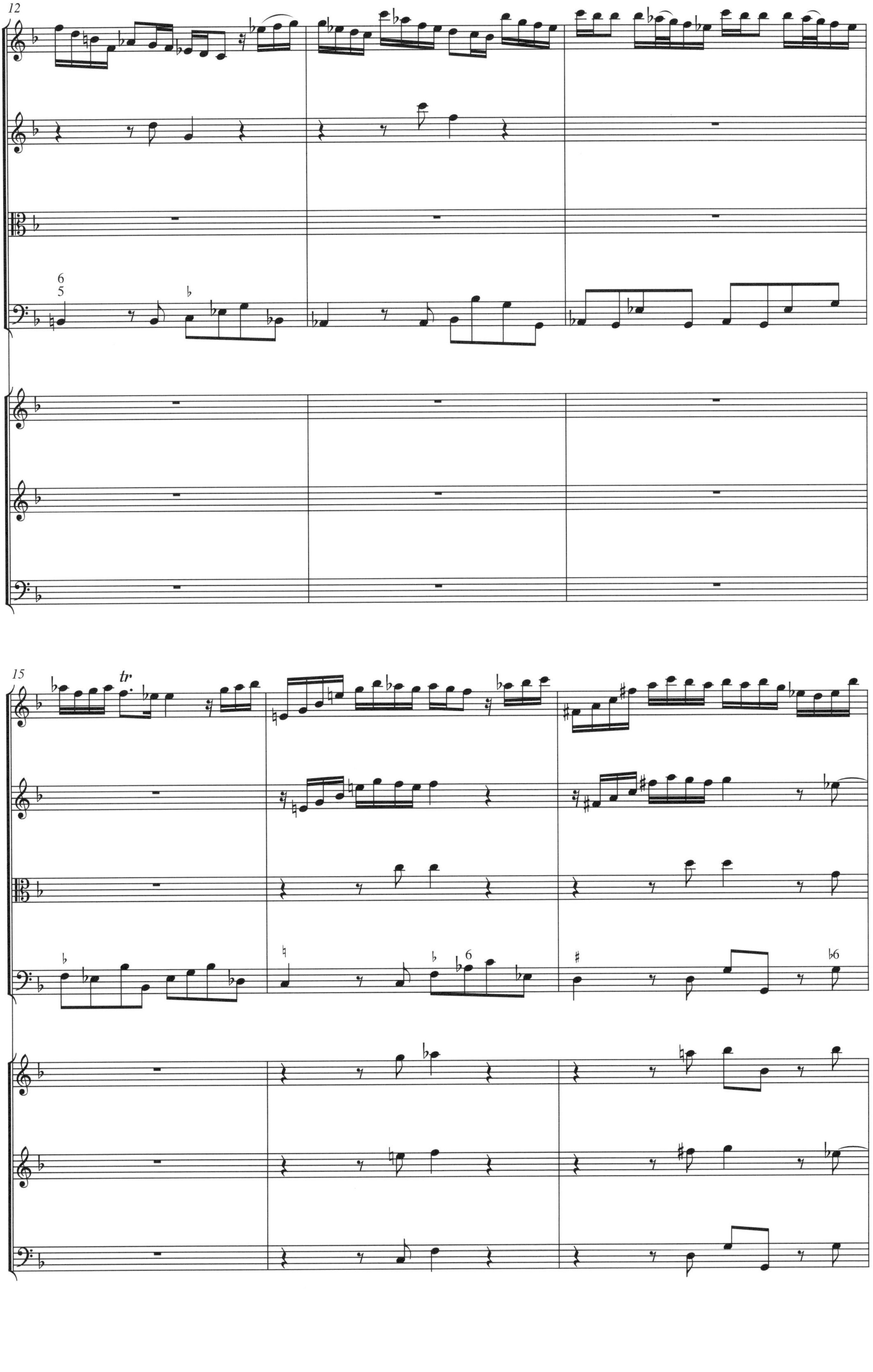
12
15

150

II

III

153

154

155

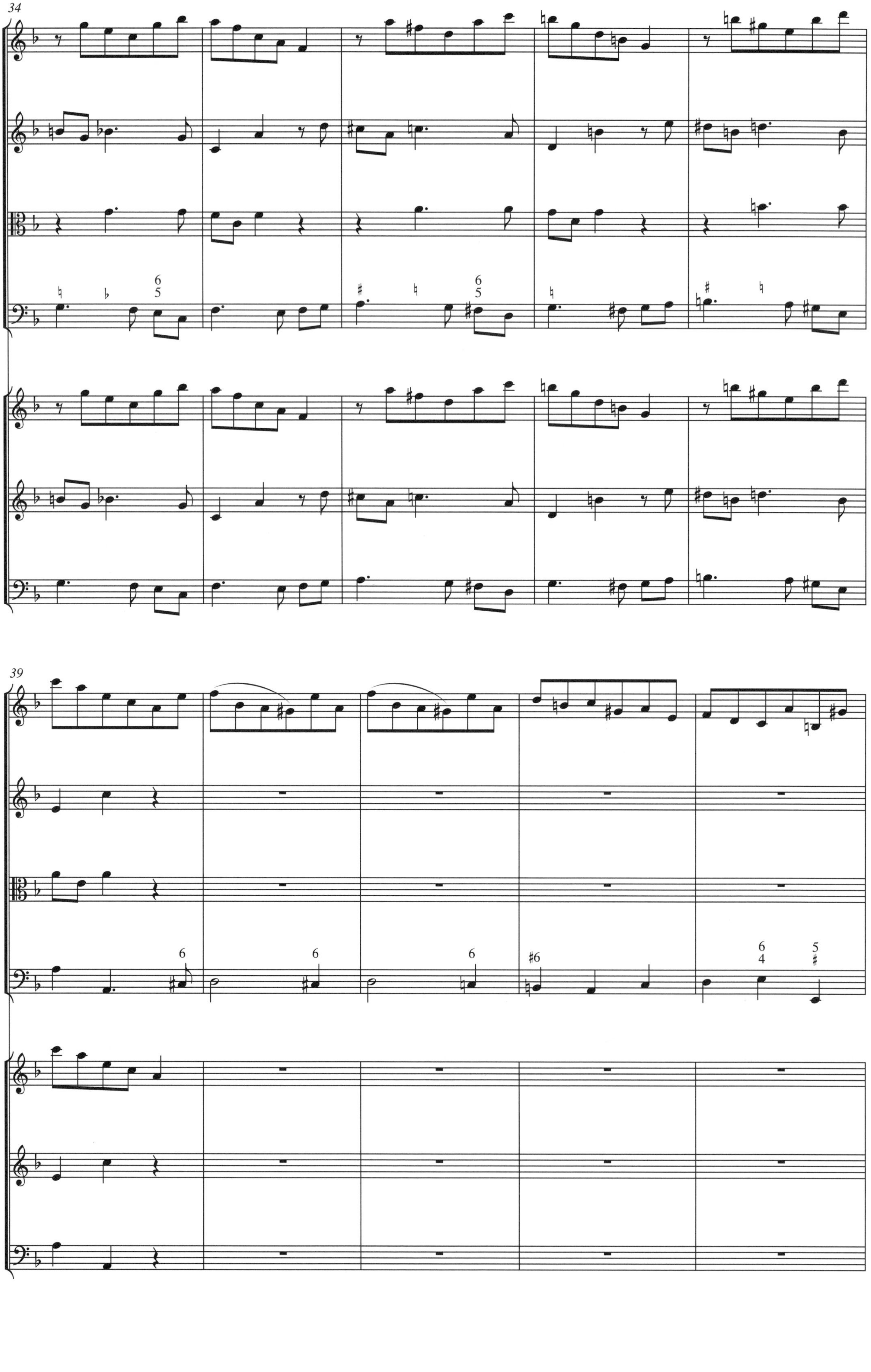
34
39

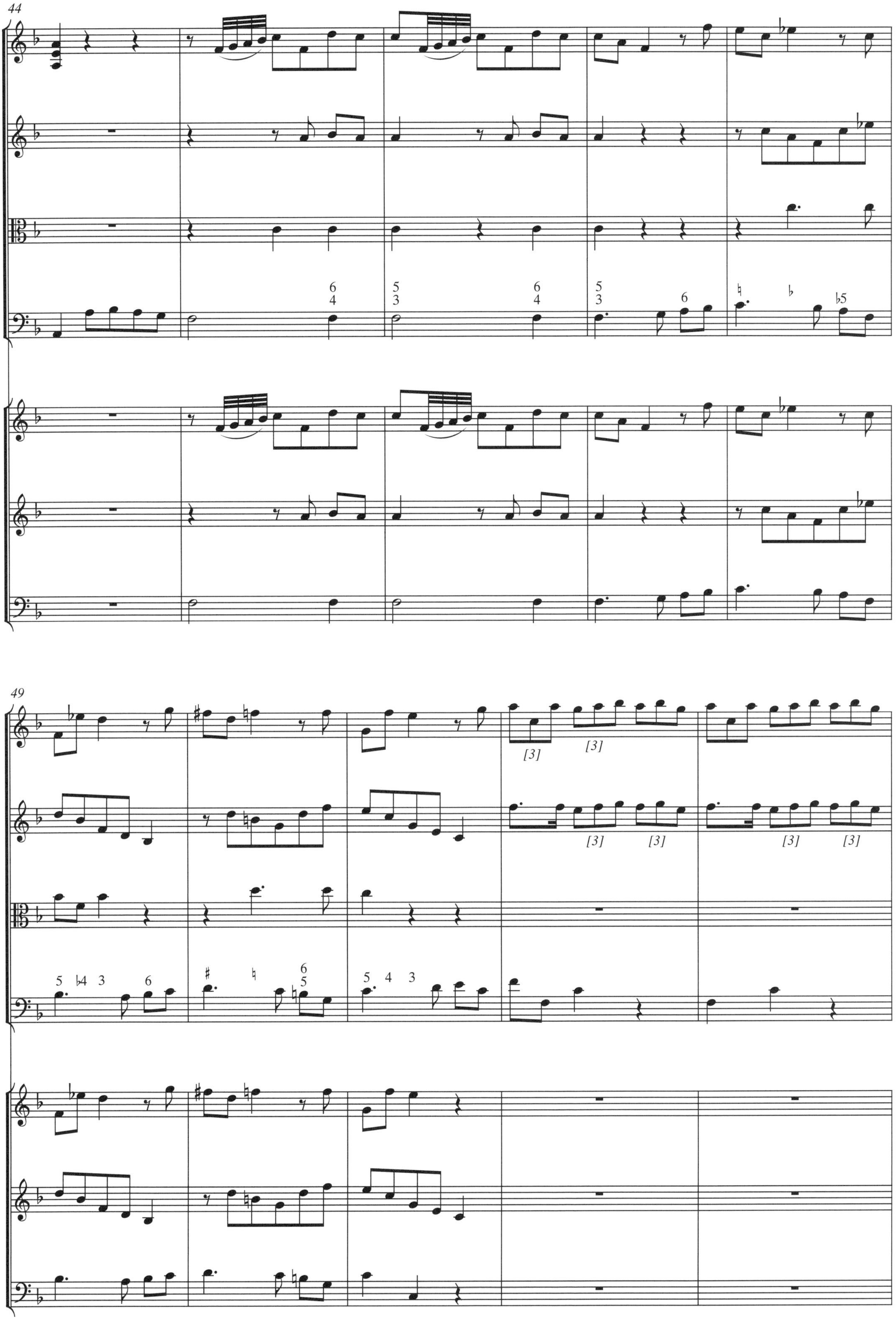
44
49
[3]

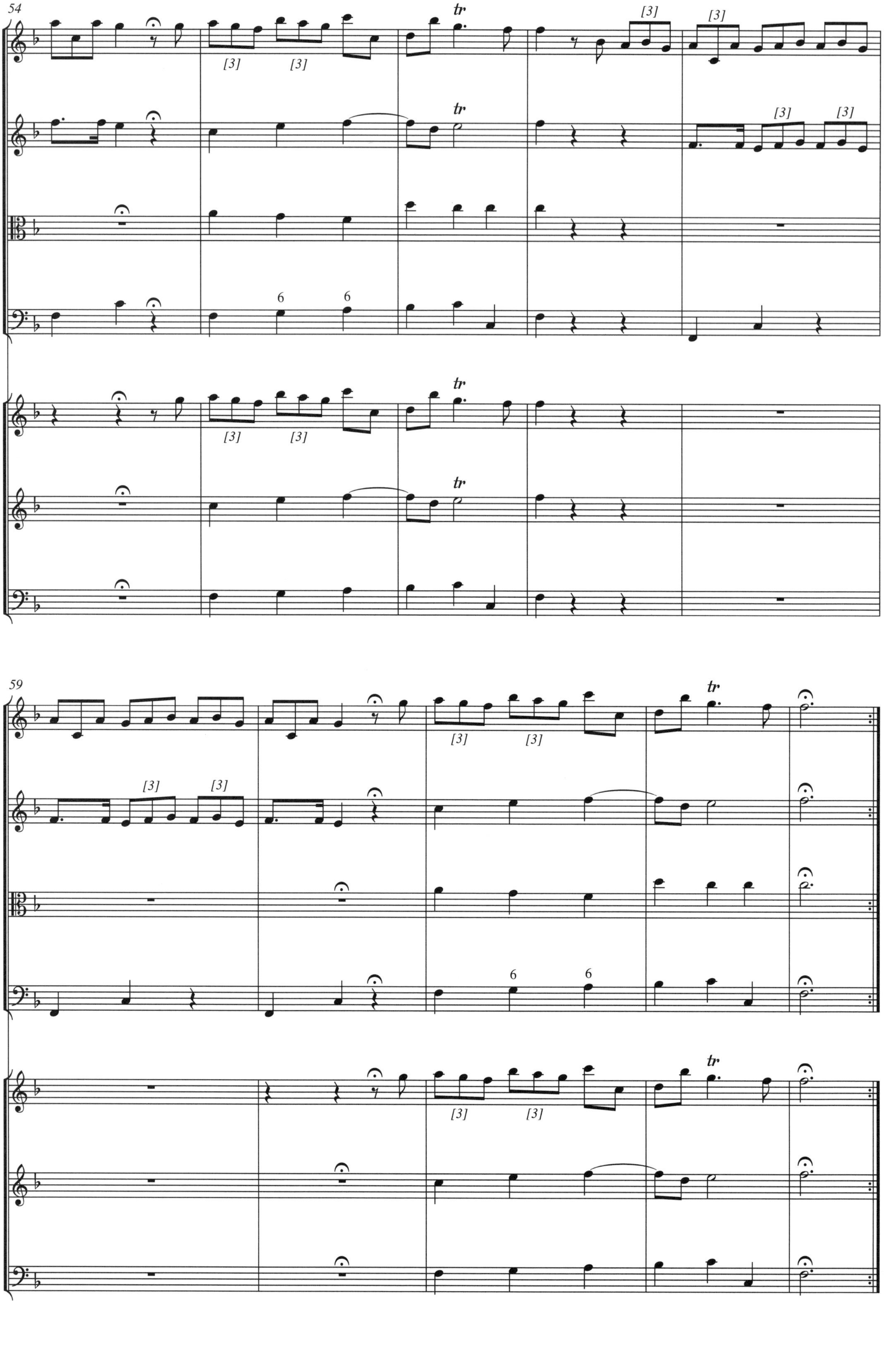

10. Concerto in D Major
I

From Francesco Geminiani, Sonata in E Major, Op. 1, No. 10

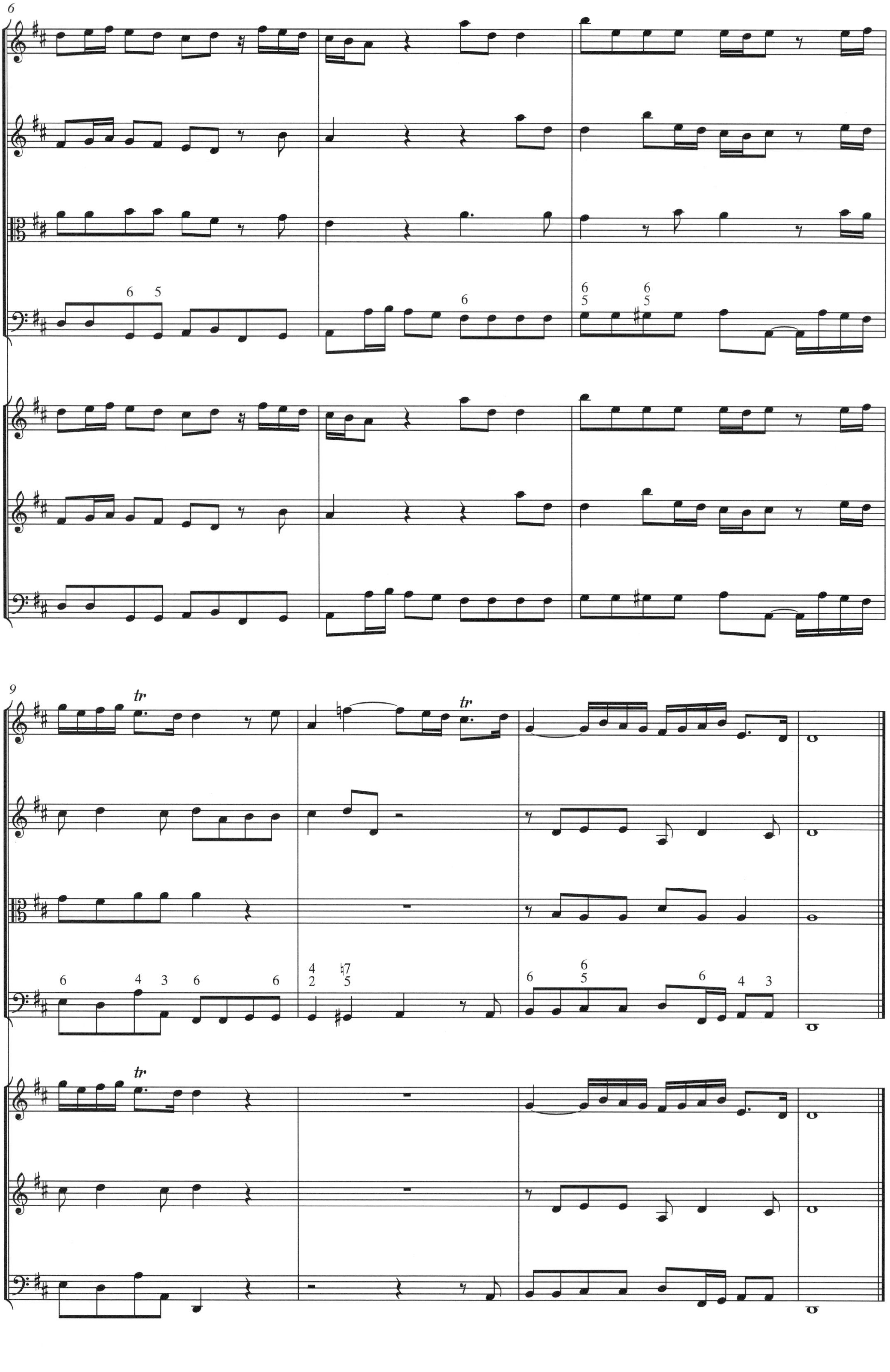
6
9
tr
tr
tr

II

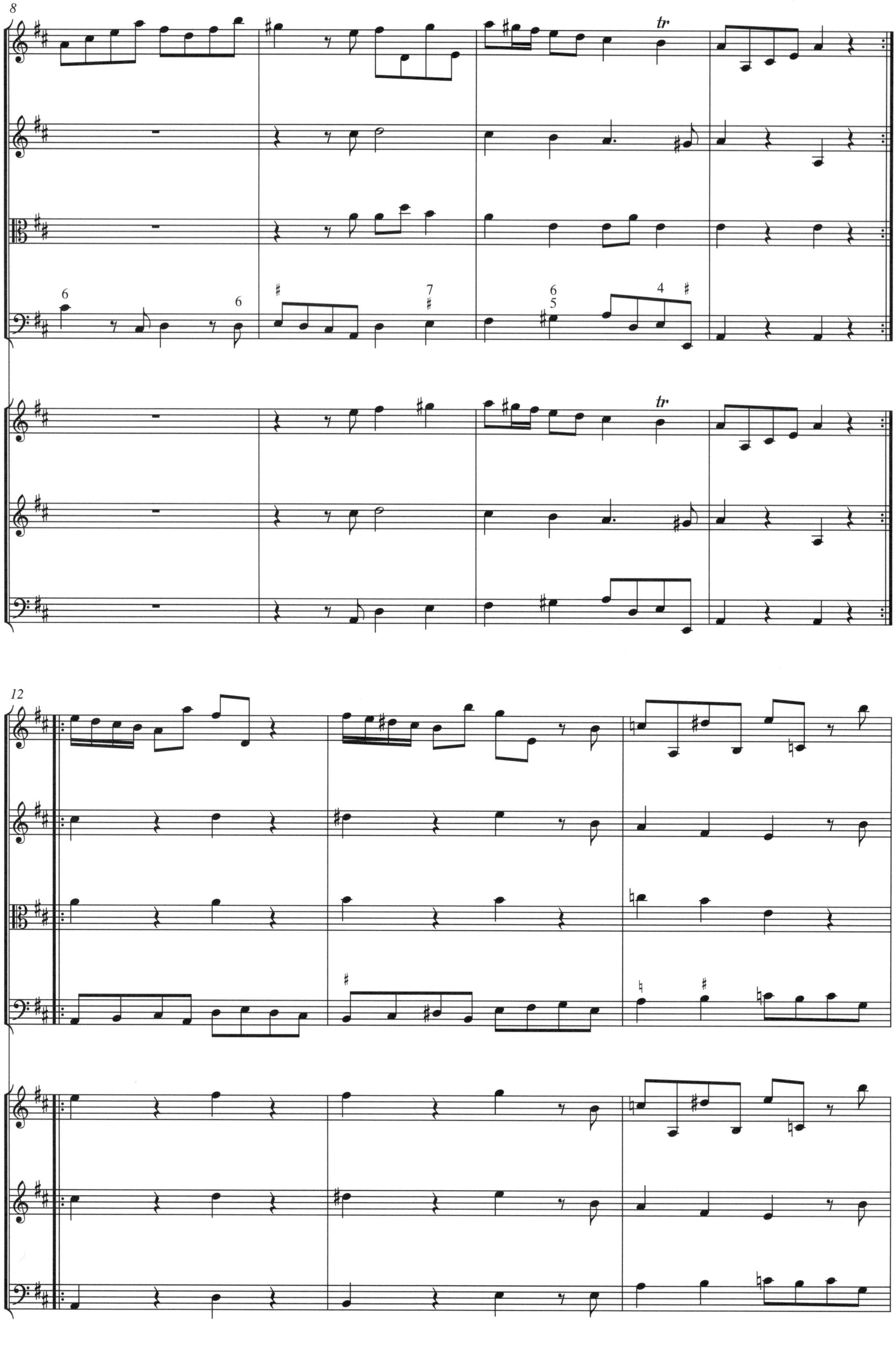
8
tr
tr
12

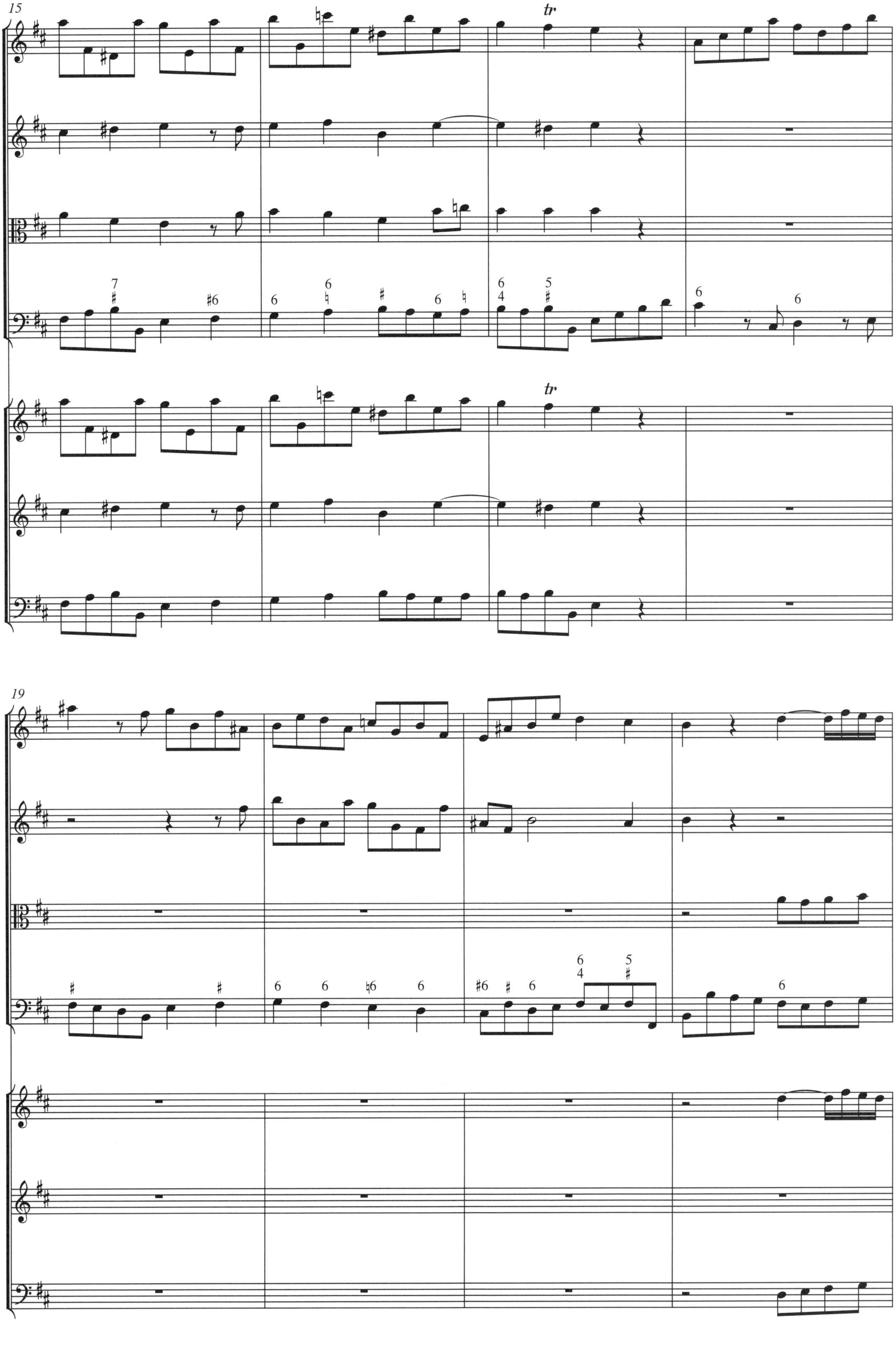

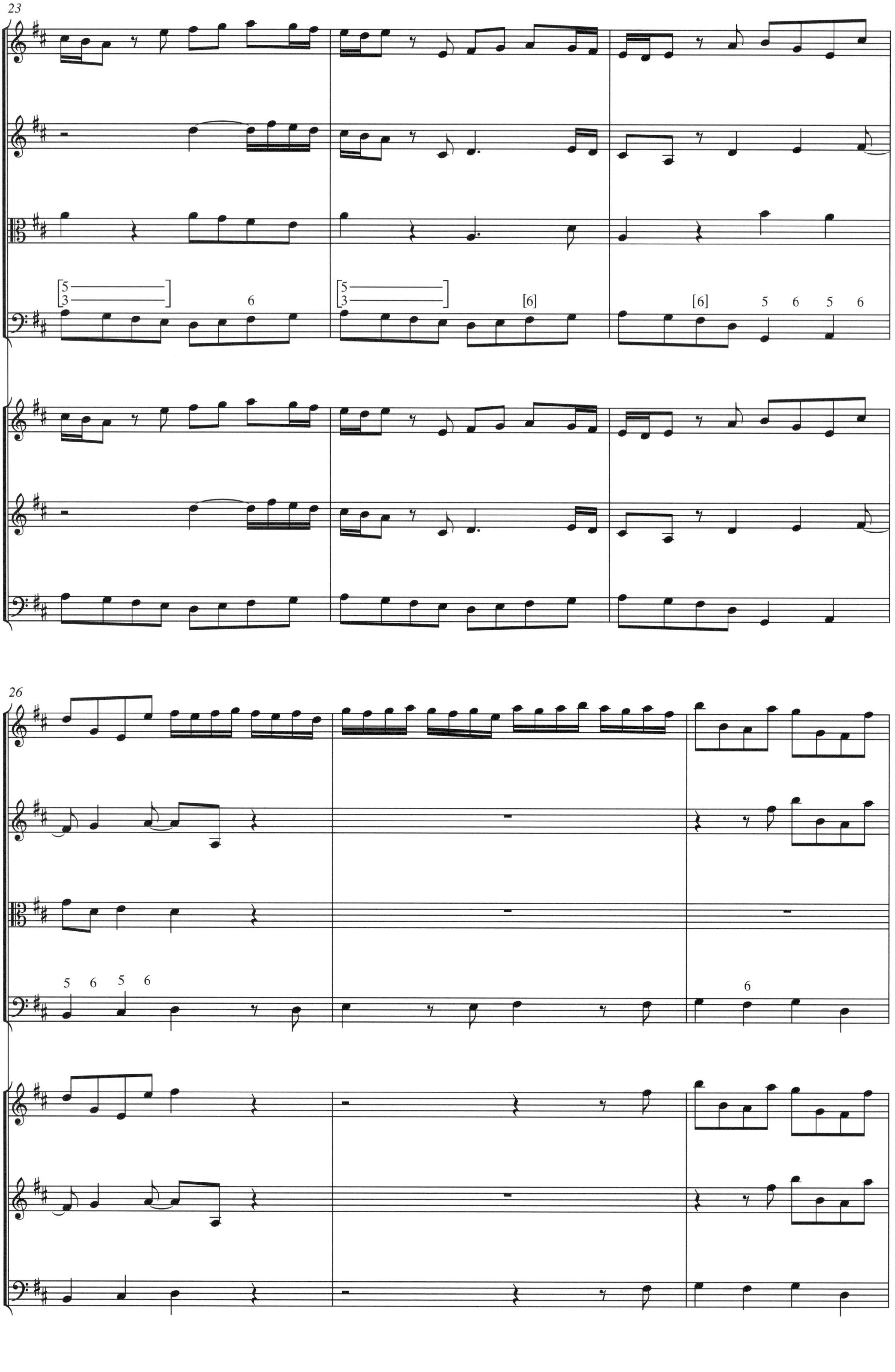
23
26

III

Adagio

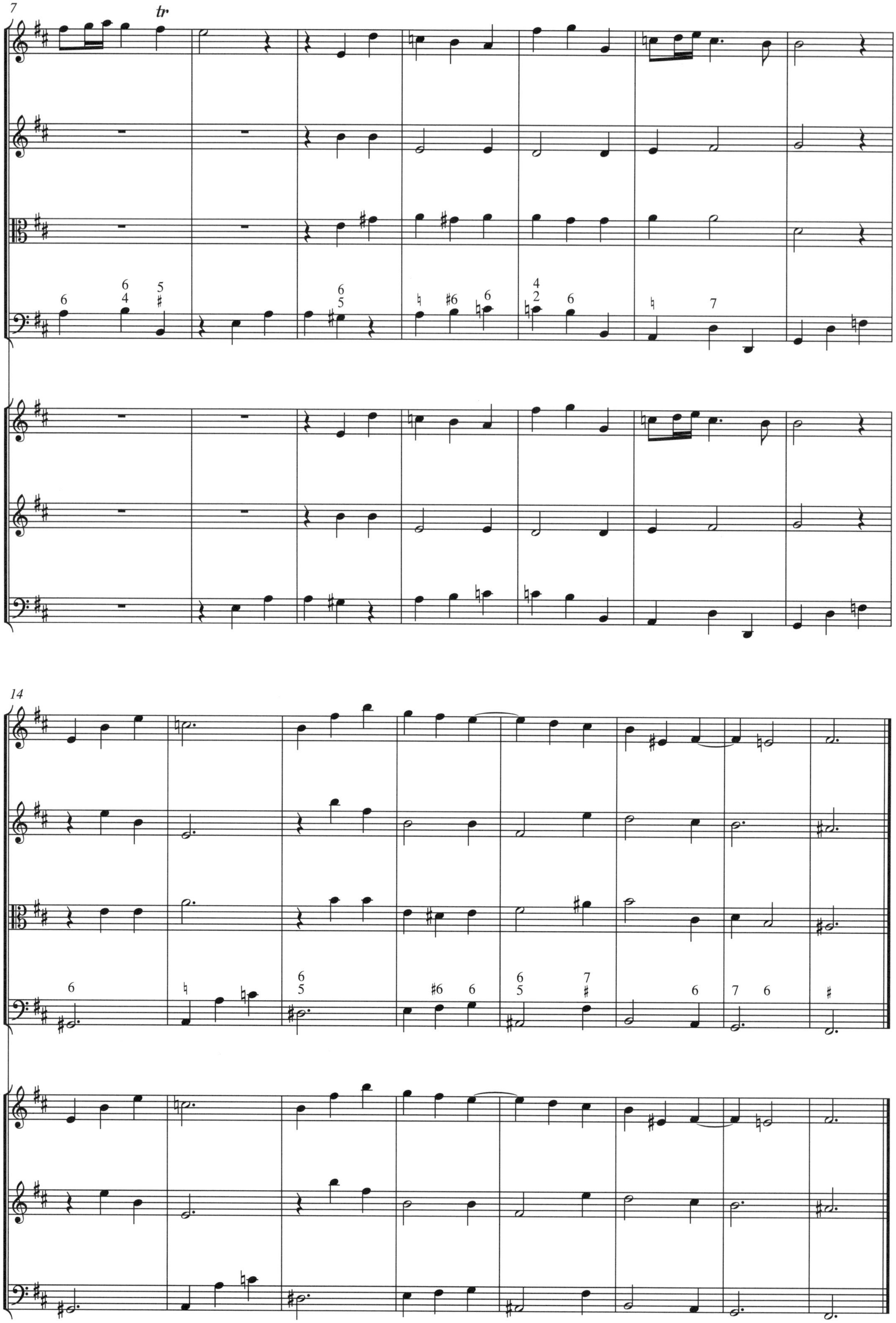
tr

IV

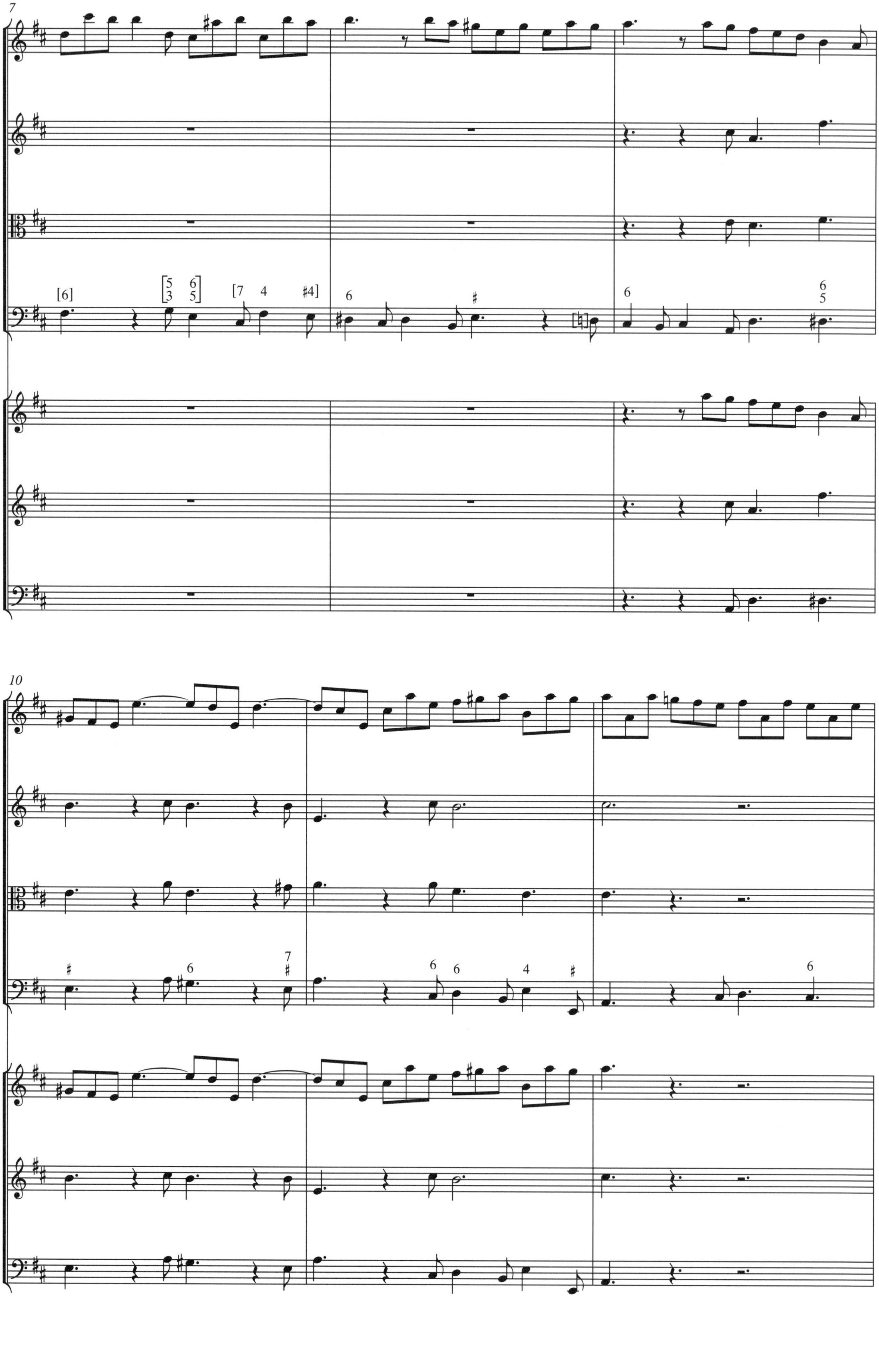

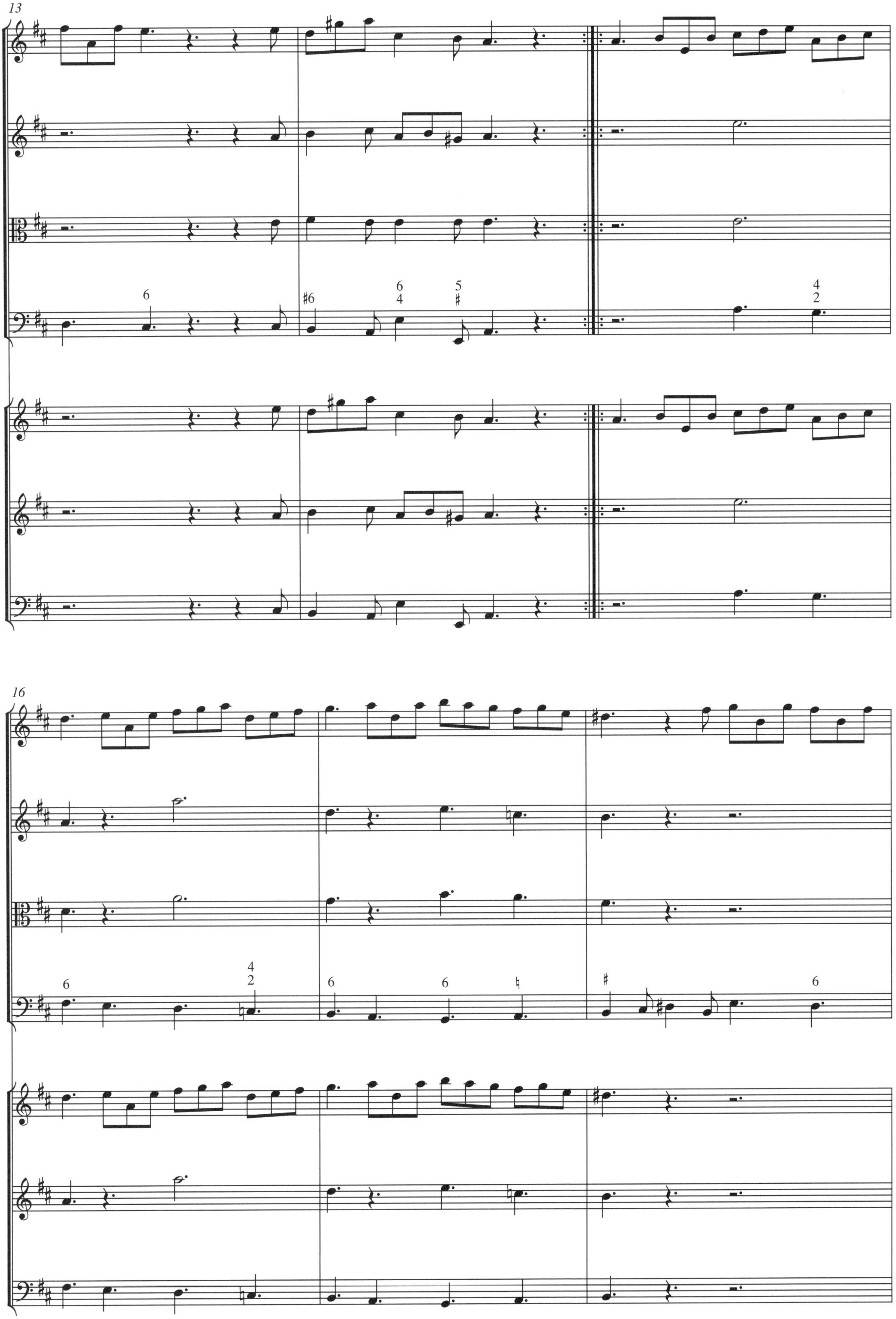
13
16

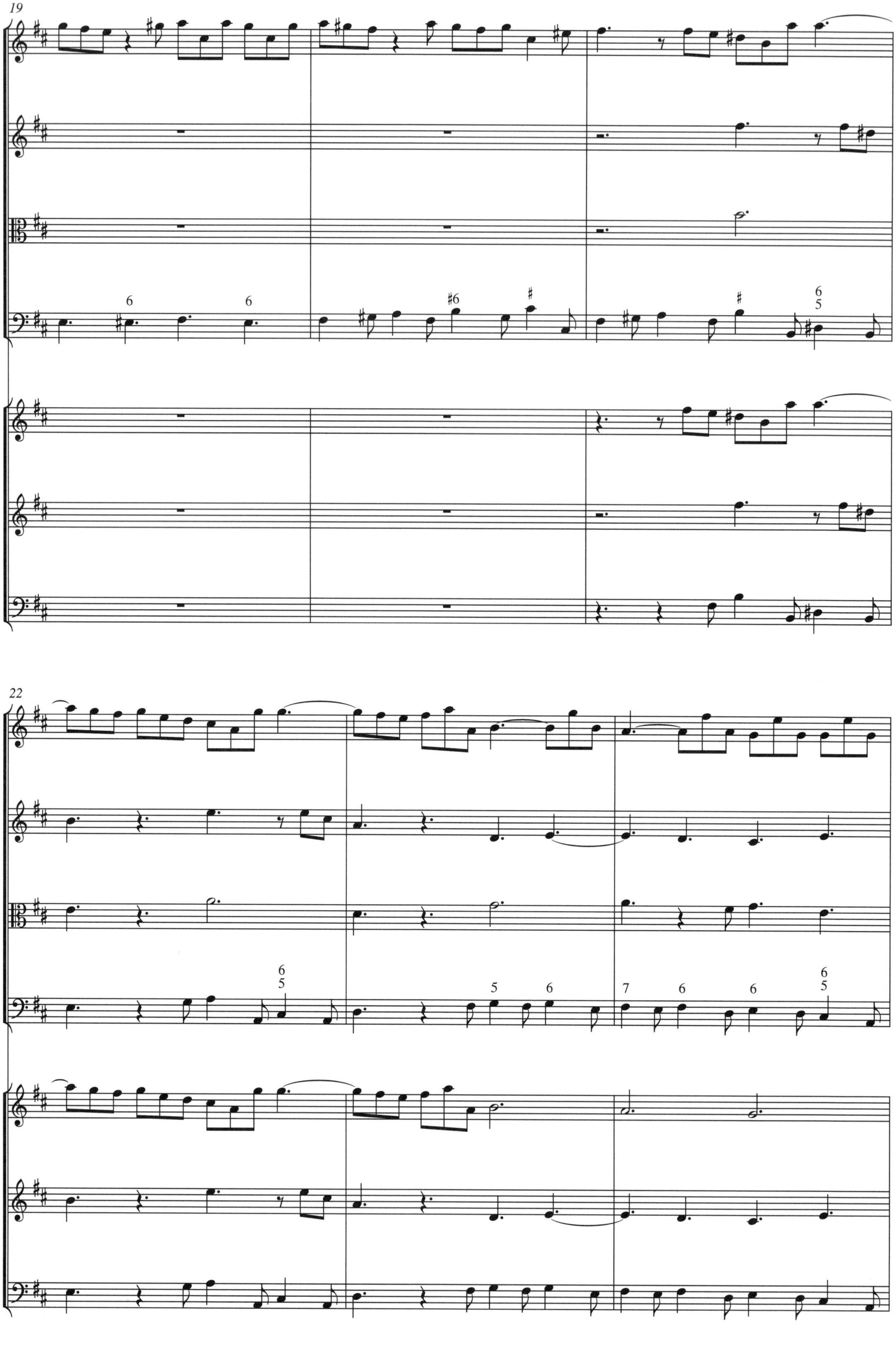
19
22

171

11. Concerto in D Minor
I

From Francesco Geminiani, Sonata in D Minor, Op. 1, No. 12

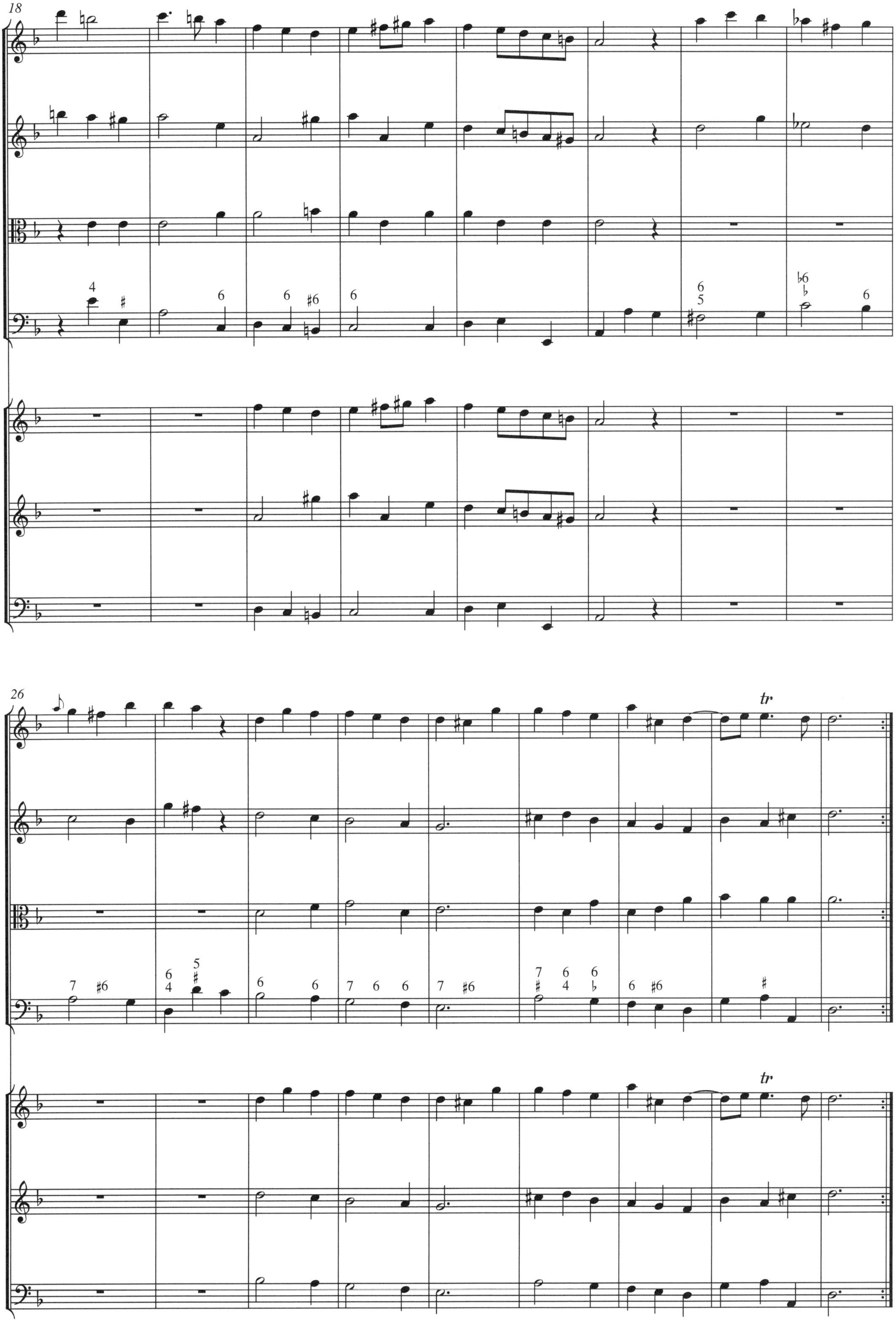
18
26
tr
tr

II

175

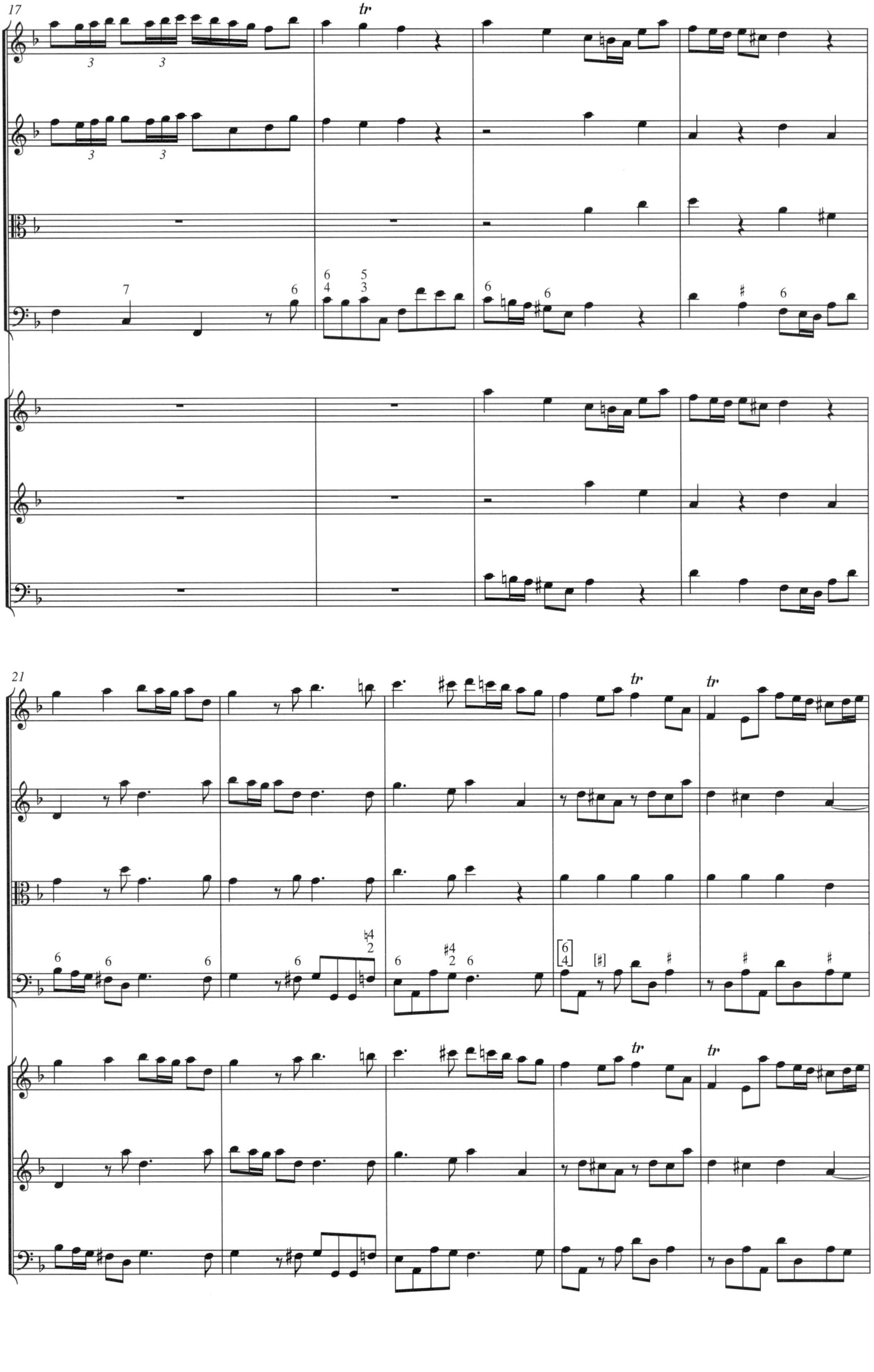
17
21

177

III

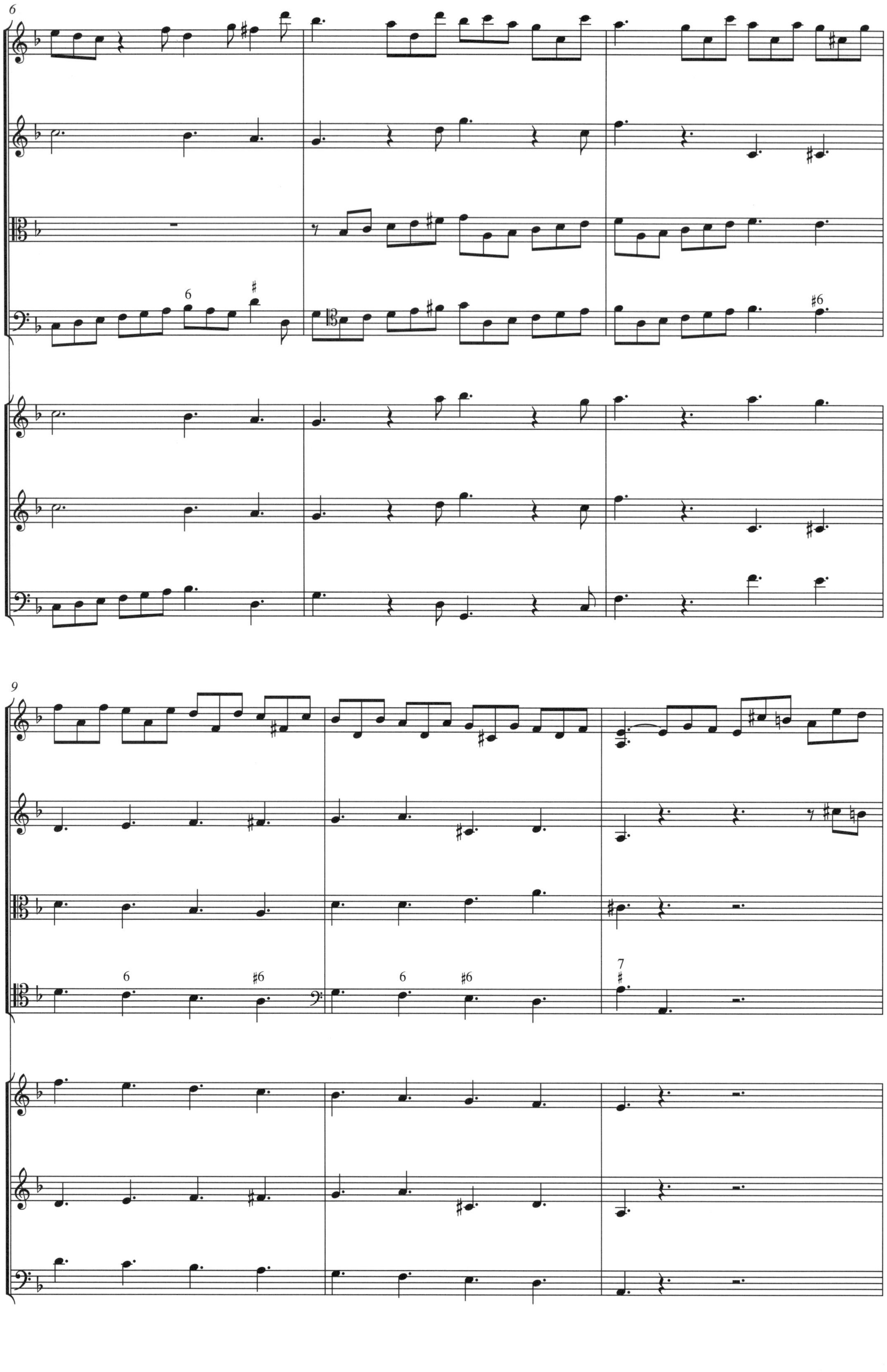

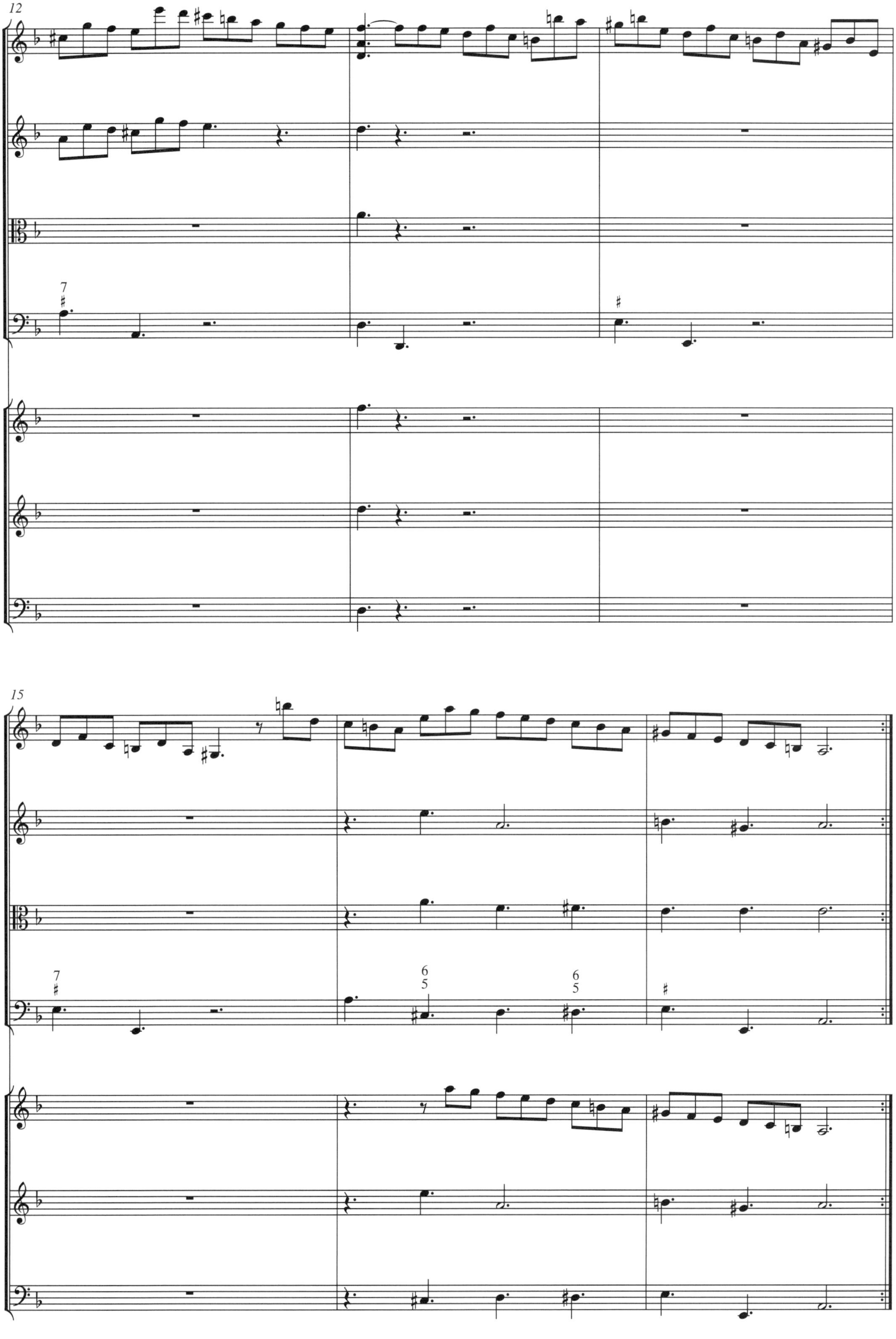

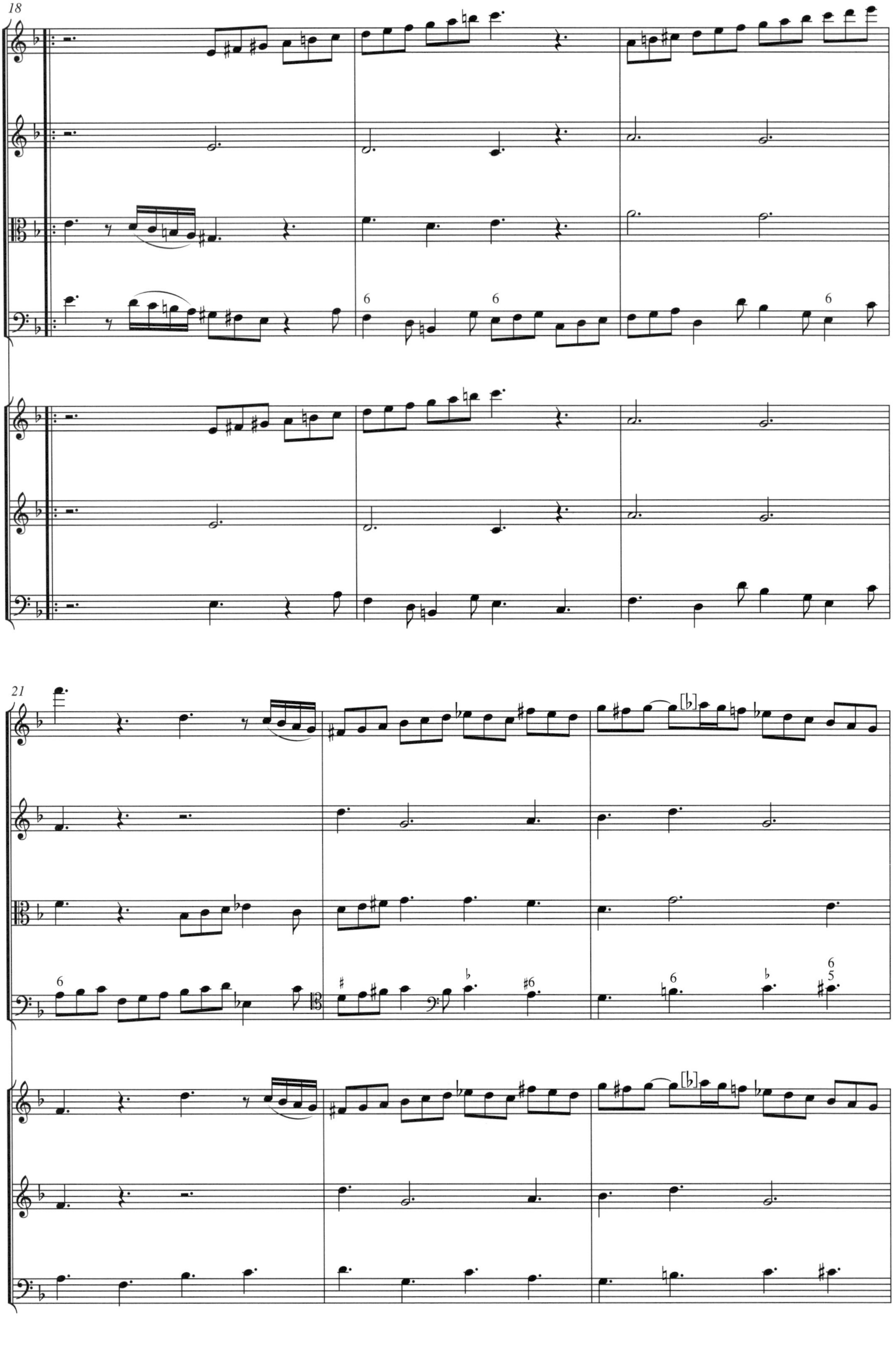
18
21

181

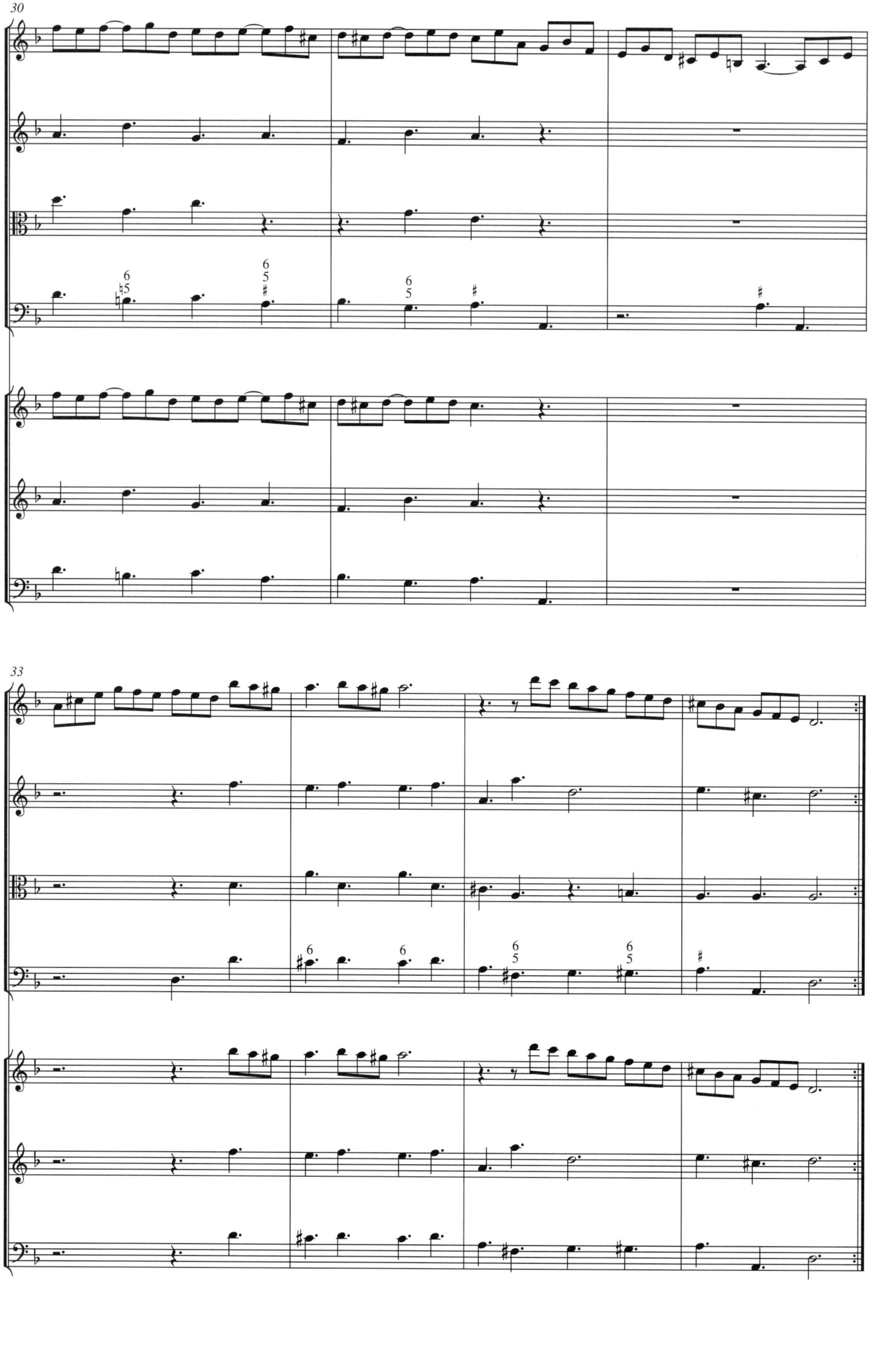

Critical Report

Sources

There is only one source for the music of this edition: the second of two workbooks owned, used, and largely transcribed by Charles Avison. The workbooks were discovered in 2000 and 2002 after being hidden from view for over two centuries. They are currently owned by the Charles Avison Society of Newcastle, England (Avison Charitable Trust) and are housed in the Charles Avison Archive, part of the larger Newcastle Collection at the Newcastle City Library. The library also holds facsimile copies of both workbooks. With more than six hundred pages of music and text, the two workbooks offer new perspectives on Avison and his role in the development of the orchestral concerto in the eighteenth century. For further information, including the dramatic events leading to the discovery of the workbooks, see Mark Kroll, "Two Important New Sources for the Music of Charles Avison," *Music and Letters* 86 (2005): 414–31.

Considering the strong ties between Avison and Geminiani, it is not surprising to discover that Geminiani's name appears in the workbooks more often than any other composer. In Workbook I, we find Avison's copies in score of Geminiani's Concerti Grossi, opp. 2 and 3 (published in parts in 1732 and in score in 1755), as well as Avison's score versions of Geminiani's arrangements of Corelli's Sonatas for Violin and Basso Continuo, op. 5, which Geminiani had published in parts in 1726 (sonatas 1–6) and 1729 (sonatas 7–12). Workbook II contains not only the arrangements of Geminiani's Sonatas for Violin and Basso Continuo, op. 1, but also Avison's concerto versions of Geminiani's Sonatas for Violin and Basso Continuo, op. 4, and his copies in full score of Geminiani's Concerti Grossi, op. 7, which had previously been published only in parts.

The pages of Workbook II were numbered, possibly in the nineteenth century, and this system will be used here. Workbook II has a total of 328 pages; the eleven concertos of this edition appear on pages 5–77. Watermark studies indicate that Avison's workbooks are of eighteenth-century manufacture and were probably first used between 1730 and 1740. At least five different hands can found in these workbooks, including those of Charles Avison and his son Edward. The concertos of this edition appear to have been written by Charles Avison in his neat and precise handwriting.

Editorial Methods

The concertos copied into Avison's Workbook II do not bear titles, nor is there any acknowledgment of the original Geminiani sonatas from which they are derived. For this edition, generic titles, including the key of the arrangement, have been supplied, and the Geminiani sonata upon which each concerto is based is also identified.

Roman numerals are added tacitly to designate movements. The source is neither clear nor consistent in indicating whether a portion of music should be considered an independent movement or a section within a multi-tempo movement. The scribe of the concertos used thick-thick barlines to indicate both the end of a movement and, on occasion, the end of a section within a multi-tempo movement. In most cases, the end of a movement is followed by blank staves, and the next movement begins on the following page. Movements in binary form, however, tend not to have blank staves at the end, presumably because the form of the movement and use of repeat signs already suffice to delineate the end of the movement. For this edition, movement divisions are determined by tempo indications, the style of barlines used in the source, the presence of blank staves following barlines, and the form of the movement. Thick-thick barlines are converted to modern final (thin-thick) barlines at the ends of movements. The few thick-thick barlines that appear within a movement are converted to thin-thin barlines and reported in the critical notes. The critical notes report cases in which a movement not in binary form ends without being followed by blank staves. A thick-thick barline followed by a wavy line appears at the end of each concerto; this edition tacitly converts this indication to the standard final (thin-thick) barline.

Three concertos—the Concerto in G Major (no. 1), Concerto in C Minor (no. 7), and Concerto in D Minor (no. 11)—contain brief sections that in some ways function more as an interlude than as a self-contained movement. In the case of the G-major concerto, blank staves separate the Grave from the following Allegro, and thus that section is treated as a separate movement in the edition. By contrast, the source does not use blank staves to delineate the end of the Grave in the Concerto in C Minor or the end of the Adagio in the Concerto in D Minor—suggesting that they serve as introductions to the following movements. Yet the 1739 edition of Geminiani's Sonatas for Violin and Basso Continuo, op. 1, ends the Grave of the Concerto in C Minor with a thin-thick barline followed by empty staves, and the edition follows Geminiani in treating the Grave section as an independent movement. The Geminiani print treats the Adagio in the D-minor concerto in a similar manner, but due to the extreme brevity of this section—a mere three measures—this edition combines this section and the following Allegro into a single movement.

Repeat signs are tacitly modernized. The source has forward-facing repeat signs in the first measure of many movements. If a movement is in binary form, such signs are removed without comment, per modern engraving practices; otherwise, the sign is reported in the critical notes. The set of variations in the fourth movement of the Concerto in G Minor uses a notational shorthand in which slurs signal first and second endings, while variant first and second endings are shown with double stems or fermatas rather than written out (see plate 2). In the edition, slurs are tacitly replaced with numbered brackets, and first and second endings are written out to clarify ambiguous passages.

As the source also does not indicate instrumentation, instrument names are tacitly added and divided into two groups: *concertino* and *ripieno*. While the basso continuo of the *concertino* group contains figures and was likely performed by cello and harpsichord, the *ripieno* basso lacks figures, suggesting that this line was performed only by cello and double bass. The placement of *concertino* above *ripieno* is preserved from the source, which results in the position of the basso continuo in the middle of the score ordering. Avison used a system of notation in which empty measures without rests in the *ripieno* group indicate the sections in which the parts of the *concertino* were to be doubled (see plates 1 and 3). These parts are written out in the edition. All original clefs are retained, including the use of the tenor clef in the *concertino* basso continuo, which indicates that the cello plays without the bass in such passages.

All original tempo markings are retained, and abbreviations are written out and modernized without comment. Some concertos have tempo indications only for the *concertino* group; in these instances, tempo markings are tacitly replicated in the *ripieno* section. If a concerto movement lacks such indications entirely, tempo markings are taken from the 1739 edition of Geminiani's Sonatas for Violin and Basso Continuo, op. 1, and reported in the critical notes.

The edition reflects the time signatures of the source with two exceptions: First, time signatures redundant by modern standards, such as the reiteration of the C between the opening Adagio and Allegro in the first movement of the Concerto in E Minor, are removed and reported in the critical notes. Second, several concerto movements in $\frac{3}{8}$ include brief interludes in $\frac{3}{4}$, but the source does not write out the meter changes. In these cases, $\frac{3}{4}$ meter and all subsequent meter changes appear in the edition in brackets.

Original key signatures are retained. As was common in eighteenth-century practice, several concertos have one flat fewer than would be expected by modern conventions. All editorially added accidentals appear in brackets. Added cautionary accidentals appear in parentheses; source cautionaries are retained only where they clarify passages. Accidentals of the source that are redundant by modern standards are tacitly removed.

Original note values are retained, with one exception: Notes that appear tied within a measure in the source have been tacitly realized as a single note of comparable duration wherever viable, particularly in those movements in which the source is inconsistent in the use of tied notes. The stem directions, beaming patterns, and rhythmic groupings of notes and rests in the source are made to conform to modern conventions. Triplet numerals are placed at the beam or stem side of notes, and triplet slurs are tacitly removed. Missing triplet indications are added and placed in brackets. Fermatas do not appear consistently in all parts in the source; when they appear in only one part, they are realized in the remaining parts without comment.

The notation of appoggiaturas is retained from the source, that is, with stems up and without slurs underneath. Appoggiaturas appear with three different note values in the source: sixteenth note, eighth note, and quarter note. These durations are mostly retained, and exceptions are reported in the critical notes. It is not possible to offer a definitive interpretation of the proper execution of these appoggiaturas. However, sixteenth-note appoggiaturas were probably played very short and before the beat (see, for example, the first movement of the Concerto in D Minor [no. 2], m. 4; and the first movement of the Concerto in D Major [no. 4], m. 2). Appoggiaturas of an eighth or quarter note in duration were probably played on the beat and took at least half the value of the main note (see, for example, the second movement of the Concerto in D Minor [no. 2], m. 21; the final movement of the Concerto in G Minor [no. 6], mm. 40 and 146; and the first movement of the Concerto in D Minor [no. 11], mm. 5 and 26). The only ornament to appear in the source is the trill, abbreviated both "tr" and simply "t." All trills appear in the edition with the abbreviation *tr*; added trills are shown in brackets. The addition of editorial slurs (dashed) and staccato markings (in parentheses) is limited to obvious parallel passages. Added ties are also dashed.

Figured bass symbols are placed above the basso continuo staff (as they are in the source). Bass figures are retained with the exception of slashed numerals (such as 6̸), and numerals with a plus after them (such as 4+), which are rendered in the edition as ♯ or ♮ as appropriate. Inflections of intervals are regularized to precede the numeral, as in ♭6 (rather than 6♭). As with accidentals, most cautionary figures are retained, and editorial bass figures—limited to those passages in need of clarification—are bracketed. Incorrect figures are corrected and reported in the critical notes, as are obvious errors and inconsistencies in pitch and rhythm.

Critical Notes

Critical notes list rejected or ambiguous readings from the source as well as elements supplied from the 1739 edition of Geminiani's Sonatas for Violin and Basso Continuo, op. 1 (hereafter Geminiani 1739). Notes are located in the score by measure number and part name. When specific notes and rests in a measure are cited, appoggiaturas are included in the note count, tied noteheads are numbered individually, and rests are counted separately from notes. The following abbreviations are used in the paragraphs below: M(m.) = measure(s), Vn. = violin, Va. = viola, B.c. = basso continuo, B. = basso. *Concertino* and *ripieno* violins are further differentiated as follows: C. = *concertino*, R. = *ripieno*, C./R. = both *concertino* and *ripieno*. The pitch system used throughout is that in which c' represents middle C.

1. Concerto in G Major

I. Grave; Allegro; Adagio; Allegro; Adagio

M. 22, barline at end of measure illegible. M. 34, Va., note 1 is c".

II. Allegro

M. 32, C./R., Vn. 1, note 4, slur over trill. M. 42, C./R., Vn. 1, note 4, slur over trill. M. 74, B.c., note 3, figures are 7 ♯6. M. 88, B., whole note.

IV. Allegro

M. 12, B.c., note 8, figure moved from note 7. M. 25, C., Vn. 1, note 6 is e".

2. Concerto in D Minor

I. Adagio

M. 6, R., Vn. 2, first beat is quarter rest, second beat 8th rest lacking.

II. Allegro

M. 5, B.c., note 1, figure is 3. M. 11, B.c., note 2, first figure is 5. M. 23, C., Vn. 1, notes 4–8 are three 32nd note triplets, dotted 16th, 32nd note. M. 24, C., Vn. 1, notes 1–5 are three 32nd note triplets, dotted 16th, 32nd note. M. 25, C., Vn. 1, notes 9–13 are three 32nd note triplets, dotted 16th, 32nd note. M. 26, C., Vn. 1, notes 1–5 are three 32nd note triplets, dotted 16th, 32nd note.

III. Adagio

M. 1, forward-facing repeat sign.

IV. Allegro

M. 36, B.c., second figure is ♭6/4. M. 37, B.c., second figure is ♭6/4. M. 38, B.c., second figure is ♭6/4. Mm. 58–61, R., Vn. 2, additional notes (see example 1) written on same staff in small, light hand. M. 61, C., Vn. 2, quarter notes d', c', b appear on same staff in small, light hand.

Example 1.

3. Concerto in E Minor

I. Adagio; Allegro; Adagio; [Tempo giusto]; Adagio

M. 1, C., Vn. 1, notes 2–10 are 16th, four 32nd notes, dotted 16th, three 32nd notes; slur over last five notes. M. 4, 𝄵 at beginning of measure. M. 22, Va., note 1 is quarter followed by 8th rest. M. 25, tempo marking from Geminiani 1739. M. 34, R., tempo marking on beat 3.

II. Allegro

M. 54, B.c. and B., note 5 barely legible, likely g.

4. Concerto in D Major

I. Adagio

M. 6, B.c., note 8, figure is 7/5. M. 7, B.c., note 3, figure is 7/5.

II. Allegro

M. 7, C./R., Vn. 1, note 5 (appoggiatura) is 8th. M. 15, Va., note 1 is g'. M. 16, C., Vn. 2, note 7 is f'.

III. Grave

M. 12, C., Vn. 1 and Vn. 2, note 1 (appoggiatura) is 8th.

IV. Allegro

M. 90, C., Vn. 2, note 3 is c".

5. Concerto in B-flat Major

I. Affettuoso

M. 8, B.c. and B., note 1 is e♭.

II. Vivace

Movement begins immediately after double barline of Affettuoso without intervening blank staves. M. 5, C., Vn. 2, note 2 is d". M. 7, B.c., note 5 is d. M. 8, B.c., note 4, figure is 7. M. 42, B.c., note 4, figure is ♭. M. 46, B.c., note 1, second figure moved from second half of beat 1.

III. Grave

M. 5, double bar (thick-thick) at end of measure.

IV. Allegro

M. 3, B.c., note 1 is b♭.

6. Concerto in G Minor

III. Allegro

Movement begins immediately after double barline of Adagio without intervening blank staves. M. 23, B.c., second figure is ♯5. M. 111, B.c., directive reads "tasto soli." M. 111, B.c., whole note instead of two half notes (changed to clarify placement of "tasto solo").

IV. Andante

Movement begins immediately after double barline of Allegro without intervening blank staves. M. 7, B.c., figures are 7 ♮6. M. 16, repeat sign from Geminiani 1739. M. 17, repeat sign from Geminiani 1739. M. 25, B.c., note 1 is dotted half note with double stem. M. 32, repeat sign from Geminiani 1739. M. 99, thick-thick barline. M. 148, right hand, note 1 (appoggiatura) is 16th.

7. Concerto in C Minor

I. Grave

M. 1, tempo marking from Geminiani 1739. M. 3, B.c., note 1, figure is ♯6. M. 6, B.c., note 2, figure is ♭.

II. Allegro

M. 1, tempo marking in a different, unidentified hand. M. 6, B.c., note 3 is quarter note. M. 20, B.c., fourth note illegible. M. 53, repeat sign from Geminiani 1739.

III. Grave

M. 1, tempo marking from Geminiani 1739.

IV. Allegro

Movement begins immediately after double barline of Grave without intervening blank staves. M. 1, tempo marking from Geminiani 1739.

8. Concerto in B Minor

II. Vivace

M. 1, tempo marking from Geminiani 1739. Mm. 27–30, C., Vn. 2, rhythm for each measure is 8th note, 8th rest, three 16th notes.

III. Adagio

M. 1, tempo marking from Geminiani 1739. M. 1, forward-facing repeat sign. M. 6, B.c., note 7, figure is ♭6/♮4.

IV. Vivace

M. 1, tempo marking from Geminiani 1739. M. 29, R., Vn. 2, rhythm is quarter note followed by 8th rest. M. 40, B.c. and B., note 2 is f.

9. Concerto in F Major

I. Vivace

M. 1, tempo marking from Geminiani 1739. M. 5, B., whole rest.

III. Allegro

M. 1, tempo marking from Geminiani 1739. M. 5, B.c., note 1, figures are stacked 5/♭4. M. 42, C., Vn. 1, note 6 is f'.

10. Concerto in D Major

All tempo markings are taken from Geminiani 1739.

I. Adagio

M. 2, C./R., Vn. 1, note 7, slur over trill.

II. Allegro

Movement begins immediately following Adagio without intervening blank staves. M. 30, C., Vn. 2, note 4 is d'. M. 31, C., Vn. 2, note 1 is d'.

III. Adagio

M. 1, forward-facing repeat. M. 19, Va., note 2 is b.

IV. Allegro

M. 8, C., Vn. 1, note 6 is a".

11. Concerto in D Minor

I. Amoroso

M. 13, Va., half note. M. 30, C./R., Vn. 2, half note followed by quarter rest.

II. Allegro

M. 1, tempo marking from Geminiani 1739. M. 21, Va., note 3, quarter note followed by 8th rest. M. 23, C./R., Vn. 1, note 1, quarter note followed by 8th rest. M. 24, B.c., note 1, figure is ♯.

III. Adagio; Allegro

M. 1, tempo marking from Geminiani 1739. M. 3, thick-thick barline. M. 4, tempo marking from Geminiani 1739. M. 4, repeat sign lacking.